Enrique Ibarra

Private forest use decisions and state forest policy effectiveness in Costa Rica

Zugl.: Freiburg, Univ., Diss., 2002

Die Bilder des Umschlags wurden freundlicherweise von "Fundación Cecropia" zur Verfügung gestellt.

1. Auflage 2003
Tel./Fax: 02228-493

Homepage: www.forstbuch.de, www.forestrybooks.com

ISBN: 3-935638-36-1

Druck: www.business-copy.com

Freiburger Schriften zur Forst- und Umweltpolitik
Band 3

Private forest use decisions and state forest policy effectiveness in Costa Rica: The role of institutions, private stakeholders and the state

Enrique Ibarra

Verlag Dr. Kessel
Remagen-Oberwinter 2003

To my parents, Eduardo and Anita

and,

to María del Mar, in loving memory

Acknowledgements

The persons and circumstances that brought me to walk this 'long and winding road' are too many to be exposed here, and would probably provide material to write a novel. It should suffice for now for the reader to know that this is the result of my own initiative, and of a twist of fate that today still makes me wonder.

To begin with, I wish to express my acknowledgement to the DAAD and to Prof. Dr. Dieter K. Tscheulin, who provided the means that enabled me to set foot in Germany several years ago.

Several persons and organizations have contributed and accompanied me throughout this research, and to them I would like to express my deep thankfulness.

First and foresmost my gratitude goes to the Heinrich Böll Stiftung, who supported and financed this research from the very beginning.

I am also deeply grateful to my tutor, Prof. Dr. Michel Becker, whose patience, focused and careful guidance provided the necessary elements for me to conceive this work. His – sometimes skeptical, but always constructive – critique showed me constantly new and enriching points of view, and so, by giving me at the same time the liberty to follow my own thoughts, he contributed decisively to the development of this research study.

I am also thankful to the Forest Faculty and its teaching staff, for their openness and friendliness and for the provision of a most intellectually inspirational academic environment. I am also specially thankful to my colleagues at the 'Institut für Forstpolitik' Dr. Dietmar Stoian (now at CATIE) and Dr. Carol Grossman for reading and commenting on sections of this document, and to Carmen Gottwald, Sergio Ruiz and Dr. Guillermo Navarro (former staff member of the Institut für Forstökonomie) for the lively discussions and insights on several subjects that helped me further elaborate my arguments.

In Costa Rica, I wish to thank Fundación Cecropia for providing logistics during the field research in the Osa peninsula in both of my research visits to the area.

Any errors contained herein are my own responsibility.

Last, but not least, I want to thank all of my very dear friends who stood by me even in my darkest hours. This work would have definitely not been possible without your support. You know who you are. Thank you.

INDEX

Graphic index

Map index

Table index

Acronyms

ACA-HN: Area de Conservación Huetár Norte

ACTO: Area de Conservación Tortuguero

ACOSA: Area de Conservación Osa

AFE: Administración Forestal del Estado

APREFLOFAS: Asociación Preservacionsita de Flora y Fauna

ASCONA: Asociación Costarricense para la Preservación de la Naturaleza

BCCR: Banco Central de Costa Rica

CAF: Certificado de Abono Forestal

CATIE: Centro Agronómico Tropical de Investigación y Enseñanza

CCT: Centro Científico Tropical

CIEDES: Centro de Investigaciones en Desarrollo Sostenible

CEPAL: Comisión Económica para América Latina

CODEFORSA: Comisión de Desarrollo Forestal de San Carlos

COSEFORMA: Cooperación de los Sectores Forestal y Maderero

COVIRENA: Comité de Vigilancia de los Recursos Naturales

CR: Costa Rica

CRA: Consejos Regionales Ambientales

DGF: Dirección General Forestal

FAO: Food and Agriculture Organization

FECON: Federación Costarricense para la Conservación del Ambiente

FONAFIFO: Fondo Nacional de Financiamiento Forestal

FUNDECOR: Fundación para el Desarrollo de la Cordillera Volcánica Central

GTZ: Deutsche Gesellschaft für Technische Zusammenarbeit

IDA: Instituto de Desarrollo Agrario

INBIO: Instituto Nacional de Biodiversidad

ITCO: Instituto de Tierras y Colonizaciones

ITTO: International Tropical Timber Organization

JUNAFORCA: Junta Forestal Nacional Campesina

MAG: Ministerio de Agricultura y Ganadería

MINAE: Ministerio del Ambiente y Energía

NGO: Non-governmental organization

NIE: New Institutional Economics

ODI: Overseas Development Institute

OIT: Organización Internacional del Trabajo

ONF: Oficina Nacional Forestal

PES: Payment of Environmental Services

POA: Plan de Ordenamiento Ambiental

PNUD: Programa de las Naciones Unidas para el Desarrollo

RFGD: Reserva Forestal Golfo Dulce

SINAC: Sistema Nacional de Areas de Conservación

SIPRAICO: Sindicato de Productores Agrarios Independientes de Osa

TUVA: Tierras Unidas Vecinales por el Ambiente

UN: United Nations

UNAM: Universidad Autónoma de México

Überblick über die Dissertation

Die vorliegende Dissertation ist Ergebnis des Forschungsprojektes „**Private forest use decisions and state forest policy effectiveness in Costa Rica: The role of institutions, private stakeholders and the state**", das aus eigener Initiative entstand und durch die ‚**Heinrich Böll Stiftung**' finanziert wurde.

Die Dissertation ist in drei Hauptteile gegliedert.

Teil eins (Kapitel 1) führt in das Forschungsproblem ein. Konventionelle Waldbewirtschaftungsmethoden bestehen trotz jüngster Veränderungen **formaler Institutionen** (Gesetze, Normen, Erlasse), die die private Waldbewirtschaftung regeln, um Nachhaltigkeit und Waldschutz zu erreichen. Konventionelle Waldbewirtschaftung wird als eine schädliche Art der Waldnutzung verstanden. **Informelle Institutionen** (Verhaltensnormen privater Akteure) stehen in Konflikt zu den formalen institutionellen Rahmenbedingungen, da sie die konventionelle Methode unterstützen. Die Kernfrage der Studie ist: ‚**Wie beeinflussen informelle Institutionen die Erreichung formaler forstpolitischer Ziele?**'

Teil zwei (Kapitel 2-3) beinhaltet den theoretischen Rahmen der Arbeit, der auf der Theorie der neuen **Institutionenökonomie** beruht. Kapitel 2 beginnt mit der Einführung des Konzeptes der ‚Rationalität'. Danach werden die Konzepte der formalen und informellen Institutionen sowie der Unterschied zwischen Institutionen und Organisationen erklärt. Das Konzept der ‚Geschäftskultur' und die Rolle des Vertrauens bei der Gestaltung der wirtschaftlichen Umwelt werden vorgestellt. Danach wird aufgezeigt, in welcher Verbindung Geschäftskultur und Institutionen zueinander stehen.

Der nächste Abschnitt des 2. Kapitels beinhaltet die Theorie der institutionellen Entstehung und des institutionellen Wandels. Besondere Aufmerksamkeit wird hierbei auf die Handlungsmacht verschiedener Akteure des Forstsektors auf die Bestimmung institutioneller Rahmenbedingungen gelegt. Diese Macht wird eingesetzt, um Vorteile bzw. spezifischen Nutzen zu erzielen. Dadurch wird die wirtschaftliche Aktivität strukturiert und der Nutzen auf die Akteure verteilt. Das Konzept der ‚**Pfadabhängigkeit**' (path dependence) knüpft an die vorherigen Konzepte durch die These an, dass der institutionelle Wandel pfadabhängig ist. Pfadabhängigkeit wird stark von historischen, sozialen und politischen Zusammenhängen beeinflusst.

Am Ende des 2. Kapitels wird ein Modell der dynamischen Beziehungen zwischen informellen und formalen Institutionen dargestellt. Dieses Modell betont die enge Verzahnung informeller und formaler Institutionen. Es wird die These vertreten, dass die Erreichung der Ziele formaler Institutionen von der „Harmonie" zwischen den beiden Arten von Institutionen abhängt. Der letzte Abschnitt des 2. Kapitels vermittelt einen Überblick über die Theorie der ‚**Governance**', die die Relevanz der Interaktion zwischen den informellen und formalen Institutionen hervorhebt.

In Kapitel 3 werden verschiedene Aspekte der Forstpolitik präsentiert. Das Konzept der **Forstpolitik**, wie es in akademischen und internationalen Kreisen benutzt wird, analysiert das forstpolitische Geschehen auf einer breiten Ebene und stellt seine Abhängigkeit von verschiedenen Sektorpolitiken (z.B. Agrarpolitik, Energiepolitik, Siedlungspolitik, etc.) dar. Besondere Aufmerksamkeit wird auf die ‚Agenda 21‘ der Rio Umweltkonferenz gelegt. Der Einfluss von Marktverzerrungen auf die Entwaldung wird dargestellt. Ein Überblick über forstpolitische Anreizinstrumente wird gegeben.

Im **dritten Teil** der Dissertation (Kapitel 4-7) werden die Ergebnisse und die Diskussion präsentiert.

Kapitel 4 stellt mittels einer Literaturrecherche die Ursachen der Entwaldung in Mittelamerika heraus. Es werden Hintergrundinformationen für den Fall Costa Rica (z.B. Entwicklungsstrategie durch Agrarmaßnahmen) geliefert. Regionale forstpolitische Maßnahmen (z.B. Konzessionen oder Waldmanagement-Pläne) sowie Anreizmaßnahmen (z.B. finanzielle Anreize) in einigen mittelamerikanischen Ländern werden vorgestellt.

In Kapitel 5 werden die jüngsten Entwicklungen der Rahmenbedingungen für die formalen Institutionen des Forstsektors in Costa Rica vorgestellt. Ein genereller Überblick über den Forstsektor, dessen Akteure, sowie über die Konflikte, die aufgrund des institutionellen Wandels entstehen, wird gewonnen. Welche Ziele der Staat auf der administrativen, rechtlichen und wirtschaftlichen Ebene anstrebt, wird erklärt und anhand der empirischen Untersuchung analysiert. Die vom Staat gewählten Anreizmaßnahmen werden untersucht. Hierbei liegt der Schwerpunkt auf den neu eingeführten ‚Bezahlungen von Umweltleistungen von Wäldern‘ sowie auf der systembedingten Nutzenverteilung.

Desweiteren wird der Konflikt, der aufgrund der Teilnahme der staatlichen und privaten Akteure an forstwirtschaftlichen Aktivitäten entsteht, beschrieben und analysiert.

Kapitel 6 beschreibt die **Waldnutzung** aus Sicht der privaten Landbesitzer im Untersuchungsgebiet in Costa Rica. Verschiedene informelle Verhaltensnormen sowie soziale Durchführungsmechanismen im privaten und staatlichen Bereich werden dargestellt. Diese Gesamtdarstellung resultiert aus den Daten, die in Kapitel 5 präsentiert und analysiert wurden. Transaktionskosten, die durch konventionelle Waldbewirtschaftung für die Landbesitzer entstehen, werden analysiert. Besondere Aufmerksamkeit wird hierbei auf die Kosten gelegt, die die Landbesitzer durch unvollständige und asymmetrische Informationen (wie z.B. Fehlinformationen bei Vertragsabschluß über Preise, Volumen des Holzes, etc.) tragen.

In Kapitel 7 wird diskutiert wie die Interaktion zwischen informellen und formalen Institutionen die private Nutzung von Wäldern bestimmt, und wie dies die Erreichung von formalen Zielen beeinflusst. Ein Hauptergebnis der Arbeit ist, dass die formalen Ziele der Forstpolitik in Costa Rica nur schwer erreicht werden, da private Akteure einen größeren Nutzen von der Beibehaltung der informellen Regeln haben. Die stärksten Gruppen im Forstsektor (Holzeinschlagunternehmer, Forstingenieure) tragen durch die Nutzung ihrer Handlungsmacht zur Erhaltung ihres ‚*Status quo*‘ bei. Ein Hauptschwerpunkt liegt hierbei auf dem formellen institutionellen Wandel und dessen Pfadabhängigkeit.

Research outline

This dissertation is divided into three main sections.

Section I (Chapter 1) presents the research problem, the research objectives and research questions followed by the methodology and methods for data collection and analysis used throughout the research. The research problem is derived from the observation that despite recent changes of the formal institutional framework to achieve sustainable natural forest management and forest protection, conventional logging persists. Conventional logging is here understood as a particularly destructive method of forest management traditionally used in the country. The central research question is 'How do informal institutions affect the achievement of formal forest policy ends (sustainable forest management and forest protection)?'.

The theoretical framework is presented in **Section II** (Chapters 2-3), and is based largely on the theory of the New Institutional Economics (NIE).

Chapter 2 begins with a discussion of the concept of rationality and its relation with the theoretical approach used in this research. Thereafter the working concepts of formal and informal institutions will be presented as well as the distinction between institutions and organizations. Following, the concept of business culture will be introduced as well as the role that trust and reputation play in determining the economic environment. Then, the connection between business culture and institutions will be discussed, followed by the relationship between the private use of natural resources and formal and informal institutions.

In the next section of Chapter 2, the theory of institutional emergence and institutional change is presented. Of particular interest is the theory on bargaining power of different groups over institutional rules as a means to obtain an advantage over specific benefits arising from institutional arrangements. Then, it will be discussed how institutions drive collective action through particular enforcement mechanisms, and how they – by structuring economic activity – influence the distribution of benefits between business partners and social groups in the production of collective goods. Next, the concept of path dependence will bring forward the theoretical proposition that institutional emergence and change is subject of a process influenced by historical, social and political circumstances. At the end of the chapter, a model of the interaction between informal and formal institutions will be introduced. This model pays particular attention to the concept of embeddedness of informal institutions in society and thus in formal arrangements, underscoring that formal and informal arrangements act in an intertwined manner rather than separately. This raises again the issue of business culture, and the fact that economic activity embodies not only formal arrangements but informal ones as well. It is posited that economic performance and the achievement of policy goals depends on the 'harmony' existing between formal and informal institutions. The final section addresses the issue of governance, which brings forward the relevance of the interaction between informal and formal arrangements in the achievement of forest policy ends.

Chapter 3 presents some concepts from the field of forest policy on which the research is based. The chapter attempts to bridge theoretical and empirical issues. It begins with the introduction of the concept of forest policy as understood in international and academic circles, which draws on a holistic rather than an isolated forest sector approach. Following, a review of the relationship between policy failures and deforestation and forest degradation is undertaken as well as of some of the measures proposed to attend the problem, which includes an overview of different forest policy instruments (incentives).

In **Section III** (Chapters 4-7) the dissertation's results and discussion are presented. In Chapter 4 a literature review is performed to take a look at the underlying causes of deforestation in Central America, which serves as a background to the case of Costa Rica and the empirical research, followed by the policy issues being addressed in the region as well as the incentive measures used in the forest sector in some Central American Countries.

Chapter 5 focuses on Costa Rica and the recent evolution of formal arrangements in the forest sector and provides an overview of the involved stakeholders and the conflicting issues that arise through recent institutional changes in the forest sector. It explains what is being attempted by the state at the administrative, legal and economic level and a look is taken at the incentive measures that the Costa Rican state has selected to achieve formal forest policy ends. Particular attention is given to the "Payment of Forest Environmental Services", and distributional issues are addressed. The conflict around the participation and performance of governmental organizations and private actors in forestry activities is also presented and discussed.

In Chapter 6 the issue of forest use – from the standpoint of private stakeholders – is addressed. It begins by listing observed informal norms of behavior at the private and public level, and thus it bridges Chapter 6 with the former chapter by highlighting several norms of behavior that in Chapter 5 are observed as interactions between formal and informal arrangements at the governmental and private level. Transaction costs stemming from conventional logging are examined and particular attention is given to the role of information asymmetries and imperfect information as sources of transaction costs.

The discussion in Chapter 7 addresses the research questions and discusses them by contrasting the empirical research with the theoretical framework used throughout this study. A main finding is that despite the changes of the institutional framework, the achievement of formal ends is hampered because private actors receive larger payoffs by complying to informal arrangements that support conventional logging than to formal ones supporting sustainable forest management and forest protection. It is found that the logging industry, by making use of bargaining power is able to maintain the *status quo* of its members despite the formal institutional change. Particularly relevant to this chapter is the discussion of the change of formal arrangements (and the path being followed) related to the model of interaction between informal and formal arrangements in the light of the empirical evidence. It is also discussed how far does this research study complements (or not) the findings of other authors for Costa Rica. Finally it will be discussed how appropriate the theory of the NIE is to address the research questions posed in the study.

I Introduction

1 Problem statement: Conventional logging vs. sustainable forestry. Crisis in the Costa Rican forest sector

This research project aims to contribute to a better understanding of the forest use criteria of private landowners in Costa Rica. Individual – private – forest use decisions are based on economic and personal goals and values such as short-term profit criteria, followed by subsistence, business and personal criteria (Solórzano 1990: 3; Schelhas 1996: 302; Jantzi et al. 1999: 32-33), which are not necessarily short-term.

Throughout the years, the strong support that agriculture and cattle ranching have received from the government as well as from bilateral and multilateral organizations has made forest-based production the less attractive land use alternative from a private point of view (Watson et al. 1998: 57-59), underpinning what has been acknowledged as an "agricultural culture". Thus, public policies skewed against forest-friendly activities have consistently contributed to an undervaluation of the natural resources harbored by forests (e.g. the long term protection of biodiversity, soil and watershed), and have driven to the performance of 'conventional logging' (Solórzano 1990: 3; Peuker 1991: 3; Repetto 1993). Between 1970 and 1990, the country's agricultural frontier was already exhausted – i.e. all the land considered suitable for agriculture was already in use – and 'conventional logging' turned to be the main cause of deforestation (Solórzano 1990: 3; Watson et al. 1998: 37, 57).

Conventional logging is characterized by a passive role of landowners in the process of application for the logging permits and the felling activities, and a corresponding active role of loggers and forest engineers. Due to insufficient financial and technical resources, many landowners cannot harvest their timber on their own, and depend on loggers and forest engineers to exploit their forests commercially (Solórzano 1990: 5; Watson et al. 1998: 22). Conventional logging is also characterized by the use of conventional heavy machinery[1] to construct roads, skid trails and landings, as well as by a lack of pre-harvest procedures like vine-cutting in areas where heavy vines connect tree crowns. The most valuable trees are selectively extracted (creaming), producing severe damages to the total managed area. According to Méndez (no date: 3) between 40-55% of the stand's area is damaged by conventional logging practices. Besides the degradation of wood resources, the damages comprise the loss of species in the undergrowth and soil compression. Timber extraction takes place without any planning of the extraction activities (felling, hauling, log landings) and lacking

[1] Logging in Costa Rica is a seasonal activity, and takes place mainly during the dry season. During the rest of the year this machinery is used for the construction and repair of roads, houses, buildings, etc. For this reason conventional tractors and trucks are used instead of machinery designed specifically for logging.

forest inventories prior or after the felling activities (see Méndez, no date: 3-4; World Bank 2000).

These three groups of private actors (landowners, loggers and forest engineers) build the core group of private actors directly involved in forest use. Even though some forest use strategies of private landowners are well identified – as well as the role that loggers and forest engineers play during forest use – so far the circumstances under which these private stakeholders negotiate and perform forest use are not adequately understood.

The Costa Rican government has recently introduced several institutional reforms aimed at improving the overall management of natural resources. Among these reforms we find efforts to decentralize government's political and administrative functions towards so called 'Conservation Areas' throughout the country, and the introduction of the Payment for Forest Environmental Services (PES). On the basis of these efforts Costa Rica has reached wide international acknowledgement. At the technical level of natural forest management, to perform logging private actors must comply to requisites like presenting – *ex ante* – forest management plans to forest authorities in order to be awarded logging permits. Forest management plans should include pre-harvest inventories, mapping of individual crop trees, use of appropriate felling and bucking techniques, etc.

Nonetheless, today's logging activities still arise large critique from not only environmental organizations and academicians, but also from landowners themselves (as the field research showed), due to large damages caused to stands despite planning of logging activities (i.e. damages are considered the same as those described for conventional logging).[2] The criticism on today's logging activities claims that despite compliance to written requisites, observable improvements of natural forest management are more the exception than the rule. Which means that conventional logging persists despite formal arrangements to improve the management of natural forests. The fact that conventional logging persists despite actual governmental efforts to promote sustainable forestry and forest protection (including those undertaken during the last decades) is a key issue underpinning this research project.

Little is known about how informal institutions drive private forest use, how do they contribute – or not – to the achievement of formal ends pursued by the state, and how institutional arrangements (formal and informal) contribute to the allocation of benefits stemming from conventional logging. An analysis of the actual informal institutional arrangements is necessary to understand their influence on the achievement of formal institutional ends related to the private use of forest resources.

While the rules of 'sustainable forestry' and 'forest protection' are well documented (as they are established and enforced primarily by the State), the set of informal rules driving conventional logging (the behavior codex of private actors and enforcement mechanisms supporting

[2] See also La Hoja, Volúmen 1, Números 1-9, 1998. Barrantes et. al (1999); Campos, et al. (2001).

conventional logging) has not been yet properly documented and analyzed. It is only recently that researchers in Costa Rica have turned their attention to institutional issues of the forest sector (see Richards et al. 1996; Segura et al. 1997; Lindegaard and Segura 1998; Segura and Johnson 1998; Segura and Vargas 1999; Campos et al. 2001), but even though these authors mention some of the difficulties faced by actual state policy strategies, they focus largely on the ongoing negotiations between the private – entrepreneurial – sector and the government. The standpoint of individual private landowners is only vaguely included.[3] Hence, existing research has largely not addressed the relationship between formal and informal arrangements driving private forest use. In general, research on the interaction between informal and formal institutions is acknowledged to be scarce (Nee 1998a: 3; Mummert 1999: 3-4).

Based on these insights this study addresses the issue of how informal institutions in Costa Rica drive private forest use and how they are linked with formal ends (sustainable natural forest management and forest protection).

1.1 Objectives and research questions

The main goal of this research is to contribute to the understanding of how informal institutions influence the achievement of formal forest policy objectives in Costa Rica. Two objectives have been formulated for this matter:

1. Documentation and analysis of informal institutions relevant for the Costa Rican forest sector, and their relationship towards formal ends.
2. Assess the potential of recent formal institutional reforms to successfully promote sustainable forest management and protection.

The main research questions focus on:

1. What are the rules, behavior codex and enforcement mechanisms of stakeholder groups involved in conventional logging?
2. Which are the dominant objectives influencing private landowners' forest use decisions?
3. How do informal arrangements support the stability of conventional logging in opposition to formal arrangements?
4. How do informal arrangements influence the achievement of formal forest policy goals (sustainable forest management and forest protection)?
5. How does the institutional framework (formal and informal) structures benefit distribution among private actors?

[3] For example, Campos et al. (2001) performed their research on illegal logging almost without landowner-interviews.

1.2 Methodology and methods

1.2.1 Research design

In this research a qualitative approach is used to answer the research questions, which focus largely on human economic behavior. For this matter a case study is built focusing on how recent institutional changes influence local private forest use. The case study is enriched by including the general discussion at the national level on the recent formal institutional changes. This qualitative approach is combined with quantitative methods that complement and illustrate the issues discussed. The detailed description of the quantitative methods used is found at the beginning of each exercise in Chapters 5 and 6.

This research study aims to fulfill the following criteria of (well done) case studies:[4]

Criteria	Research tactic	Research phase in which the tactic is used
Construct validity	Use of multiple sources of evidence	Data collection
Reliability	Use research protocol	Data collection
	Develop research data base	Data collection
Internal validity	Do pattern matching	Data analysis
	Do explanation building	Data analysis
External validity	Use replication logic	Research design

Source: Adapted from Yin (1994: 33)

Construct validity relates to the extent to which inferences can be made from the empirical research to the theoretical constructs on which the analysis is based (Yin, R., 1994: 33-34; Kvale, S. 1996: 240; Trochim 2000). In this regard, multiple sources of evidence are used throughout the research study. Reliability refers to the characteristic inherent to a scientific research that if the operations of the study – like the data collection procedures, and the same theoretical framework is used – are repeated, similar results shall be obtained (Yin 1994). Internal validity refers to the establishment of causal relationships that show that certain conditions guide to certain outcomes (Yin, 1994, Trochim 2000). External validity refers to the degree to which the conclusions obtained in the research study can be generalized to other persons and places (Trochim 2000).

This study departs from the example of the Central American region where, following Segura et al. (1997), efforts are being undertaken to improve private forest use by means of institutional arrangements that seek to enhance the different values of forest resources. The research study is performed in Costa Rica, a country that regionally plays a pioneering role in the reform of the institutional framework of the forest sector.

[4] See also Kvale (1996: 237).

Segura et al. (1997a) and Watson et al. (1998) agree that the remaining areas of primary forests in private hands in Costa Rica are concentrated in three regions: the Osa peninsula, the northern zone of the country and the lowlands of the Talamanca mountain chain. Segura et al. (1997a: 102) state that approximately 60% of Costa Rica's remaining primary forest area is located in those three regions and the other 40% is distributed in small areas throughout the country. These three primary forest areas are undergoing a process of deforestation (Solórzano 1990: 6; Segura et al. 1997a: 102; Watson et al. 1998: 9-12). The field research of this research study is performed in the Osa peninsula (see Map 2).

The reasons that led me to choose the Osa peninsula as the research area are:

1. The area is considered – together with the Talamanca mountain chain and the Caribbean – one of the best areas in the country for logging due to the availability of many rare and precious timber species.
2. The Osa has been a source of ongoing debate between landowners, loggers, the government and environmentalists over the area's suitability for logging.
3. The area harbors the last tropical primary rain forest of the Pacific coast of Central America and is one of the areas with highest biodiversity and endemism of the country (Gottfried et al. 1994; Barrantes et al. 1999), which makes it a particularly sensitive area concerning the management of natural resources.

At the same time, the Osa peninsula is comparable to other areas of the country with primary forests in several ways. Similar to the Talamanca mountain range and the Caribbean, the area is of difficult access, possesses poor infrastructure and scarce social services like health and education. Many farmers live in conditions of poverty,[5] and the involvement of NGOs and similar non-profit organizations in the management of forest resources is rather weak. Research on topics similar to those analyzed in this research study is also scarce in areas like the Talamanca mountain range or other similar areas.[6]

---

[5] On poverty see Deutsche Bischofskonferenz (1997: 13-17) and Wunder (2001: 2).

[6] See Richards et al. (1996) for a study on the result of the decentralization process in the Area de Conservación Tortuguero (ACTO) and the Area de Conservación Huetar Norte (ACA-HN).

Map 1. Costa Rica, research area

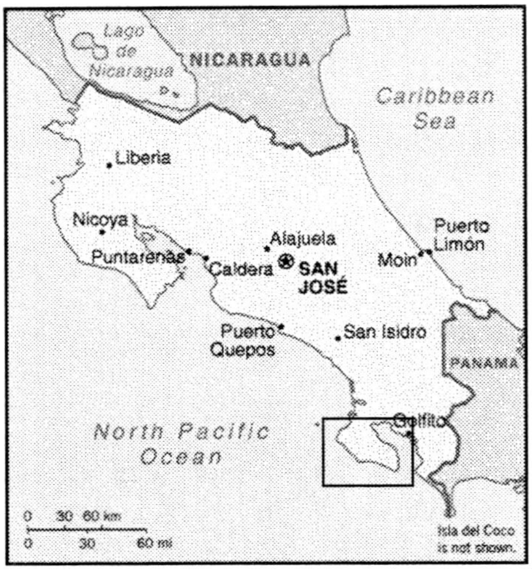

Source: http://www.lib.utexas.edu/maps/americas/costa_rica_sm97.gif

Map 2. Visited locations in the Osa peninsula

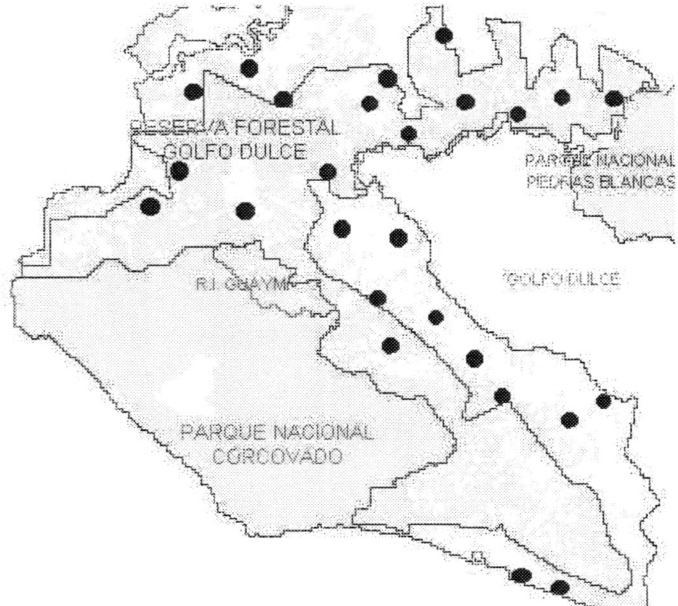

Source: Fundación Cecropia. Dots: own approximation

For data collection a multi-stakeholder approach is applied. This research includes an analysis of the standpoints of experts, landowners, loggers, forest engineers, government officials, and environmentalists concerning private forest use and forest policy objectives.[7] I use a multi-stakeholder approach based on two reasons, first because the decisions and points of view of private landowners can be better understood when the agents surrounding them are included in the analysis, and second, because the achievement of forest policy objectives can be better understood when the main actors are conceived as part of a larger picture. This has the advantage of allowing an integral analysis, instead of a partial one.

The analysis performed in this research study is based on the theory of the New Institutional Economics (NIE). This theory has the advantage of allowing the researcher to integrate socioeconomic and political aspects influencing private decision making.

1.2.2 Methods of data collection

Following Vayda (1996), human actions (behavior) and their effect on the environment should be analyzed establishing causal relations rather than through the assumption of established conceptualizations of human behavior. For that matter I used structured and semi-structured interviews for this research. "*The research interview is based on the conversations of daily life and is a professional conversation,...,* its *purpose is to obtain descriptions of the life world of the interviewee with respect to interpreting the meaning of the described phenomena*" (Kvale, 1996: 5-6).

The members of the different groups were interviewed using convergent lines of inquiry to obtain their points of view on the same issues. Prior to each interview I introduced myself formally to the interviewee and explained briefly the purpose of the interview. The interviewees were assured that the interview has a confidential character, and that their names would neither be mentioned in the study nor revealed to others, unless they explicitly allowed me to do so.

An interview method applied repeatedly was '*condensation of meaning*' to summarize the information obtained from the different questions. Here, the essence of the answers related to the research question were spoken back to the interviewee to confirm the veracity of the interpretation. This kind of dialog continued until there was only one possible interpretation/answer to the research topic being discussed (see Kvale, 1996: 189,190).

Concerning strategic answers, I assume that the interviewees did tell what they think. Firstly, because, I explained to them clearly that I am an independent researcher and the purpose of the research, which is not linked to any particular organization in the country. Therefore, it should have been clear to them that it is unlikely that they might obtain something specific from answering the questions in one form or another. This way, the incentive to behave

---

[7] Robertson (2000) uses a similar approach and calls it multi-layered.

strategically during the interview was reduced. Second, the method of condensed meaning allows to identify contradicting answers and these could be cleared during the conversation.

Short structured expert interviews were also performed via e-mail and fax.

Additional methods I used during the field research are:

Notes taken during the interview as a result of the method of condensation of meaning.

A *memory protocol* was used to complete the notes that could not be taken during the interviews on particularly interesting comments given by the interviewees. Such notes were taken immediately after the interview to reduce the danger of forgetting what was said. An average of 30 minutes were devoted to summarize the interview.

Direct observations were concentrated on issues such as farm/house characteristics, attitude of the interviewee towards particular themes, etc. These were written down after the interview was performed in combination with the *memory protocol.*

A *research logbook* was kept to summarize the events/impressions of the day and of the week that appeared of particular relevance to the research questions addressed on the field.

Many interviews were *taped.* This includes the expert interviews (all), key informers (3), forest engineers (2), government officials (2). Even though I transcribed many of the interviews (all those marked with the symbol "*" below) for analysis, the method I used more intensively to analyze the interviews was a *repeated hearing* of the tapes so as to capture the nuances that a live conservation has – and that are lost during the transcription.[8] I also attended – and taped – three different public events where the points of view of several NGOs, the government and landowners were brought forward. The records of these events were also subject of repeated hearings.

Additional to the interviews, other sources of evidence comprise primary and secondary literature and data[9] including the revision of newspapers and unpublished documents and data from governmental organizations and NGOs.

1.2.3 Methodological details to the interviews

The field research is divided in two stages. The first field research was performed between November 1999 and April 2000. During this research phase expert interviews were performed. The expert interviews served to identify the research area and to identify relevant issues of the forest policy in the country as well as to identify relevant stakeholders. A pre-study was performed during this stage in the research area (the Osa peninsula) between

[8] See Kvale (1996: 160-166).

[9] Primary literature refers to those publications written by academicians for academicians, while secondary literature is written for a general audience. Secondary data refers to the data that the researcher has not collected personally, that is, that were collected by others for a different problem from the one being analyzed.

February and March 2000. The pre-study included 33 test interviews with landowners. The results of the test interview helped to improve the interview guidelines and rearrange them to better focus on the research questions during the next phase. The second field research was performed between March and May 2001.

The members of the interviewed groups comprise experts, landowners, loggers, forest engineers, government officials (and government functionaries[10]), representatives of NGOs and environmentalists. *Structured interviews* were used mainly with landowners, loggers and forest engineers, whereas *semi-structured* interviews were used with experts, government officials, representatives of NGOs and environmentalists.

- **Experts**. The interviewed experts comprise members of academic and research organizations, members of NGOs, and the representative of a governmental organization. They were selected following two criteria. First, after revised publications on topics relevant for this research. Second, after the recommendation of the experts themselves about others who could give further insights about the discussed issues. Experts were interviewed during the first and the second stage of the field research. The interview guidelines were adapted to the expertise of the individual interviewees, but always keeping a convergent line of questioning. The interviewed experts belong to the following organizations:

Academic and research organizations

- Centro Agronómico Tropical de Investigación y Enseñanza (CATIE): Manuel Gómez (e-mail interview).
- Centro Científico Tropical (CCT): Vicente Watson and Raúl Solórzano (former executive director of SINAC). *
- Institut für Forstökonomie, Forstwissenschaftliche Fakultät der Albert-Ludwigs-Universität Freiburg: Dr. Guillermo Navarro.
- Universidad de Costa Rica. Facultad de Biología: Dr. Jorge Lobo and Dr. Mauricio Quesada (currently researcher at UNAM).*
- Universidad Nacional. Centro Internacional de Política Económica y Desarrollo Sostenible: Dr. Olman Segura. *

Non-governmental organizations

- Cooperación en los Sectores Forestal y Maderero (COSEFORMA): Guillermo Arias Murillo, national coordinator. *

[10] There is a substantial difference between a government official and a government functionary. The government officials have a higher status due to which they cannot be dismissed. A government functionary can be dismissed.

- Fundación Cecropia: Eric *Russman*, ex-executive director and Hector González, executive director. *
- Fundación de Desarrollo de la Coordillera Volcánica Central (FUNDECOR): Ing. Pedro González, regional director, Sarapiquí. *
- Junta Nacional Forestal Campesina (JUNAFORCA): Felipe *Vega*, executive director. *
- Red de Reservas Naturales Privadas: Marta Marín, president. *

Governmental Organizations

- Fondo Nacional de Financiamiento Forestal (FONAFIFO): Ing. Jorge Mario Rodríguez Z., executive director. *

– **Landowners**: The main requisite for a landowner to qualify as an interviewee was the availability of forest within his/her property. During the first stage I chose the interviewees (33) systematically by following the main road between Puerto Jiménez and Mogos (the distance between these two places is approximately 70km) and along secondary and tertiary roads branching off this main road in distances up to 30 km. The interviewees were selected following distance intervals of more or less 5km, and, in the case where there was no house in sight I drove further until a house was found. An interview was only conducted if the owner of the house also owned a forest, if not the next house was visited and so on. When necessary, landowners were also reached by foot (in walking distances that lasted – in one occasion – up to one hour). During the second field research I envisaged to interview all the landowners who had an approved management plan in 1999. Of this group comprising 63 landowners, 44 interviews were completed. Map 2 depicts the visited locations. These locations coincide with those visited during the first stage. The interviews during this second visit lasted between 40 and 60 minutes.

The landowner interviews were conducted using a questionnaire, which is divided in two parts. The first part is oriented to gather demographic, social and economic data to elaborate a socioeconomic profile of the landowners. The second part of the interviews addresses qualitative aspects of forest use, focussing on the motivations of the landowner to set up and implement a forest management plan in his/her property (why questions). Central issues were initiation of a management plan, partners of negotiation, and his expectations concerning the performance of conventional logging in his/her property.

– **Loggers**. Loggers were selected after the information given by landowners on who performed the management plan, hence all of them have been involved in logging activities in the Osa. Eight loggers were interviewed. All of them live outside the peninsula. The loggers I interviewed in their offices in San Jose, Cartago, Río Claro and Paso Canoas did not have anything against notes being taken during the interview, though they did not wish to be recorded. The rest – approached mainly on the field at the log landings – had an awkward attitude towards notes being taken, so I refrained from doing so while I talked to them. In these cases I used a *memory protocol* only.

- **Forest engineers**. Like in the case of loggers, forest engineers were selected according to their partake in the elaboration of forest management plans in the Osa during the same year. Five forest engineers were interviewed and two allowed the interview to be recorded. One forest engineer did not wish to be recorded so I took notes during the interview. Two did not wish that notes were taken in which case I used a *memory protocol*. Originally I wished to interview eight, but three did not wish to give an interview.

With loggers and forest engineers the following issues were discussed: How did they become engaged in the elaboration/execution of management plans? Is he (logger or forest engineer) engaged in other productive activities? Under what conditions do they negotiate with the landowners? Who is in charge of planning and monitoring the activities foreseen in management plans? Why/Why not?

- **Government officials**.
  - Ministerio de Recursos Naturales, Energía y Minas Lic. Elisabeth Odio Benito, 1[era] (ex-) Vice-Presidenta de la República y (ex-) Ministra del Ambiente (fax interview). The purpose of the interview with the minister was to clear the reasons behind the governmental decision of changing formal requisites for landowners to access logging permits. It was pursued to perform a live interview, but the minister did not have enough time and refrained from giving an appointment, but she acceded to answer the interview if sent by fax. The questions were answered by a subordinate in her name.
  - ACOSA's sub-regional director, Luis Barquero. The purpose of the interview with Mr. Barquero was to gain an overview of the problems that ACOSA is actually facing, including the lack of material and human resources and how does this affect the performance of ACOSA regarding the enforcement of governmental forestry guidelines. Mr. Barquero allowed the interview to be recorded.
- **Government functionaries**. The main criteria to select the interviewees was that they were involved in the approval and/or monitoring of management plans, hence of logging activities. Most were reluctant to give an interview, that is, the quality of the conversation was not good. Three ACOSA functionaries provided good interviews though. One of them allowed me to tape the interview but wished to remain anonymous. The other two were awkward towards notes being taken, in which case I used a *memory protocol*. All of them provided 'insider' information to the research area and played a valuable role for this research as key informers.
- **Environmentalists**. Four members of the COVIRENA group were interviewed. The criteria for their selection was that they either live in the area or were active in the

monitoring of logging activities in the Osa. One allowed the interview to be recorded, whereas one allowed notes to be taken. The other two were awkward towards both methods, so I used a *memory protocol.*

1.2.4 Data analysis

Using the methods described above the research data base was created, which enabled to trace causal relations, determine patterns of behavior and assess how the stakeholders relate to one another.

To allow the analysis of the landowner interviews the data were broken down in keywords following the research protocol. I summarized this data in a matrix-like table that allowed pattern matching within stakeholders. These patterns are shown in the chapters below where the empirical data is presented and analyzed.

The information obtained from the second part of the landowner interviews was cross-checked with the interviews performed with the loggers and forest engineers, government functionaries and officials and COVIRENA to identify causal relationships driving forest use. The role of landowners, loggers, forest engineers, COVIRENA and governmental organizations in the process leading to – and during – logging was determined this way. Of particular interest was to establish if the arguments of the landowners coincided or diverged from those given by loggers and forest engineers.

The data analysis and conclusions drawn are based on the theoretical propositions of the theory of New Institutional Economics (NIE).

At the end of this document the main findings of this research study are discussed in comparison with the results of other studies performed in Costa Rica. The thesis is concluded with an assessment of the appropriateness of the theory of the NIE to tackle the issues addressed in this research study.

II Theoretical Framework

2 Institutions

2.1 Chapter overview

The theoretical framework on which this research is based pertains largely to the theory of the new institutional economics (NIE). A salient characteristic of this theory is that it breaks with the omniscient individual assumed in the classical and neoclassical economics, the 'homo economicus'. In its place, a common human being is brought into play. Despite this fact, the NIE still posits that individuals will tend to act rationally – but still, limited by their own knowledge. Thus, the NIE builds further on the concept of rationality, and assumes that institutions provide information for individuals to make decisions. For this reason, this chapter begins with an explanation of the concept of rationality.

The following section introduces the reader to the formal concept of institutions. The basic definitions are presented on which the theoretical framework is built. These definitions include – besides that of formal and informal institutions – organizations, and business culture. Business culture is an important concept because we deal with it everyday in economic activity, and it contributes thus to the way institutions evolve. This concept shall be helpful to explain the relationships prevailing between business partners analyzed in this research.

Institutional emergence, institutional change, collective action and path dependence are the subjects of the following sections. This concepts should provide the instruments to explain why the institutions ruling forest use in Costa Rica have taken the form they have. To support such an explanation one needs a theoretical basis that explains how institutions emerge and change. Institutions ruling the use of natural resources – like those ruling private forest use – aim at the provision of specific goods and services. The institutions addressed in this research aim at the provision of collective goods that stem from natural forests, and that are, in one way or another, affected or enhanced by the use that private actors give to such resources, hence the problem of collective action is also addressed. The NIE posits that institutional change does not take place by chance, but evolves continually following a path of change influenced mainly by historical, social and economic conditions.

The use that private actors give to forest resources is largely a result of the institutional framework ruling the use of such resources. This institutional framework comprises formal and informal institutional arrangements. For this reason, the relationship suggested in the theory of the NIE between formal and informal institutions will be addressed by means of a model. The final section addresses the issue of governance, which brings forward the relevance of the interaction between informal and formal arrangements in the achievement of forest policy ends, especially towards the management of collective goods.

2.2 Rationality

According to the Webster's Dictionary, rationality means the quality or state of being rational, and to be rational means to have reason or understanding.

Maybe one of the most influential conceptions of rationality in economic theory (if not the most influential) is the neoclassical postulate of rational – satisfaction, and benefit maximizing – agents. According to this model of rationality, a rational economic agent is able to discern between all the possible alternatives available to him and to choose those that maximize his satisfaction (utility, profit), implying that he has an exact knowledge of the world surrounding him, and that he is aware of the future consequences of his actual choices. Hence, according to this model, any economic agent is bound to commit no mistakes, as he is provided with a thinking capacity through which he always makes the best of all possible decisions, i.e. the transaction costs of exchange are zero and thus institutions become irrelevant (North 1995). To make this possible, the assumption must be made that the individual's preference function provides him with an ordinal measure of utility so that he can order the different available alternatives according to the amount of satisfaction they provide. Thus, the individual's preference function must be so that preferences are reflexive, transitive and complete. Lets elaborate some basic thoughts on these qualities. Lets assume a landowner with a choice between three different forest products *x*, *y*, and *z*, and imagine that one of these goods is timber, the other is a non-timber forest product, and the third is watershed protection. Which is which is not relevant at this moment. The landowner's preference function is

1. reflexive if $x \leq x$, i.e. two consumption goods 'x' are considered the same by the landowner;
2. transitive if (for the choice between three goods) $x \geq y \geq z \Rightarrow x \geq z$;
3. complete if (i) $x \geq y$, (ii) $y \geq x$, (iii) $x \geq y$ and $y \geq x$, which means that the landowner is indifferent between *x* and *y*.

Actually, we – human beings – have neither an exact knowledge of all the facts and alternatives available to us, nor do we possess a thinking structure – nor the thinking ability – to effectively maximize our utility every time we choose between available alternatives, even though we might wish to (Williamson 1984). As a matter of fact, our attention can only take care of a few problems at a time. Other than assumed in neoclassical economics, individuals do not have a complete overview of the available alternatives to them and they cannot always decide between 'comparable' alternatives and are mostly not aware of the consequences that a particular decision may have for them in the future. This means that preferences need be neither reflexive, nor transitive, nor complete (Elster 1989a: 1-35; Simon [1983] 1993: 22-33). We discriminate the information that we perceive from our surrounding environment and establish subjectively what is important to us and what is not. Based on that election process we decide what to do. The information and knowledge we possess about those things within our range of interest is limited, therefore we decide and make choices on the basis of limited knowledge and information: we decide on bound rationality (Simon [1983] 1993).

Bound rationality implies that we may not be optimizing our utility at all, and it cannot even guarantee for the consistency of our decisions. For example, if there were two possible alternatives to choose from, x and y (with y being the best of them), but we know more about x than about y, it is likely that we might decide ourselves for x even though y was the best option. Very rarely are we aware of all the implications that our present decisions will have in the future. This is due to the fact that the future is always uncertain, therefore, a decision that we make today – and that we consider to be the best one – might prove flaw in the future. Thus, had we known what was coming our way, we may have not taken such a decision. Stock markets are probably the best example of this. An environmentally degraded location due to human action is another example. Because individuals are rationally bounded and information is costly to obtain, transaction costs arise (Sen and van Kooten 2001: 18-19). Furthermore, because information is asymmetrically distributed, individuals have an incentive to act opportunistically, i.e., in their own self interest with guile. Opportunistic behavior can manifest in many forms including cheating, lying and stealing, and can of course be observed in much more subtle forms like the incomplete and/or distorted disclosure of information to obtain an advantage in an economic transaction (Williamson 1984: 198-9). Opportunism is thus an element that increases uncertainty in economic transactions. Therefore, bound rationality and opportunistic behavior are primal background elements of why institutions matter.

2.3 Institutions: concepts and definitions

Institutions are ubiquitous in social life. Institutions are humanly devised rules that constrain/structure human interactions (social, economic and political) in specific ways through the provision of information and incentives to encourage compliance to institutional ends or discourage individuals from not complying to them (Elster 1989: 148; North 1990; Knight 1992: 56). An institution requires two basic conditions for its functioning. First, the set of rules is shared by the members of the relevant groups. Second, it is endowed with enforcement mechanisms applied by either third parties – like the state – or by group members through social control mechanisms (Knight 1992: 2-3, 54, 68).

Formal institutions, like Forest Laws and regulations, are enforced by the state to guarantee that forest users – landowners, loggers, private enterprises, cooperatives etc. – will comply to them. Informal institutions – social conventions, norms of behavior and self-imposed codes of conduct – are rather self enforcing, i.e., there is no particular organization or authority to make sure that group members will follow them – say, rules of etiquette, friendship or respect for elder people, and conceptions through which private agents perceive and use forest resources. Hence the enforcement of informal institutions is a by-product of social interaction and is endogenous to the group (Knight 1992: 54; Khan 1995: 76; Eisenberg 1999). But an institution need not be strictly formal or informal. Actually many institutions comprise characteristics of both (Knight 1992: 3, 59), which is precisely the case of economic activity driving the use of natural resources.

What distinguishes institutions from organizations? Institutions are the "rules of the game" and organizations are the "players". Organizations are groups (political, religious, business, social or educational) created with the intention of achieving particular objectives within a given institutional framework, and organizations – through the constant pursuance of goal achievement – are themselves relevant agents of institutional change (North 1998). As organizations exist to take advantage of the opportunities offered by the institutional framework, institutions are useful if they encourage cooperation between the members of organizations in order to achieve their desired ends, and to produce cooperation, institutions must reduce uncertainty. Even though uncertainty is always present in any economic activity, some business environments can be considered less uncertain than others, depending on several factors, like the information available to trading partners, and the reliability of the business agreements between them. In short, uncertainty is strongly related to the business culture prevailing in a specific economic environment.

A basic theoretical assumption throughout this research is that the decisions private actors make regarding the use of natural resources – like forest resources – do not take place in a social vacuum, but within a particular social context. Culture is here understood as "*the transmission from one generation to the next, via teaching and imitation, of knowledge, values, and other factors that influence behavior. Culture provides a language-based conceptual framework for encoding and interpreting the information that the senses are presenting to the brain.*" (North 1990: 37).[11] The values that society assigns to natural resources are directly related to the uses (productive, recreational, religious, etc.) given to them, and such values are directly influenced by culture. This means that culture actively contributes to form the set of institutional and social-historical influences that determine individual as well as collective economic behavior (Zafirovski 2001: 69-71). Therefore, not only resource endowments, but also culture plays a dynamic role in determining how a society values and uses its forest resources. Hence culture will also contribute heavily to how landowners decide to use such resources. Here the intention is not to draw a line between culture and economic activity, but since cultural values influence and shape all – formal and informal – institutional arrangements in society (Sen and van Kooten 2001; 11), our attention must turn to the fact that both – culture and economic activity – affect the use of forest resources in an intertwined manner (Nee 1998a; OECD 1999; Humphrey and Hugh-Jones 1992: 13, cited in Zafirovsky 2001: 73).

Culture in everyday economic activity plays a fundamental role, as it helps actors to develop trust in their business partners and thus to build stable expectations and relations. The building

[11] See also North (1995: 18) and Greif (1998: 78).

of expectations in economic transactions is the product of a dynamic process based on past and present experiences. Therefore successful (negative) experiences will contribute to increase (decrease) the level of trust in the economic environment and will have a positive (negative) effect on the reputation of the actors participating in ongoing exchanges, which will positively (negatively) stimulate economic activity (Hardin 1982: 214; Casson 1991: 3-23). Thus trust and reputation are essential components of business culture (Robinson [1970] 1975: 24; Casson 1991: 170-172; Nee and Ingram 1998: 23). They are directly related to the emergence of transaction costs. Since information in economic transactions is costly to obtain, information asymmetry and uncertainty influence the credibility of transaction agreements and difficult their enforcement. In view of this, different business cultures imply differences in the credibility of business agreements and so the costs of transacting will vary accordingly (Nee 1998a). In this regard, trust and reputation have public good characteristics because those participating in economic transactions are bound to obtain information from others with previous experiences with specific groups and/or firms, and based on this information expectations on potential business transactions are built. But by business culture is not meant a monolithic entity, because society comprises different groups and firms with different interests, and each one is prone to develop its own characteristics, which can be similar or deviate from one another (Williamson 1998). Thus some groups or firms will have a reputation of being more reliable/trustworthy than others and will be able to develop more stable business relationships than others (Casson 1991: 225-237).

2.4 The evolution of institutions

2.4.1 Institutional emergence and institutional change

A basic theoretical proposition underpinning this research is that – despite the general assumption that formal and informal institutions facilitate the maximization of the aggregate welfare of the members of a group by enabling cooperation to solve social dilemmas regarding the provision of collective goods (Elster 1989: 153; Nee 1998a), optimal social outcomes are not necessarily always obtained, hence sub optimal outcomes are possible and can even persist over long periods of time (North 1989: 667; Knight 1992: 10).

In the theory of NIE it is posited that people create institutions to reduce uncertainty in social interaction and facilitate cooperation (North 1990; Bates 1995: 34). In the case of collective goods, the emergence of formal institutions is conceptualized as an effort to overcome the problem of collective action, where institutions are created to resolve recurring problems of cooperation in society, therefore formal institutions emerge underpinned by the intention of enabling cooperation between different actors and produce specific social outcomes (Elster 1989: 153-154). Toye (1995: 63) adds that even though this is the main goal of the creation of institutions, it is not always achieved.

In this regard, it is considered that institutions that structure economic and political organization are the result of the effort of specific groups oriented to restrict and guide – to their advantage – the actions of other groups with whom they interrelate (Stinchcombe 1986: 156; Knight 1992: 126-127; North 1995: 20). This brings forward the issue that institutions and their socioeconomic outcomes are the result of the social conflict between actors competing over particular objectives and the distribution of specific benefits. In this regard formal institutions are less the result of casualty and more the result of the distribution of political power between different groups in society (Khan 1995).[12]

Institutions can have different origins. First, they can emerge from custom, that is, everyday accepted social norms of behavior (Eisenberg 1999). Second, they can be designed intentionally. Third, they can emerge as the unintentional result of the pursuit over strategic advantage. The basic point is that the development of formal and informal institutional rules is a means to an end (Knight 1992: 126). A complementary condition is that enforcement mechanisms are developed to induce compliance. By definition, actors will not dedicate efforts to create an institution if the costs of doing so are larger than the expected benefits (Heckathorn 1988: 549, 553; Knight 1992: 43). Not only people and organizations will try to design – or participate in – institutions that give them advantage over others, but given the fact that the creation of institutional arrangements involves a transaction cost, the cost of institutional development can significantly affect the final welfare outcomes of such institutional arrangements (Hardin 1982: 20-22; Tuomela 1992: 165). In small groups, these costs are related to the costs of information and those of drafting and enforcing contracts (Knight 1992: 43). An example of this is the establishment of a logging contract between a logging firm – or individual logger – and a landowner. In larger groups like governmental organizations, the high transaction costs of collective action (for example, in relation to particular uses of forest resources) are one of the main reasons why group members cannot agree on new rules to improve the group's welfare (Eggertsson 1990: 214).

Informal institutions arise first, through the regular repetition and adoption of behavioral patterns by groups that end up being norms, and second, when the group members are ready to punish those not complying to those norms (Knight 1992: 131; Eisenberg 1999: 8). Informal institutions are intrinsic to social life as they provide the norms through which social interaction takes place like norms of courtesy, friendship, and loyalty, but – as explained for business culture – they can also determine specific ways of doing business and in this specific regard they contribute to build expectations on both social and economic exchange (Knight 1992: 56-58).

Some informal institutions may – apparently – not follow particular ends, like rules of etiquette, of which Elster (1989: 121) says that "*rules of etiquette, norms of dress and the like do not seem to have any useful consequences. On the contrary, the rigid grip of these norms on the mind seems to create a great deal of pointless misery*". He acknowledges though the argument that norms of dressing can contribute to confirm one's identity in social groups,

[12] This brings us to the issue of bargaining power over institutional design, which will be addressed below.

even though many can adopt a particular form of dressing to try make others believe they 'belong'.

Formal institutions designed to structure social interaction aim mostly to achieve particular tasks, like bringing the post, organize firms and structure trade. Task oriented institutions[13] restrain the behavioral possibilities of individuals considerably, because they describe the tasks they must perform in order to accomplish specific ends.[14] Institutions designed to achieve specific tasks concerning the use of forest resources are normally the rules within organizations (Mummert 1999: 6).

It is due to the fact that institutions structure social interaction that they also reduce uncertainty and enhance group performance, because within a defined set of rules, actors know what to expect from particular forms of exchange – either social, political or economic – (Knight 1992: 24-25, 55-58; Nee and Ingram 1998: 19; Nee 1998a). Institutions – formal and informal – provide information. Nonetheless, in the specific case of formal institutions, they need not be Pareto-efficient in the sense that they will always minimize transaction costs and contribute to a fair distribution of benefits among different economic agents, because formal institutional arrangements can be the product of specific groups trying to maintain their own private well being (North 1990: 5-6, 48; 1995: 18, 20; Toye 1995: 54, 61,64). But the fact that those obtaining the larger shares of exchange have a stake in designing institutions to their own advantage does not mean that institutional design reflects exactly the preferences of those particular groups, rather, the final form of institutional arrangements is the product of the conflict of interests between the involved actors and their bargaining power (Knight 1992: 27).

While some formal institutions determine what one is able to do, other institutions – by embedding transactions in governance structures designed to mitigate hazards intrinsic to transactions – create the necessary conditions for individuals to undertake enterprises from which they would otherwise refrain (Williamson 1998). Contracts are a good example of this. The fact that contracts represent a binding promise between business partners encourages individuals to engage in exchanges that otherwise they would not perform due to the risk of being swindled (Elster 1989: 148). Hence contracts are a kind of formal institution that, through the establishment of explicit liabilities, provide incentives and sanctions to the involved actors to comply to the contractual terms. Nonetheless, contracts alone do not provide total security to an exchange since the reliability of any contractual transaction

[13] This expression is found in Mummert (1999).

[14] According to Marshall (1983: 188, cited in Mummert, 1999: 5) rules penalize, prohibit, require, obligate, prescribe, inform, guide, empower, permit, license, enable, facilitate, entitle, command, define, designate, constitute, distribute, describe, exempt and identify.

depends on the level of trust between the partners and the effectiveness of the monitoring and sanctioning mechanisms supporting the agreement (Bates 1995: 32, 41).[15]

Even though formal institutions are designed to achieve specific ends, the fact is that institutional design seldom renders the exact results as originally intended; first, agents cannot foresee the future consequences of their present actions, second outcomes usually diverge from original intentions because the individuals designing institutional arrangements have limited capabilities to fully address the complexity of the problems to be solved. In this regard it is considered that institutional emergence and change has mostly unintended consequences in the long run (Elster 1989: 91-101; North 1989: 667). Knight (1992: 44-47) contends that actors designing institutions are confronted with several sources of uncertainty about the possible outcomes of institutional design. The first source is the possible array of the available institutional designs of which they can make use. The second source of uncertainty is the actual consequences of their present choices. The third source is related to the future consequences of the institutional choices made today.[16] Uncertainty here should be understood as "*a condition wherein one cannot ascertain the probability of an event and therefore cannot arrive at a way of insuring against such an occurrence*" (North 1990: 126). Even though uncertainty is ubiquitous, if we admit that institutional design is performed (and lobbied) by those agents prone to obtain the larger profit share from exchange, we can further theorize that those agents also have better information and knowledge to influence institutional design and change to their advantage than other agents with no experience or less knowledge of the issues at stake (North 1990: 74-8). As a result, while all the agents are likely to bear desired as well as undesired consequences of institutional design, probably the distribution of positive as well as negative outcomes will be asymmetric.

2.4.2 Institutional design and bargaining power

If one considers that individuals and/or groups have bargaining power over institutional design and change, it follows that some actors are more powerful than others and are willing to use this power consciously (Harsanyi 1962). Thus, the reason why it is contended that institutional arrangements need not lead to Pareto optimums is that the more powerful can make the less powerful comply to a set of rules and so they will be better off at the cost of the rest. In this regard, the less powerful comply to the rules not because they agreed to them, but because they have no other choice. Actors can constrain the actions of others if they can affect their expectations of what they are going to do in a particular situation (North 1990: 48; Knight 1992: 126-127).

---

[15] The uncertainty related to the compliance of contracts is known as the principal-agent problem, and will be discussed below with more detail.

[16] Knight (1992: 45) adds a fourth and fifth sources of uncertainty which are "*(4) the future institutional alternatives available to them, and (5) their future preferences regarding future alternatives and outcomes.*" While these sources of uncertainty cannot be denied, it should also be acknowledged that the future is by definition uncertain, which gives these sources a tautological character.

Bargaining over – formal and informal – rules[17] means that actors will negotiate over specific payoffs. Therefore, when a particular strategy or course of action is bound to provide certain advantageous payoff for an actor 'A', it is said that A has a greater bargaining power than actor 'B' if A can effectively constrain the alternatives available to B, hence A is bound to obtain the greater payoff from bargaining over rules (Elster 1989: 150; Knight 1992: 131-132; Knight and Ensminger 1998: 107). Bargaining power will be now illustrated following Knight's (1992: 129) two-person bargaining game:

		B: L	B: R
A	L	Δ_A , Δ_B	x_A , $x_B+\varepsilon_B$
	R	$x_A+\varepsilon_A$, x_B	Δ_A , Δ_B

In this two person game, if $\Delta_{AB}<x$, the two equilibrium outcomes that solve the bargaining game are the strategy combinations L,R and R,L. The value 'Δ_{AB}' represents the payoff (loss) that the players receive if they fail to achieve one of the equilibrium outcomes. Also, $\varepsilon_{A,B}>0$, where 'ε' represents the distributional advantage accruing to either one of the actors when a specific equilibrium outcome is chosen. Of course, the goal of each actor is to achieve 'ε'. From this example it follows that bargaining asymmetry exists in either case:

$$\Delta_A < \Delta_B \text{ or } \Delta_A > \Delta_B$$

This means that A will have a bargaining advantage if B has more to loose than A if no agreement is reached. Likewise, B will have more bargaining power if A stands to loose more than B from a breakdown of the negotiations. In the end, bargaining power can be defined as a superiority in resource endowments (Knight and Ensminger 1998: 106).

Since human history is a story of persons and groups with unequal bargaining strength pursuing to maximize their own well being, there is no reason to believe that – tangible and intangible – resources are distributed symmetrically (North 1990: 134). Now, when actors bargain over particular rules that will determine benefit distributions, their bargaining power will basically depend on the resource asymmetries between them, their credibility, their aversion towards risk and their time preference.

---

[17] Knight (1992: 126-70) elaborates basically on the theory of the emergence and change of informal institutions and how agents' bargaining power over the rules of such informal arrangements influences the final outcomes. But Knight (ibid. 171-2) also contends that the mechanism (bargaining power) underlying the creation of informal arrangements is basically the same for formal arrangements, because formal institutions are created on the foundation of informal arrangements. Considering this, the issue of bargaining power is meant here in the general sense applicable to both formal and informal arrangements.

Intangible resources like intelligence, previously – accumulated – experiences, and available information are factors that strongly determine the bargaining power of actors (Elster 1989: 141). Tangible resources include a wide array that go from illiquid, i.e. those hard to sell immediately, to the very liquid – like cash. Of course, assets that support the actors in the case of lengthy, costly and even unsuccessful negotiations are determinant of bargaining power (Knight 1992: 129, 132).

If some actors can really influence institutional design and thus constrain the behavior of others, the effectiveness of their attempt will depend on the credibility of their commitment. Therefore, in the example above, if A wants to convince B to choose L, the commitment of A in playing R must be credible to B. In the case A follows the establishment of self-enforcing rules, the way to convince B is partly through repeated plays of the game, and partly through the self-constraining of A to its own commitment (Knight 1992: 65; 130-131). Related to the commitment strategy is retaliatory action, thus A can threaten retaliation against B if B fails to choose what A wants (that is, L). Actors will refrain from choosing a particular strategy if they believe the sanctions coming their way will be real, and not just empty threats (Elster 1989: 139; 1989a: 164; Ostrom 1990: 43-44). Credible threats have the effect of increasing the costs of adopting a different strategy – R in the case of B – (Knight 1992: 135). In terms of our game:

$$\Delta_B > x_B + \varepsilon_B - c$$

Therefore, if B believes that the threat of retaliation is real, then the preferred strategy will remain L. The key issue here remains: How credible are threats? Threats are credible as long as actors can affect the benefits obtained by others from their own courses of action (Knight 1992: 135).

Risk aversion is influenced by resource ownership. There is an inverse relationship between resource ownership and risk aversion, i.e., the more resources A has, the less risk averse he/she will be. This can also give credible signs to B about A's commitment, because should the negotiations turn unsuccessful, A stands to loose less than B, hence B has a reason to believe in A's commitment. Related to risk aversion and commitment is time preference, which in turn is also affected by resource ownership. This means that the more well-off actors can simply be more patient should bargaining turn out time consuming. In this regard, if A is the more well-off, he/she will also be less dependent on the result of the negotiations (and has less to loose should the negotiations fail) and his/her discount rate is likely to be low. On the other hand, if B is the less well-off, has less resources to support himself/herself during the negotiations, and bargaining turns out to be costly and time consuming, his/her discount rate is likely to be higher than that of A, and B will probably be willing to accept a rule that gives him/her less advantage than otherwise (Elster 1989: 138; Knight 1992: 133).

The creation and approval of some new law is the product of a decision making process that involves intentional bargaining over institutional constraints, and where the final outcome is a function of the political setup. In other words, the institutional framework conditions the bargaining power of different groups within a particular state (Weingast 1989). While the interest of economic actors is to establish norms that give them a distributional advantage in economic transactions, the interest of the state (or those in office) is – at least partly – to further their own interest, namely, an economic interest in the payoffs of being in office and a political interest in staying in office by providing the political outcomes necessary to satisfy those actors they need to maintain political power. In this regard, depending on the 'clientele' at which state officials aim to stay in office, so will be the process of institutional creation and change. But it should be considered that those in office can influence the bargaining power of different groups in society if – as a payoff – they (actors in office) can increase their chances of maintaining power (Knight 1992: 188-194). The bargaining power of different groups will also depend on their capacity to establish alliances and the presence – or absence – of external forces in the policy-making process (Silva 1997). Therefore, depending on the political setup and the bargaining power of polities, the state can engage in producing either efficient institutional arrangement or institutional arrangements that increase unnecessarily transaction costs – like restrictive entry rules, useless inspections, increase information costs etc. (North 1990: 63). Nonetheless, due to the fact that governments change and thus there is an intrinsic difficulty for those in office to find successors that further their political projects, a problem of credibility, and particularly of state commitment arises (Weingast 1989). This problem is illustrated in the following example:

1	2	3
A	B	C
B	C	A
C	A	B

There are three political parties 1, 2 and 3, and there are three different policies A, B, and C. Each political party has different preferences concerning the different policies, and should any of them come in office, so will be their political agenda. Hence, the party 1 prefers policy A to B and policy B to C. Party 2 prefers policy B to C and C to A. According to this, parties 1 and 2 prefer policy B to C and could reach an agreement. But if party 3 wins the election, the preferred policy will be C in spite of what parties 1 and 2 may wish.

The intransitivity of political preferences across political parties is therefore considered one of the main sources of the lack of credibility of state commitment in the long term (Weingast 1989).[18] Retaking the theoretical argument that institutional design is actively influenced by those actors (polities) prone to obtain the larger shares of economic exchange, the following

[18] Buchanan and Tullock ([1965] 1982: 328-34) discuss a similar example from the point of view of voters.

section will explain how the organization for the provision of collective goods is likely to happen.

2.4.3 Collective goods and collective action

Like in the case of institutional emergence, individuals will find it worthwhile to cooperate in a specific activity if they obtain a benefit from it (Heckathorn 1988; Eisenberg 1999: 4). Assuming a situation in which the members of a group have the choice of engaging or not in a particular activity, the group is bound to have a problem of collective action if some cooperate while others not, and if it is worse for all if no one cooperates, as this will preclude the production of a collective good that will improve collective wealth. Because of the difficulty of getting people together to cooperate for their mutual benefit, collective action problems arise (Hardin 1982: 133; Elster 1989: 126, 131). The problem of collective action is closely related to the problem of free riding (Ostrom 1990: 6; Tuomela 1992). For example, someone belonging to a group confronted with the choice of either cooperating or not in the provision of a collective good may think: 'if all the others cooperate, then my contribution is not that important – because the provision of the collective good is guaranteed – and I can even benefit from refraining myself from cooperating, as I will not incur any costs and still perceive the benefits'. On the other hand, if the same person perceives that his/her participation is indispensable for the collective good to be provided, then this member will probably not attempt to free ride because there may be nothing to free ride from.

To illustrate the problem let me take a look at the prisoners dilemma game. This is a modified example of Hardin's (1982: 25-27) illustration of the problem underlying collective action as a prisoner's dilemma game in a setting 'individual vs. collective'.[19] The usefulness of the prisoner's dilemma to explain collective action is that it allows to represent strategic decision making on the side of the players who – driven mainly by narrow self interest – will hamper the provision of collective goods.

In the example, the players are a private landowner and a community – of which he is also a member – of size 10, and where the community involves mainly other private landowners (farmers and tourist entrepreneurs). The landowner's property includes a primary forest which he wishes to log, and if possible transform it into a grazing area. Assuming a tropical setting with poor soils, after the land use is changed, future returns to cattle decline until benefits are nil. At this point the landowner will wish to move on to clear another parcel. The community is interested in the conservation of the forest because the property is part of a watershed from which several other landowners downstream obtain a benefit, as it provides irrigation to their farms, recreational possibilities and game. Tourist entrepreneurs benefit from the landscape, recreation possibilities, wildlife and generally from the protection of the watershed itself.

---

[19] Similar examples are found in Elster (1989) and Ostrom (1990).

Let me assume now a non-cooperative setting where all players possess complete information. With complete information is meant a situation where all players are aware of the structure of the game as well as of the possible outcomes of different strategies. Let 'A' be the landowner and 'B' the community. It is assumed that the provision cost of the collective good (watershed conservation) is 1 for each member and that for such contribution a gross benefit of 2 – per capita – is obtained, and that the net benefits of each contribution (1) for the provision of collective goods are distributed symmetrically. In a non cooperative setting, the dominant strategy of the landowner is to change the land use, while the dominant strategy of the community is to free-ride from the watershed protection provided by the landowner's forest. The alternatives are that the community (player B in the game matrix) pay the landowner (player A) for the maintenance of the forest cover, in which case, each obtain a payoff of 1 (in the case of the community 1 represents the per-capita payoff). In the case that the community free-rides from the watershed protection provided by the landowner's forest it will obtain 0,2 while the landowner will gather -0,8. In the opposite situation, the community pays him for the maintenance of the forest cover but the landowner considers that there is enough forest around his property so he decides not to cooperate, in which case he will obtain 1,8 (the highest payoff) and the community 0,8. In the last case both actors set their dominant strategy forth (non-cooperation), and no one becomes any benefits.[20]

	B cooperation	**B** non-cooperation
A cooperation	1 ; 1	-0,8 ; 0,2
A non-cooperation	1,8 ; 0,8	0 ; 0

The dilemma of cooperation on the side of the landowner can be seen when we look at his payoff matrix. Given that the dominant strategy of the landowner (narrow self interest) is to obtain as much benefit as possible, his strategy will follow the payoffs 1,8 ; 1 ; 0 ; -0,8. Likewise, the community will follow the payoffs 1 ; 0,8 ; 0,2 ; 0. From this example it can be seen that – in a non-cooperative setting – the dominant strategy of both actors is non-cooperation. Hardin (1982: 27) shows that the result of the prisoner's dilemma for two players can be generalized for 'n' players and (in non cooperative situations) the above result – deception – stands. This result is evidently not Pareto optimal since everyone could be better off if cooperation were achieved. Nonetheless the result can be still considered an equilibrium because – in the assumed setting – no player has an incentive to change his/her strategy. Each

[20] The results of the matrix are quite easy to calculate. Let me take for example the cell (-0,8 ; 0,2). Here the landowner provides the collective good while the collectivity free ride, he pays 1 and 2 is the net benefit for the whole community since it did not incur any costs. So the collective benefit is 2/10=0,2. Since the landowner paid 1 the result he obtains is: –1+0,2= -0,8.

will expect the other to cooperate and take advantage of that. This result can be obtained in several situations; in a one-shot game – i.e. the game is not repeated, or there is an end game – when information on the other players is scarce and when the number of players is large so that organization turns more difficult. In these situations non-cooperation tends to be the dominant strategy for all actors (North 1990: 13). The problem arising when actors have little information about each other (or fail to communicate) is that they will probably fail to build reliable expectations over business transactions, hence they do not have a particular reason to trust each other. One must be clear that one shot games and end-games tend to describe static situations, and social/economic relationships are anything but static, and that economic agents are usually not so naive to think no one else – but them – will behave strategically (Knight 1992: 56, 140).[21] It is therefore recognized that if the actors know – or have an information asset on – each other and are partners in ongoing business relationships, it is very likely that they will acknowledge that through cooperation they can actually obtain improved benefits without diminishing those accruing to the others (Hardin 1982: 132; Knight 1992: 128; North 1995: 21; Eisenberg 1999: 5; Steele 1999: 13). As long as – formal and informal – norms, and the mechanisms supporting them, enable cooperation for the achievement of collective benefits they can be considered a form of social capital (Nee 1998a).

The demand for some collective good depends partially on the economic outset of the agents. For example, some may consider environmental protection a superior good because the well-off are more prone to donate considerable amounts of money for it than the poor, or that those donating for conservation act basically on a moral basis enabled by their own wealth (Hardin 1982: 86).[22] But the motivation to cooperate in the provision of some collective good can be attributed to a number – combination – of reasons like self interest, solidarity, altruism, social norms, misinformation (and even ignorance) and not just a single one (Elster 1989: 131). Though the motivation to cooperate in collective action is associated with the expected benefits of that action, these benefits need not be exclusively pecuniary, as other motivations can provide a benefit for those contributing. For example, many derive a benefit when they donate to help the poor, or people suffering a natural catastrophe, or to the development of some project in a third world country.

Even though it has been explained that self interest is bound to hamper collective action when agents act out of sheer narrow self interest, this may not be always true in the case of leadership. Professionals that engage and formally work in particular organizations – say environmental organizations – may follow their self interest of making career in a specific area and would not be interested in offering their work and knowledge to some cause if the payoffs were not large enough for them. On the other hand people contributing – e.g. with

---

[21] See also Hardin's (1982: 126-31) comments on the – static – analysis of Cournot's duopoly model in regard to strategic behavior.

[22] The issue is put in an unorthodox but very clear manner in Brecht´s Dreigroschenoper: "erst kommt das Fressen, dann kommt die Moral" (cited in Hardin 1982: 119).

money or personal engagement – to some particular cause may act out of a combination of moral and personal interest,[23] or because the issue at stake is an historical one and they wish to be a part of it like the rest.[24] In a related way, people can also act out of a lack of information and misled by how leaders present and discuss an issue.[25] But people can also have a distorted image of how important their contribution to the production of a collective good might really be, assigning thus a higher importance/weight to it than it actually has. Hence should they come to know that a yearly contribution for some organization that aims at controlling poaching or illegal logging (for example) does not amount for even a millionth of the required costs to effectively abate the problem they would probably not contribute at all to any organization, nonetheless they may still contribute under the assumption that their contribution 'is making a difference'. But this is not necessarily good or bad, it depends on the circumstances. For example, this distortion is bound to be short lived when people donate to a particular cause but nothing happens. On the other hand when donations are given to organizations successful in lobbying a cause at the governmental level – so that the lobbied issue is included in the governmental agenda – a multiplier effect can be perceived, and the distorted perception can have some grounds on reality since for every monetary unit donated for political lobby real governmental action addressing the problem – with a value many times larger than the original donation – can be obtained. Hence, while a single donation can fall short in directly addressing the provision of some collective good, a little can sometimes help achieve much, provided the 'entrepreneurs' remain consequent to the cause they are representing (Hardin 1982: 101-124, 135).

It can be seen that an individual's decision to cooperate or not in some activity is not as simple as calculating potential benefits, it has also to do with the perception one has on the other members of the group. Characteristic of the prisoner's dilemma explained above is that it is implicitly assumed that the players are bound to bear the same costs and benefits when cooperation obtains. In case one cheats on the others, while the others cooperate, he/she is bound to obtain larger benefits but the costs are always distributed evenly among the other players. Besides, the game – as described – depicts a situation of internal organization (or provision), that is, a situation where first, there is no third party involved in monitoring the

[23] For example, after September 11th 2001, the developed countries – under the leadership of the USA – called for common action to combat terrorism. In this initiative it was acknowledged that to effectively combat terrorism, poverty must be abated to assure security in industrialized countries. That is, poverty is not to be abated because industrialized countries find it unfair that others live in misery, but because they fear for their own security. Therefore, a combination of motivations of self interest and social justice can be assumed to underpin the coalition against terrorism.

[24] Hardin (ibid.) draws on the example of the civil rights movement in the United States during the sixties, where certainly many people participated in demonstrations and several other activities out of self conviction of doing what they thought was right, but it cannot be discarded that many others also participated because everyone else did, and people usually wish to live up to their time.

[25] Probably one of the saddest – and scariest – examples that one can think of is the fascist movement in Europe during World War II.

behavior of the players and second, all the players have the same interest in the provision of the collective good.

The provision of collective goods – like those stemming from forests – pose several difficulties for internal provision (organization) since it is likely that not all of the involved actors will obtain the same utility from the provision of the collective good simply because some are bound to benefit more from its provision than others. For example, a tourist entrepreneur is likely to obtain more – monetary – benefits from the conservation of biodiversity in a specific forest location than a farmer in the same location. But the situation turns even more complicated when the costs and benefits of provision within the group are not transferable or not even comparable. These difficulties arise because there are interest asymmetries within the group. Hardin (1982: 67-83) defines four main sources of asymmetries involving the provision of collective goods:

1. Nonfungibility, which means that the provision of the collective goods is not readily exchangeable for money, and leads to an asymmetry between costs and benefits because each individual will tend to value the good differently. This has to do with the fact that usually, once provided, a collective good can be enjoyed or not, but it cannot be traded.
2. Asymmetry of demand for the collective good arises because the group itself is asymmetric and some members are willing to pay more than others to have the good provided at the level they wish. This is much the case with non-fungible goods like environmental protection.
3. Asymmetry in the content of the collective good means that the members of a group may wish the provision for several different reasons and because of this they value some attributes of the good more – or less – than others. For example, for some the protection – or sustainable use – of a forest may only mean that some trees shall be left standing while others may consider that it must include the protection of the whole ecosystem within.
4. Asymmetry between gains and losses (hysteresis in valuations) means that people value gains differently than losses. Hysteresis means that persons tend to value losses more than gains, i.e., one will value more the loss of something already owned than the – uncertain – benefit of having something still not possessed. This means that persons are more likely to act against the production of collective bads – e.g. the construction of a sewage deposit in the neighborhood – than for the provision of collective goods – e.g. sustainable forestry and forest protection.[26]

The existence of asymmetries within groups is not necessarily negative as they may help explain how group organization arises towards the provision of collective goods. In particular,

[26] Even though the destruction of forests provides society with several collective bads like runoff and the destruction of marine ecosystems. But the costs accruing to the rest of society may not be perceived symmetrically by the group.

groups with demand asymmetries are likely to build a core group – say of size k – [27] due to which the collective good will be provided (Marwell and Ames 1981: 302; Hardin 1982: 38-46; Tuomela 1992). This means that the core group will either undertake the provision of the collective good (a self enforcing institution), or that it will undertake the necessary lobbying for its provision. The problem of collective action does not necessarily imply that everyone without exception must cooperate, in fact, cooperation cannot be assured if all the members of the group are narrowly – and symmetrically – self interested (Hardin 1982: 52, 133). In a typical case, additional – marginal – collective benefits will be low in two extreme situations, when only few persons cooperate and when almost everyone cooperates. Thus, when only some group members cooperate the good will not be provided,[28] and when everyone cooperates the good will be indeed provided, but the marginal contribution of the last members is not noticeable (Elster 1989: 129-130). For example, if people try to organize to keep a park clean, the effect of only a few visitors taking the litter with them will not be noticeable if everyone else leave their litter behind in the park, and if almost everyone take the litter with them, the effect of some littering the park will be hard to notice as well.

Organization for the provision of collective goods like the example above (a clean park) assumes the internal provision of collective goods, i.e., the provision of the goods exclusively by the members of the group. But the private provision of collective goods – like those provided by forests – may be perceived too expensive by private agents to undertake by themselves. In such case "*k*" may wish to engage the government – or some other intermediary organization – for the provision of the collective good (external provision) rather than providing it internally as long as the group obtains positive benefits (North 1990: 87). Following the example introduced at the beginning of the section, the members of the group can either rely on each other to monitor compliance to the provision of the collective goods provided by the forest – internal direction – or they can rely on the monitoring of an external agent – external direction. The reason to engage a third party – say the government – is that it may be easier for the third party to regulate internal group action than for the group itself, and because under the problem of collective action explained before voluntary cooperation cannot always be expected (Hardin 1982: 51-52). Nonetheless, Ostrom (1990: 14-21) argues that in the case of some collective goods,[29] resource use and monitoring can be more effective if

---

[27] Mancur Olson (1962, cited in Hardin 1982: 38- 41) defines a group as privileged if there is at least a subgroup of size $k<n$ that could benefit more than the total costs of provision for the entire group. In this regard the existence of k will assure the provision of the collective good.

[28] Collective goods depending on the existence of a minimum – demanding – group size are called step goods. Step goods are not provided continuously as the group size increases, therefore, a minimum group size is required.

[29] Ostrom (1990) analyzes the governance of common pool resources in different settings where internal governance is successful, and where it is not. Some cases of successful self governance refer to groups of users where the members know each other, communication between them exists and the group agrees on a set of rules as to who, when and how much resources are allowed to be used, and since the members are all direct users, monitoring is a by-product of their resource use. Her analysis includes the use of common pool (tangible) resources like inshore

undertaken by the users themselves, provided the participants communicate and trust one another and realize that they are bound to share a common future. Therefore, engagement of a third party (the government) can be not only expensive but also ineffective. Ostrom underscores that there is no single solution to the problem (internal or external), but many mixtures able to cope with the task. The organization of the provision of collective goods can also be the result of entrepreneurship, i.e. persons who, for the sake of their own career, find it in their self interest to work towards the provision of collective benefits (Hardin 1982: 34, 106-107, 134; Mummert 1998). Hence such – political, environmental – entrepreneurs are bound to obtain a mandate as long as they are successful in matching their personal interests with the motivations of their target groups (moral, guilt, take advantage of a lack of information, misunderstanding,[30] etc).

As explained at the beginning, institutional arrangements (formal and informal) aimed at the provision of collective goods should also be endowed with an enforcement mechanism to induce group members to compliance. The enforcement mechanisms of an institutional arrangement can be manifold and can include punishments for non compliance as well as retributions for complying behavior.

The most salient aspect of institutions is their capacity to influence behavior through the use of incentives and sanctions. Formal and informal sanctions make undesired behavior costly for offenders and discourages potential offenders (Knight 1992: 59). The state can use force against tax offenders by making them pay fines or sentencing them to jail. But it can use tax exemptions as well to motivate individuals towards particular objectives, for example, donations for charity or environmental protection. Firms can ultimately punish shirking employees by firing them. Churches can punish severe religious offenses with excommunication (Elster 1989: 148; North 1990: 43). Likewise groups uphold and produce norms through either social approval – like popularity, prestige, etc. – and disapproval – like ostracism, violence, etc. (Nee 1998a). When rule trespassers are aware of the consequences of their course of action it is likely that they will also include in their strategy (or the expected benefits of their actions) the possibility of being discovered and punished. In this regard the credibility of institutional sanctions against offenders is a crucial factor in either inviting or making individuals refrain from breaking established rules. This means that institutions are only relevant as long as their enforcement mechanisms are credible (Knight 1992: 61-62; Eisenberg 1999: 8-14). Relevant institutions are those that show endurance over time, which raises the focus of the next section, path dependence.

---

fisheries, meadows, forests and irrigation systems. Monitoring can prove more difficult for local agents alone when the collective goods are non fungible, like the environmental services provided by forests.

[30] That is, taking advantage of people's perception of the real effectiveness of their contributions.

2.4.4 Path dependence

The concept of path dependence refers to a process in which specific forms of institutional arrangements (and thus of economic organization) are chosen contingent of historical circumstances. Therefore, under certain conditions some technology or policy might be chosen over another even though the choice made might not necessarily be the most efficient in the long run, but the circumstances under which the choice is made can make it appear the best at the time. That is, the choice is sensitive to the initial conditions, and once an institutional arrangement is chosen it will be difficult to abandon. In this regard it is said that an institution is locked-in (North 1990). The concept of path dependence brings forward the issue that what we have today is partly consequence of decisions made in the past. In particular, path dependence is closely related to the evolution of the political and economic system, i.e. unless it is interrupted by a revolutionary movement, because within the established institutional framework societies transmit specific values to their citizens (language, customs, laws, etc.) who also inherit a specific – natural and man-made – capital stock and particular forms of using it (Liebowitz and Margolis 1995). Path dependence contributes thus to form business culture.

North (1990) argues that history matters if we wish to explain economic performance and supports his argument based on a comparative historical analysis of the economic performance of England and Spain during the 16th century and the institutions that they heired to their colonies. While England had a strong, centralized state dominated by the parliament and a strong system of property rights, in Spain the polity was strongly divided and the parliament was dominated by the crown, which led to a pervasive bureaucracy and a diffuse system of property rights. Thus the English system led to the evolution of a polity able to cope with fiscal crises and the financing of warfare that allowed the expansion of its circle of influence in the western world, while Spain faced recurrent fiscal crises, insecure property rights and confiscation of assets that drove the Spanish empire into three centuries of relative stagnation. Consequently Latin America inherited from Spain a system of centralized governments where institutions are designed mainly by wealthy leaders for their own advantage and where personal relationships determine much of the political and economic exchange (North 1990: 112-117). Contrasting historical circumstances, Khan (1995: 76-77) brings forward the example of South Korea and Taiwan of the 1960s, where political power was strongly centralized but – contrary to what one could expect from North's argumentation – both countries were quite successful in adapting their economies to a highly competitive standard by coordinating technology acquisition. In view of this Khan (ibid.: 76) contends that "*the evidence suggests that the political balance of power conditions both the problems institutions have to solve and the costs of solving them in particular ways*". Hence institutions do not arise independently of the polity. North (1995: 20) argues further that path dependence is to a large extent the consequence of the actions of individuals and organizations (polities) that – as a result of the existing institutional framework – have achieved strong bargaining power and have thus a crucial stake in perpetuate and adapt the system to further their own interests (see also Bates 1995: 43).

Path dependence can be conceived in different ways. Liebowitz and Margolis (1995) distinguish between three different types of path dependence and name them first-, second-, and third-degree path dependence, each case requiring additional conditions.

In the first-degree case, the choice made represents no harm to efficient outcomes[31] and thus it is rather indifferent if some institutional arrangement (say a policy goal) is chosen over another because the outcome is optimal, even though it may not necessarily be the only optimal choice.

In the second-degree case of path dependence, the choice is made based on imperfect information, hence decisions considered optimal today may appear suboptimal in hindsight, but the inferiority of the path cannot be recognized on the basis of the available – imperfect – information. Outcomes obtained in this case can be regrettable and costly to change (North 1989: 667). Though information is never perfect, choices and their outcomes need not always be regrettable. Sometimes once a path is locked-in the cost of institutional change can preclude adjustment even when preferable alternatives are identified, otherwise change might happen provided the discounted social benefits of the alternatives are perceived higher than the costs of undertaking institutional adjustments. Hence second-degree path dependence is a consequence of deficient foresight, i.e., the uncertainty of the future consequences of decisions made today. Otherwise, second-degree path dependence can also be a consequence of the limitations of institutional arrangements in identifying better alternatives.[32]

In the case of third-degree path dependence, conditions lead to a choice that is known ex ante to deliver a suboptimal outcome – despite available information on better alternatives – and, though the possibility of choosing the alternative institutional arrangement exists, the suboptimal choice is taken. Explanations of why third-degree path dependence might happen – despite the fact that relevant costs and benefits are recognizable – point to market failures like missing markets and the lack of coordination capacity of economic agents.[33] Another reason explaining third-degree path dependence can be attributed to vested interests that, in order to protect their own stakes, hinder the adoption of – other – institutional arrangements capable of increasing overall social wealth and take an advantage from their organizational

---

[31] Liebowitz and Margolis (1995) refer to discounted social benefits when they talk about efficient/optimal outcomes. Hence an optimal social outcome of an institutional arrangement is one where its discounted social benefits are higher than an alternative one.

[32] Recall the sources of uncertainty involved in institutional design brought forward by Knight (1992).

[33] Another reason brought forward is that some of the affected parties have not yet been born, but his would imply that in order to arrive at optimal institutional arrangements, knowledge on the preferences of future generations should be available, which is impossible.

and resource superiority and the lack of organizational capacity of other agents (see, for example, Clarence-Smith 1995; Greenhill 1995).

The example of a firm may illustrate the concept of path dependence. The firm has a set of fixed assets and has chosen a production technology, which after some time is inferior compared to a new one in the market. Nonetheless, under the old technology the firm can still produce at a lower average variable cost than with the new technology, which still keeps its break-even point lower than otherwise. In this case the old technology can be said to be locked-in by the firm and the case is one of first-degree path dependence. In the case of second-degree path dependence the firm manager realizes at a later point that the technology chosen is inferior than another already available in the market, but due to incomplete information the inferior technology seemed to be the best alternative 'ex-ante' because of the ignorance about better alternatives. If the costs involved in a change of technology are prohibitive the inferior technology will be locked-in. In the case of third-degree path dependence, suppose the firm manager is a close friend of the industry offering a technology inferior to others in the market; the manager can obtain a series of personal economic advantages by purchasing that technology and not another more efficient. Hence, knowing ex-ante that the technology is inferior, he decides to take it – most probably against the will of the firm's shareholders – and it will be locked-in, that is, unless the shareholders have notice of it and fire the manager before he can undertake anything.

Thus, while the first case shows a situation where the choice has no particular inefficient effect in terms of overall wealth, the second case establishes that intertemporal effects transmit errors that not necessarily can be amended, and the third case establishes the possibility of path improvement, but change leading to improvement is somehow not achieved (Liebowitz and Margolis 1995). For the purpose of this research, the second and third degree path dependence are the most interesting cases because the first case describes a situation that can happen merely by chance and no regrettable loss is incurred. In the second case, it is clear that any decision made at any point in time involves some degree of uncertainty because information is never complete; but the second-degree path dependence does not seem to attribute any particular intention behind the choice of some specific institutional arrangement. It could be assumed, like in the first case, that a choice can by chance turn out good the same as it can place the involved actors at disadvantage, hence unfortunate choices can be easily attributed to good intentions, but one should consider that the intentional election of a – political – course of action is also underpinned by ideological beliefs and thus by the consideration of what is considered best (Silva 1997; Knight and Ensminger 1995). Instead of considering just one or the other case of path dependence, a way out can be to assume that institutional outcomes can be a combination of the second and third degree path dependence (see for example Kahn 1995).

2.4.5 The relationship between formal and informal institutions

One of the most salient aspects of the relationship between formal and informal institutions is that while formal arrangements can be changed relatively quickly, informal arrangements do not change as fast (Nee 1998: 85-87). For example, England and Spain faced much difficulties in their attempt to establish their formal institutions in their colonies as informal arrangements persisted over time hampering formal ends pursued by these colonizing powers – adoption of religion, avoidance of traditions against "civilized" life and good economic principles etc. – (Robinson [1970] 1975: 28; Landes 1998: 232).

While formal arrangements are produced to serve the interests of those with the bargaining power to establish new rules (North 1998: 249), informal rules that have an effect on the allocation of resources influence the power asymmetries in the conflict over the establishment of formal institutions (Knight 1992: 174). As mentioned before, an institution embodies a web of interrelated – formal and informal – norms that structure social, political and economic interaction, and thus influences group performance (Nee and Ingram 1998: 19). Knight (1992: 171) posits that formal institutions are designed and created on the foundations of informal institutions. In this regard it can be also proposed that informal institutions are embedded in formal arrangements. Institutions play a crucial role by transmitting information to agents on which expectations on present and future transactions are built. In this respect individuals make decisions according to the incentives (payoffs) and disincentives (sanctions) provided by the institutional framework ruling the activities in which they are involved, and the transmission of such information occurs at the formal and the informal institutional levels (Knight 1992: 55-59, 72; Eisenberg 1999; 9-11).

Formal institutions provide the framework of legitimate action within which informal norms and networks operate (Nee 1998). In particular, institutions do not result by coincidence, they are shaped by historical, economic and social conditions, and they usually emerge out of the interests of those obtaining the larger shares of exchange (North 1990; Knight 1992; Nee 1998a). While formal institutions are approved and enforced by the state through the influence of governmental and non-governmental organizations to solve problems of collective action, informal institutions emerge from social networks as a consequence of the conflict over distributional benefits and are enforced through ongoing social relationships (Knight 1992: 123-124; Nee and Ingram 1998: 19, 21, 28). Informal rules are implicit or explicit norms of behavior reflecting both the interests and customs of a group or community and – unlike formal rules – their monitoring and enforcing occurs as a by-product of social interaction, i.e., within the group (Nee 1998: 86-87). Because informal institutions are embedded in formal arrangements, it results that when the normative content of formal institutions is in conflict with the interests and preferences represented in informal arrangements, the achievement of formal ends is hampered (Nee 1998a: 9). The contradiction of the normative content between informal and formal institutions is a primal source of institutional conflict (Mummert 1999).

Institutional conflict is bound to arise as long as the payoffs of complying to informal arrangements are larger than those expected from formal arrangements. In this situation, the actors will fail to perceive the informal institution as subordinated to the formal one (Stinchcombe, 1986: 258-259; Eisenberg 1999: 12; Mummert, 1999: 4-10). Institutional conflict is discussed largely as an issue of the stability of informal institutions against formal institutions.

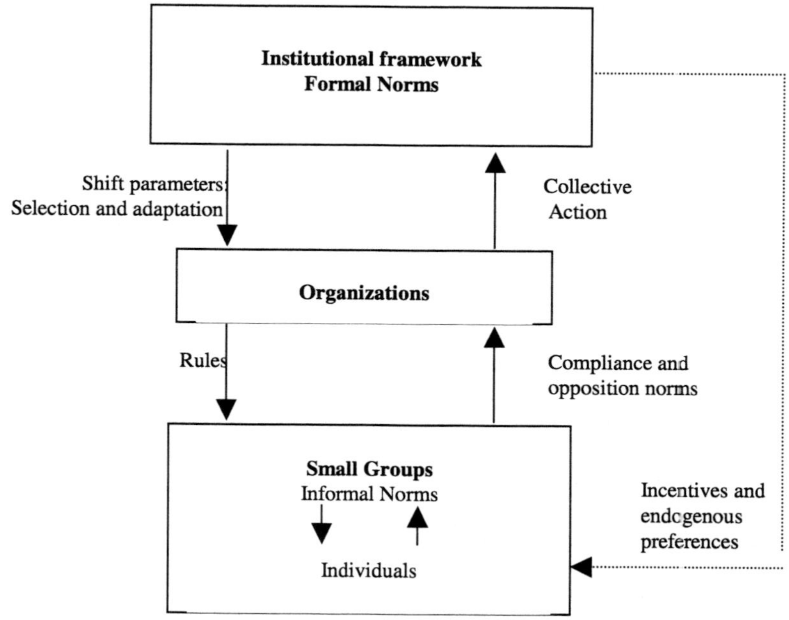

Source: Nee and Ingram (1998: 31)

A main requisite for institutional stability is that the institutional rules (information) are socially shared. Lack of information within the group can arise from ambiguity in the normative content of the rules and from the group size. Uncertainty increases with the group size. This means that as the group grows larger uncertainty also grows among its members as to whether actors have the same understanding of the rules governing their interactions. Another source of institutional stability is the incentive structure derived from compliance and non compliance to the rules. The effect of – formal and informal – institutional sanctions is principally to diminish the payoffs of non-compliant behavior and in this respect the credibility of potential sanctions is determinant when individual actors evaluate the possible payoffs of alternative strategies (Harsanyi 1962; Knight 1992: 59-64; Mummert 1999: 16). A crucial element of the stability of norms is that they are likely to persist in situations where such norms aim at the production of collective goods from which the group members depend (Nee and Ingram 1998: 29).

The relationship between formal and informal institutions is represented below following Nee and Ingram's (1998: 30-37) integrated model of institutions, embeddedness and group performance. This model also ties up the theory presented until now.

In this model, the arrows pointing downward indicate constraints imposed by hierarchically superior levels on inferior levels. The institutional framework includes; a) the formal norms that constrain organizations; b) organizational norms, a type of formal norms that constrain groups; and c) informal norms that constrain the members of groups which in turn affect individual action.

The arrows pointing upward show how formal institutions are built upon informal norms, i.e., how the inferior levels create and support superior institutional levels. Actors located in inferior levels, i.e., social networks and small groups, create and enforce informal rules. Organizational rules are established at the organizational level through a bargaining process where, due to power asymmetry among actors, the bargaining process will be dominated by those with more resource endowments. On the other hand, organizations influence the emergence and change of formal norms through political action, and their performance determines performance at the macro level.

The relationship between formal and informal institutions can be characterized as coupled when formal rules are congruent with the preferences and interests of actors in subgroups (social networks). Congruence between formal and informal norms is likely to produce mutual reinforcement between them and will tend to promote high performance in organizations and economies. Formal and informal institutions are decoupled when the normative content of formal rules is at odds with the interests and traditional values of actors of social networks. Moreover, informal norms will evolve into opposition norms when formal institutions and their enforcement is weak in contradicting group interests (Nee 1998: 87-88; Nee and Ingram 1998: 34-37). Of these three cases, the last one is the worst, because agents will actively resist formal rules.

According to the NIE, the change of the institutional framework is path dependent, which produces changes at the organizational level, where firms and entrepreneurs adapt themselves – their organizational structure – to capture the new profit opportunities offered by the change of the institutional framework. Hence those organizations that do not adapt are negatively affected by selection pressures. This means that organizational failure to adapt to the changes of the institutional framework selects out those organizations. As a result of the problem of demand asymmetries and entrepreneurship related to the problem of collective action, actors will try to influence the change (or the maintenance) of the institutional framework to their advantage. Corporate actors facing increased competition will usually respond by lobbying their governments to maintain their privileges. For example, recently in Germany the representatives of pharmacies countrywide are lobbying to impede that consumers can buy medicines through the internet, because they consider this would represent a loss of sales for them. But on the other hand, probably those pharmacies that adapt themselves to the new rule and go online will not suffer as much a loss.

Groups perceive a feedback from the formal norms defining the institutional framework in the form of incentives (disincentives) that influence their endogenous preferences thus reinforcing or inducing the change of informal norms.

A salient aspect of the close coupling of informal and formal institutions is that through the reinforcement occurring at both levels trust is developed. In this regard Nee and Ingram (1998: 34) argue that in developed market economies formal rules regulating economic transactions are supported by informal norms of fair exchange and honesty. When this is the case, transaction costs tend to be lower because the monitoring of third parties is overtaken by individuals enforcing informal norms. In this sense close coupling of formal and informal norms results in enhanced group performance.

The other side of the coin is when formal and informal institutions are decoupled, that is, when the normative content of formal arrangements differs from the interests of the subgroups conforming an organization. In the case of organizations lacking competitive markets for their output (for example government agencies) formal organizational rules have partly a ceremonial character designed to provide legitimacy to those organizations and thus satisfy external constituencies. But independent of this formal structure, informal arrangements also arise to structure daily business within the organization. Thus when the formal rules are at odds with the interests of the members of such groups it cannot be expected that groups follow formal ends. An example of this is presented by Nee and Ingram (ibid.) in the case of federal agents accepting bribes as a cover-up of investigations. Since this was sometimes a requisite to get inside the case, it soon developed into an informal norm not to denounce agents accepting bribes. Those agents who broke the rule were rapidly ostracized.

Decoupling between formal and informal institutions and opposition norms would mean in terms of the theory presented hitherto, that the norms established by the more powerful groups may well be built on the informal institutions that pertain to those groups, but can, however, be at odds with the interests of the rest. Two cases can be identified. First, weakness of formal institutions will make individuals perceive that the payoffs they can obtain by complying to informal arrangements are larger, and so they will have no incentive to change. Second, in the specific case of opposition norms, Heckathorn (1988) posits that the implementation of institutional arrangements perceived as unfair by specific groups can reach a point where those at odds with the norms may find it worthwhile to rebel against implementing agents and deprive them of control over collective sanctions in an attempt to defend their own interests.

2.5 Achieving policy ends: On governance and institutions

According to 'The Governance Working Group of the International Institute of Administrative Sciences' (1996),[34] "*Governance refers to the process whereby elements in society wield power and authority, and influence and enact policies and decisions concerning public life, and economic and social development. Governance is a broader notion than government, whose principal elements include the constitution, legislature, executive and judiciary. Governance includes interaction between these formal institutions and those of civil society. Governance has no automatic normative connotation. However, typical criteria for assessing governance in a particular context might include the degree of legitimacy, representativeness, popular accountability and efficiency with which public affairs are conducted*". One can see that in the concept of governance both formal and informal arrangements meet, thus the concept brings forward the issue at the heart of this research. Following Nee and Ingram's (1998) model we can deduce that governance conditions that contribute to harmonize the normative content of both informal and formal institutions have improved chances of successfully implementing forest policies.

Therefore, the implementation of incentive measures concerning the use of natural resources promises success when the proposed measures involve the participation of policy makers as well as the active partake of wider sectors of the civil society (i.e. not only of those directly related to the exploitation of forest resources like landowners, loggers and sawmills, but also others like local communities, NGOs, tourism entrepreneurs etc.), and where the participation of the different actors takes place through coalitions able to coordinate collective action (Ostrom 1990). But coalition building among sectors towards specific (e.g. sustainable) uses of forest resources is difficult because the benefits forests provide are spread asymmetrically throughout a large number of actors. Likewise, the costs of particular forms of sustainable forest use are likely to be borne by a much smaller group of persons. Coalition building among different stakeholders is thus likely to happen when different groups share or have similar interests. When the interests (stakes) are distributed in such a form that those with larger economic and political assets share similar interests with those with less resource endowments, the more powerful may increase the probability of successful coalition building and organization by investing their resources in the organization and development of rules that will structure the interaction of the interested groups towards the management of resources (Ostrom 1999). But one must remember that when those with larger resource endowments are to undertake a coalition with lesser endowed groups, they will not necessarily invest in the design of institutional arrangements that leave them at disadvantage. On the contrary, if more powerful groups have a stake in the management of a particular resource, it is very likely that they will use their bargaining power to tailor institutional design to their advantage (North 1990: 68; Ostrom 1995: 41; North 1998: 249).

---

[34] See: http://www.grdc.org/u-gov/work-def-html

Since forest resources provide goods and services at the private and public level, the implementation of incentive measures is challenged by the fact that these must take both private and public interests into account. As explained before, the goods and services provided by forest ecosystems (environmental services) are to a large extent collective goods, where the exclusion of third parties from the benefits provided by forests – say watershed protection, landscape protection, biodiversity protection, carbon fixation, etc. – is very difficult if not impossible. While some environmental services (watershed, and landscape protection) provide local benefits, other environmental services (like carbon fixation and the conservation of genetic capital) provide global benefits.[35] Hence private forests embody a mixture of private goods – i.e. timber and other resources appropriated privately – and collective goods like environmental services, recreation, protection against floods etc. Thus the challenge faced by the implementation of policy measures consists in driving private actors to a use of forest resources that takes both private and public benefits into account. This task requires to distinguish between appropriators and providers. An 'appropriator' refers to any actor that actually withdraws or uses the resources subject to management. Those responsible for the provision of common pool resources or public goods are the 'providers'. Specifically, this term refers to those who take action to ensure the long-term provision of the goods or services. Providers and producers can be the same actors but not necessarily (Ostrom 1990: 30-31).[36]

According to Ostrom (1999: 2) "*destruction or degradation of common pool resources is most likely to occur in open-access forests where those involved and/or external authorities have not established an effective governance regime to regulate the following:*

- *who is allowed to appropriate forest products;*
- *the timing, quantity, location and technology of appropriation;*
- *who is obligated to contribute labor or funds to provide or maintain the forest;*
- *how appropriation and obligation activities are to be monitored and enforced*
- *how conflicts over appropriation and obligation activities are to be resolved; and*
- *how the rules affecting the above will be challenged over time with changes in the extent and composition of the forest and the strategies of participants*"

The ensuing question is twofold. First, how policies that aim at the conservation and the sustainable use of private forests will distribute the benefits stemming from the production of collective goods? Do policy measures induce collective action regarding particular uses of public forest resources? The OECD (1999) argues that this task requires taking all (known)

---

[35] Dasgupta (1996) refers to the global commons.

[36] A straightforward example is that of an irrigation system. If landowners are responsible for its construction and maintenance, then they are both appropriators and providers. If the government constructs and maintains the irrigation system, then the landowners are only the appropriators.

relevant factors into account as well as foreseeing a difficult process of implementation due to the many interests and different stakeholders. Ostrom (1990; 1995; 1999) argues that institutional stability is a basic requisite for the successful management of common pool resources.

In regard to institutional stability, Ostrom (1990; 1995; 1999) explains that enduring institutions ruling the use of common pool resources (in this case collective goods) usually have the following characteristics:

1. The definition of *clearly defined boundaries* about what rights accrue to individuals or households regarding the use of common resources should ease that users can identify those without use-rights and take action against them. This is a primal requisite to organize collective action. It is necessary to determine 'what accrues to who' so that actors can establish what are they managing and for whom. Without this requisite the problem of free-riding is unlikely to be addressed. The bottom line is that for actors to have an interest in coordinating structures of appropriation and provision, appropriators must be able to exclude others from the use of common pool resources or effectively perceive the benefits from the production and maintenance of public goods.

2. *Congruence between appropriation and provision rules and local conditions.* The congruence principle foresees that the benefits derived from appropriation rules are proportionate to the costs involved in the provision of goods and services. This principle also focuses on the issue of the rules that restrict the time, place, technology and quantity of resource units and their relation to local conditions and to provision rules about labor, money and/or materials. A set of rules must be established about who, where, at what time, through what means and how much resource units can be used (that is unless the number of appropriators is so small that the actions of one do not affect the others). Such rules must take into account local conditions, thus, institutional arrangements designed for a whole country usually fail to account for specific local needs and resource attributes.

3. *Collective choice arrangements* where most individuals affected by operational rules can also participate in modifying these rules. The process by which institutional arrangements are set and changed is determinant of institutional legitimacy and thus of general acceptance (Mummert 1999: 11). The establishment of a set of rules does not guarantee that the involved actors will – under every circumstance – comply to them. No external authority can guarantee for overall private compliance to institutional arrangements, and this sort of enforcement alone is not enough to explain compliance to rules. It is rather when local actors are able to change and adapt the set of rules to the particular circumstances of their venue that compliance is more likely. This is also likely to involve them more actively in monitoring and designing sanctions for offenders (see also Nee and Ingram 1998: 28-29). The most evident advantage of appropriators' partake in the design of rules is that they are able to learn from experience what is enforceable and what not, and the information provided by experience will allow them to develop contingent

strategies to existing rules. Williamson (1984: 211) contends that participation of different actors may rather have the function of avoiding their demoralization ensuing from being ignored during the process of making rules, hence even though the final outcome may not necessarily reflect the interest of each and every group with a stake in the issue, being heard has itself a soothing effect and contributes to keep groups involved.

4. There is an *active involvement of local actors in monitoring*. Hence monitors auditing resource condition and appropriator behavior are accountable to the appropriator and/or are the appropriators themselves. Monitoring is a by-product of actors' resource use and their self interest in the maintenance of the availability of those resources for themselves (see also Dasgupta 1996: Ch. 5).

5. *Rule offenders are likely to be punished* (depending on the seriousness of the offense) by either other appropriators, officials accountable to offending appropriators or both. Robust institutions are characterized by active monitoring and sanctioning by the participants themselves, which also keeps the costs of monitoring low. Despite the level of acceptance of an institutional arrangement, individuals always will be tempted to cheat if this promises benefits above the expected. Nonetheless, punishment need not be initially extreme. A monitoring system should actually contribute to set signals to users that shirking behavior will be discovered and punished proportional to the fault committed, thus non-complying behavior must not necessarily be treated as a criminal case and should be weighted according to the circumstances. Self commitment can be increased when it can be differentiated when someone breaks a rule due to a dire emergency and when not. However increased punishments should be considered for actors who repeatedly break the rules. This involves an issue of fine-tuning of punishments and hence the question of what is the right way to deal with different offenses to rules? "Fairness is particularly critical when the unforeseen is a consequence of opportunism" (see also Williamson 1984: 211; Toye 1995: 59).

6. *Conflict (low-cost) resolution mechanisms* are available for appropriators and officials. Mechanisms for discussing what is and what is not allowed must exist to reduce interpretation errors of existing regulations. Conflict resolution is closely related to principles 3, 4 and 5, and even when these principles are followed, the application of rules in specific situations – despite case differentiation and discretion – is bound to arise conflict. While rules are assumed to be clear in theoretical propositions, this is rarely the case in field settings. Different individuals will interpret – the same – rules differently as to who, how and when. Individuals will want to have their own interpretation of rules anticipating the fact that they might be caught breaking them. Besides, rules can also be broken in good will, i.e., without meaning harm to anyone. Nonetheless, a discussion mechanism to resolve what is an offense and what not is necessary if individuals are to comply to a set of rules. Nonetheless, the existence of conflict-resolution mechanisms does not guarantee that actors will be able to maintain an institution over long periods of

time, but on the other hand it is difficult to imagine the prolonged existence of an institution without such mechanisms.

7. There is a minimal *recognition of the rights of participants to organize* around the use of resources, which means that appropriators are able to adapt institutions to their own needs, and that institution tailoring is not challenged by external authorities. Thus it is difficult to imagine a long-lasting institutional arrangement where external authorities insist that only they have the power to make and enforce rules.

Ostrom (1999) explains that these requirements are not to be taken as a checklist, because enduring institutions vary substantially from one setting to another, which makes empirical generalizations difficult. Nonetheless, stable self-governing institutions ruling the use of common pool resources researched by Ostrom tend to have the above listed characteristics, while fragile institutions will tend to have only some of them.

Stable self governing institutions refer to those sets of rules that endure without extensive intervention from third parties (like the government). Despite the explicit requirement of local participation in the design and enforcement of institutional arrangements, Ostrom (1995: 41) also warns from romantic views about local solutions being better than anything else organized at the national – or international – level because local organizations depend partially on national and/or international organizations to access information and support for the organization and implementation of institutional arrangements. She also points out that one should avoid putting one's faith in a single type of institutional agreement (either purely local, national or international), but that one should seek for multi-level arrangements that enhance the likelihood that actors will use resources[37] sustainably rather than otherwise.

Ostrom (1995: 42) also warns from losing the connection between local provision and use when massive external resources are available due to the simple fact that people are not as careful with other peoples' money as with their own and because processes supported by external funding make it difficult to build on existing local knowledge and institutions. "*A central part of the message in asking for external funds is that what has been accomplished at the local level has failed. Massive external technical knowledge and funds are needed to achieve "development" or to "save biodiversity"*" (ibid.: 42). In the best scenario, external resources are invested in the purpose for which they were raised, but they also require costly monitoring. Moreover, external project funding tend to generate profit-seeking-behavior (and all type of opportunistic behavior[38]) on the side of those with political connections. Furthermore – despite the importance of governments in the institutional mix – governments that dominate decision making processes through extended external funding also tend to reduce the effectiveness of local organizations. Ostrom underscores the importance of local

[37] With 'resources' Ostrom (1995: 41) refers explicitly to biodiversity.

[38] Including corrupt exchanges between officials and private (contracting) agents as well as free riding on the side of those receiving the benefits. This also contributes to increase the lack of trust between public and private agents.

institutions in the 'institutional mix' responsible to achieve the sustainable management of resources. Despite the fact that small-scale institutions are not enough, they are necessary in a multi-level governance system.[39] Ostrom (1995) refers to multi-level governance as the institutional diversity necessary to cope with the variety of actions needed to manage complex biological systems, like those in tropical forests.

[39] See also Castle (1996).

3 Private landowners and society's goal of sustainable forestry

3.1 Chapter overview

This chapter presents working concepts within the field of forest policy on which the research is based. It begins with the introduction of the concept of forest policy as understood in international and academic circles, which goes beyond an isolated forest sector approach and considers the effect that policies intended for fields like agriculture, trade, etc. have on the use of forests. In this regard, particular attention is given to the concept of forest policy contained in Chapter 11 of the Agenda 21 of the UN Rio Conference "Combating Deforestation". Following, a review of the relationship between policy failures, deforestation and forest degradation is undertaken as well as the measures proposed to address the problem. Different forest policy instruments (incentives) are reviewed, which later enable to pinpoint those chosen by Costa Rican authorities.

3.2 Forest policy: A working concept

The concept of forest policy has evolved from an isolated forest sector approach – in which actors were considered as being either inside or outside the forest sector – to a holistic (multi-sector) approach that seeks to consider all the actors in society (e.g. agriculture, energy, foreign trade, transport, tourism, NGOs) and the influence that their activities can have on forest resources when a definite course or method of action is selected (Nießlein 1985; FAO 1995). In this regard it is acknowledged that the use of forest resources is related to a wide array of environmental, social and economic issues and specifically that their state is the result of the configuration of international and national policy and economic development (UN 1992; 1992a; FAO 1995).

The loss and degradation of tropical forests over the past decades has raised much concern in the international community due to the potential negative effects that this may have not only at the regional level but also at the global level, i.e. on the global climate and on the availability of potentially useful – endangered – species. The fact that half of the world's terrestrial species are found in tropical forests (which correspond approximately to 6% of the earth's land area) shows the pressing need of protection and conservation of biodiversity (Arnold 2001; Ferraro 2001). In this regard, several agreements have come to light providing guidelines for the protection and maintenance of forest areas.

In particular, the UN Forest Principles and the Chapter 11 of Agenda 21 to combat deforestation (approved during the Rio Conference of 1992, see UN 1992; 1992a), as well as the United Nations Framework Convention on Climate Change and the Convention on Biological Diversity provide a framework for the design and implementation of national forest policies as well as for international cooperation. All these agreements underlie the principle of country-sovereignty over forest resources, and their overall goal is to encourage 'the greening of the world' by contributing to the "management, conservation and sustainable use of forests and to provide for their multiple and complementary functions and uses"[40] through national policies and international cooperation. The sustainable use of forest resources is understood as one that meets ecologic, social (including cultural and spiritual) and economic needs of present and future generations.[41]

The UN forest principles and the Agenda 21 underscore the need of an appropriate land use planning as a basic policy to achieve the sustainable management of forest resources. Additional policies that contribute to the establishment of framework conditions to achieve policy ends are of utmost importance and are – as will be shown later – incentives in their own right. In this regard, the OECD (1999: 58, 64-65) brings forward three policy elements considered to be particularly important to achieve framework conditions:[42]

- Information provision: Lack of adequate information and its dissemination is one of the main barriers to the achievement of policy ends. The collection of basic information about the resources under threat, the pressures to which they are exposed and the benefits they deliver is a necessary and vital first step to design appropriate policies for their conservation and sustainable use. The planning process will be improved if clear objectives and priorities have been defined in advance, taking account of the interests of stakeholders. The provision of reliable and accurate information on forests and forest ecosystems is considered necessary to promote public understanding and informed decision making.
- Capacity and institutional building: It is stressed that national policies and strategies should provide an appropriate framework to develop and strengthen institutions and programs for the management and conservation of forests (primary, secondary, and forest plantations).[43] Closely related to the assembly and dissemination of information is the creation of adequate capacity for the design, implementation, monitoring and enforcement of incentive measures. Capacity has to be built and nurtured on several levels. It relates not only to knowledge and conceptual competence, it depends heavily on the existence of an appropriate institutional and legal framework and the corresponding enforcement capacity. The institutional framework in a number of countries is such that aspects of the same problem are handled at different governmental levels or by different departments, leading to confusion and the generation of contradictory policies. Thus, capacity and institutional building should aim at the avoidance of these problems.

---

[40] See: Report of the United Nations Conference on Environment and Development. Annex III. 1992

[41] See also Pierce et al. (1995).

[42] See also: UN (1992; 1992a).

[43] In this agreement, like in several others, the term 'institution' is used to refer to organizations. Please recall that institutions define the rules of the game while organizations are the players.

- The partake of indigenous and local communities and other stakeholders involved in the use of forest resources[44] is required for the definition of national forest policy objectives and the planning and implementation of forest policy instruments. The active involvement of local stakeholders in the process of design and implementation of policy measures can only be expected if they perceive they can benefit from the design and implementation of those policy measures. A key issue – identified as essential for the success of any incentive program oriented at the sustainable use and/or protection of forests – is that the involved stakeholders participate on a voluntary basis, which assures their extended cooperation.

These policies should consider land tenure arrangements that incentive the sustainable management of forests and at the same time contribute to maintain different cultural identities and social organizations. At the same time, the need to develop mechanisms to protect biodiversity and recognize the environmental services provided by forests is brought forward (UN 1992a).[45] For this matter, industrialized countries are urged to cooperate with developing countries in taking actions that promote reforestation, afforestation and forest conservation through technical cooperation and financial assistance.

A requirement underlying the international position on cooperation to achieve the sustainable use of forests and their conservation is the local (country) development and implementation of institutional arrangements that show a commitment to achieve sustainability (OECD 1999; Seymour et. al. 2000). The World Bank (2000) recognized that one of the main shortcomings of its 1991 forest strategy to reduce deforestation in tropical moist forests was its failure to address country-specific governance issues. In particular, poor governance, political alliances between private stakeholders and governing elites, together with corruption and limited enforcement capacity at the regional and local level, posed the biggest hindrances for the World Bank's policy objectives. At the same time, assistance strategies focused on isolated forest-sector issues rather than providing linkages to macroeconomic and multi-sector issues (for example to exchange rates and enhancement of export incentives, removal of import quotas, removal of subsidies, price reform, fiscal tightening, planning of infrastructure and agricultural development). Hence, due to weak governance, environmentally degrading activities and socioeconomically inequitable exploitation of natural resources persisted notwithstanding World Bank's partake.[46] In view of this, it is considered that multilateral organizations like the World Bank and the International Monetary Fund should move to a 'conditionality approach', i.e., to envisage as potential borrowing countries those who show commitment to institutional reform prior to lending agreements (Dubash and Seymour: no date; Seymour et. al. 2000; World Bank 2000).

[44] Including industries, labor unions, NGOs, etc.

[45] See also ITTO (1993: 1993a).

[46] On the potential effect of Structural Adjustment Plans on forest resources see also Kaimowitz et al. (1998).

3.3 Policy failures and deforestation

As already mentioned, the allocation of resources devoted to effectively grow, maintain and protect forests depends on the combination of different policies such as environmental, industrial, agricultural, price, wage, investment, land tenure, trade and energy policies, terms of international agreements, etc. (FAO 1995). Policy linkages that affect forests negatively can be summed up in four main areas: 1-market failures and incentive structures, 2-policy failures, 3-forest policies and 4-impacts of timber trade on forest use and the environment (FAO 1995).[47] These areas should not be understood as having isolated impacts by themselves, because they can easily overlap each other, thus the negative influence of one area – e.g., timber trade – can arise due to the influence of other area – e.g. market failures and incentive structures.

It is widely acknowledged that one of the underlying causes of deforestation and forest degradation is the market failure to compensate landowners for the economic value of the (public) environmental services that their forests provide. Incomplete and missing markets as well as governmental intervention failures (subsidies and credit lines for productive activities that directly compete with forestry activities and forest conservation) have led to a widespread overuse and sub-valuation of forests (Repetto 1993; Adger and Brown, 1994; Pearce 1996; IISD, 1999; Richards 2000).

While the market enables the private appropriation of the benefits that stem directly from the use of forest resources (direct use values), indirect use values – e.g. forest environmental services – are generally not considered by the market, which leads to the production of externalities. Due to the uncertainty in the future, the market is also unable to account for the value of preserving resources today for future use contingent on increased information and knowledge about the possible uses of natural resources (option and quasi-option values). Finally, another obstacle for the market mechanism is its inability to account for existence and bequest values, that is, when individuals (and organizations) derive a satisfaction from the mere existence of natural forests (and the ecosystems and species they contain) independently of any use given to them by humans and wish that these resources are available to future generations (FAO 1995; OECD 1999: 27-31; Sen and van Kooten 2001: 20-23). Moreover, albeit market oriented mechanisms have the potential to influence particular forest uses, market instruments are not neutral. Market transactions are permeated by power and domination, therefore the final outcomes of transactions within a market system will rarely be the result of a neutral process, where every actor/group has the same chance to defend his interests (see North 1990; Knight 1992; Zafirovski 2001: 96).

[47] These categories can also be identified as 'the underlying causes of deforestation' (IISD 1999), as will be shown latter on for the case of Central America.

Though the influence of macroeconomic policies on the use of forest resources is difficult to assess (Angelsen and Kaimowitz 1999), it is considered that their influence on demand and supply conditions has an impact on forest resources. For example, currency devaluations, by enhancing the production of tradable commodities – and thus the commercial use of forests – can encourage forest harvesting and increase deforestation rates (Kaimowitz et. al 1998). Likewise, public investment decisions like the expansion of road networks can provide access to forest areas previously inaccessible, inducing encroachment and extended forest exploitation (Adger and Brown 1994; Mahar and Schneider 1994; FAO 1995). Similarly, agricultural policies can have perverse effects on forests by providing credit and subsidies that actively favor land conversion (Kishor and Constantino 1993; Adger and Brown 1994; Mahar and Schneider 1994). Ill defined property rights can provide a strong incentive to cut down the forest if this is a requirement to prove land tenure (Peuker 1991; Kishor and Constantino 1993; Repetto 1993; Pearce 1996). Therefore, it has been argued that the correction of intervention failures, the creation of local and global environmental markets as well as the implementation of local-level financial incentives are key measures to counteract these trends (Anderson and Schneider, no date; Peuker 1991; Kishor and Constantino 1993; Repetto 1993; Pearce and Brown 1994; Pearce 1996; OECD 1999; Richards 1999; Richards and Moura Costa 1999).

Examples of forest policy instruments that can negatively influence forest management by inducing over exploitation – and even land use change – are credits, subsidies and measures to induce forestation and wood production (Peuker 1991; Gillis 1992: 134). In particular, timber pricing and management policies can distort production costs twofold. First, stumpage prices do not include the economic values mentioned before.[48] Second, the costs of timber felling (and even those of land conversion) are often subsidized or distorted inducing over use and extended waste. This is much the case when policies artificially create entry barriers that hold back more efficient economic agents from participating in forestry activities (FAO 1995).

Countries can use restrictive trade policies to protect their own forest-based industries. Tariffs and quotas seek to provide protection for domestic industries by limiting the type and volume of traded products. Likewise subsidies and standards discriminate against imports of timber products. Taxes and bans on log exports seek to enhance value-added processing and restrict harvesting. But despite the support of trade liberalization, it is considered that open markets tend to concentrate benefits on more efficient groups at the expense of less privileged segments of society (FAO 1995; Uusivuori and Laaksonen-Craig 2001: 101). While trade policies can play a role in promoting incentives for sustainable forest management, several issues still raise questions. First, trade interventions address only indirectly deforestation and forest degradation (FAO 1995; Uusivuori and Laaksonen-Craig 2001: 100). Second, distortions can already exist in timber trade that encourage forest degradation, thus further

[48] See also Gillis (1992: 135) and Repetto (1993).

interventions may add to such environmental effects and even have counterproductive results. Thus, to take advantage of trade-strategies, countries need first to address domestic policy and market failures influencing deforestation and forest degradation (FAO 1995).

3.4 Incentive measures

As already explained, the correction of policy measures should contribute to send the correct signals to the actors involved in activities that directly affect forest resources. For example, when subsidized credit for cattle is curtailed cattle ranchers should have less interest in expanding grasslands. Likewise, when the market falls short in providing for the proper identification and assignment of the economic values mentioned above, incentive measures are one option to induce private actors towards the increased practice of forest friendly activities. A combination of incentives (financial and non financial) may be the most efficient way of influencing actors' behavior toward a sustainable use of forest resources – and natural resources in general (FAO 1995; OECD 1999: 28-31).

There is not a unique way of classifying incentive measures. For example, the OECD (1999) classifies incentive measures in three categories: framework incentives, regulations and economic incentives. Ferraro (2001) uses the term 'direct and indirect approaches' to distinguish between incentive measures. Direct approaches refer mainly to property rights while indirect approaches envisage economic and financial measures. Richards (1999; 2000) and Richards and Moura Costa (1999) undertake a detailed classification of financial incentives in four categories: transfer payments, market approaches based on public benefits, private/public investment flows and property rights approach. They point to each category as being mainly domestic or international.[49] Each classification overlaps more or less one another and address practically the same issues. To provide an overview of the different incentive measures (without attempting to list all the possible variations), these will be grouped here in three broad categories: framework incentives, economic/financial incentives and property rights enhancement.

3.4.1 Framework incentives

Framework incentives aim at the enhancement of social sustainability (as defined in section 5.3.1). Considering that economic agents act on bound rationality, they take particular decisions depending on the information available to them (Elster 1989: 13-51). *Information* availability plays a key role in the way institutional arrangements lead individuals in the process of bargaining and decision making. Hence, due to either incomplete or asymmetric information, economic agents can take decisions that – should more (differentiated) information had been available – they otherwise would have not made (Knight 1992: 27-28, 32). On the other hand, increased information can act as an incentive by giving individuals increased

[49] Yet on another classification see Crossley et al. (1997).

bargaining power to reach improved terms of negotiation (OECD 1999: 100). In this regard, information provision can be considered a powerful incentive if it can induce agents towards desired formal ends. But information provision goes even further than just 'making information available' to other agents. The state plays definitely a central role in the provision of information through its role as counselor and advisor of private landowners (Nießlein 1985: 84-89). In this regard, through properly built governmental officials, governmental organizations have the opportunity to come into close contact with landowners in a sphere that goes beyond mere controlling, and that can actively contribute to the building of landowner organizations that work closely with governmental organizations and at the same time are able to enhance the position of landowners against the influence of other – traditionally more powerful – actors. *Capacity building* at different levels (governmental and local) is closely related to the provision of information if it can contribute to strengthen institutional settings and their enforcement, assuring that the set of rules is understood and known by the relevant groups. Likewise, the *involvement of local actors* in the design of policies and implementation of incentive measures may contribute to the local appropriation of policy ends if the involved actors perceive they are obtaining positive benefits from them, which contributes to assure extended local participation (OECD 1999).

3.4.2 Economic/financial incentives

In the absence of financial incentives, the transition from unsustainable logging to sustainable logging – despite the enhanced production of public benefits – is likely to reduce private benefits, which can stand in the way of a change in the behavior of the involved actors. To realize the public goods derived from sustainable forest use and forest protection private actors generally have to be compensated for the forgone income. In cases where sustainable forest use is privately profitable (for example based on logging and/or ecotourism) and forests are consequently protected, a policy problem does not exist. It is there, where public and private values do not coincide that policies and incentive measures are needed. (OECD 1999: 35).

Table 1. Classification of economic/financial incentive mechanisms for tropical forestry

	Domestic	International
Transfer payments	'polluter and beneficiary pays' taxes; differential land-use taxes *Forest pricing*: concession bidding; performance bonds (deposits)	debt-for-nature-swaps; Global Environment Fund; environmental funds; international timber trade taxes; area-based payments to management units
Market-based approaches	Water commoditization; ecotourism charges	carbon offset trading; certification of forest products; bioprospecting deals; fair trade
Private/Public investment flows	Micro-finance to local users	tradeable development rights

Source: Adapted from OECD (1999); Richards (1999), Richards and Moura Costa (1999) and Richards (2000)

Transfer payments

At the domestic level, transfer payments procure to induce a change of behavior of economic agents by making them internalize positive and negative externalities (that is, social costs and benefits). This is precisely the spirit of 'polluter and beneficiary pays' taxes on, for example, fossil fuels, which are used to provide financial content for the payment of forest environmental services (Heindrichs 1997).

Differential land taxes can contribute to discourage deforestation related to land speculation by taxing newly cleared land and pastures more heavier than forests. But despite their potential, differentiated taxes are seldom used (Kaimowitz et al. 1998, cited in Richards 2000: 1004). In the case of state forests, competitive bidding for forest concessions is an appropriate way of increasing rent recovery (for the state) and provide user incentives (by giving scarcity signals to concessionaires[50]). One should consider that this measure is prone to render the desired result when the market for forest commodities is strongly competitive and chances for collusion between agents is low (Richards 2000).

Performance bonds (deposits) require the concessionaire to deposit a lump-sum in an account of the respective Forestry Department who will monitor logging activities throughout the concession period. When the Forestry Department determines compliance to the covenant terms it will return the sum to the concessionaire in payments plus interests. This incentive measure procures to cope with the problems of long-term forestry (discount horizons), but due to weak public administrative capacity, this measure is also seldom used (Richards 1999; Richards and Moura Costa 1999).

At the international level, transfer payments seek to protect public good values of forests (mainly biodiversity) and can be used as an indicator of the willingness to pay of the international community (Richards 1999; 2000). Debt for Nature Swaps (DFNS) refers to the purchase of – discounted – foreign debt, which will be converted to local currency and the proceeds will be used to fund conservation activities. Usually Debt for Nature Swaps include an agreement between a donor NGO and the debtor country. The key to the deal is that the creditor bank agrees to sell the debt at a price below its face value. Debt-for-Nature Swaps have been used mainly to purchase land for conservation (Resor 1997; Richards 1999; 2000). Their main shortcoming has been high transaction costs (and thus reduced effectiveness) due to a lack of organizational capacity and strategic planning of the involved organizations combined with unstable political and economic conditions. Moreover, the lack of local participation in the process of decision making and inequitable distribution decisions in the development and establishment of protected areas is strongly criticized. However, this last critique can be applied to almost every incentive measure (Resor 1997; Richards 1999).

[50] Much like forest fees, but concessions are considered easier to collect (Richards 1999).

The Global Environmental Fund (GEF) was created in 1991 to provide financing to the International Convention on Climate Change and Biological Diversity. One of the main problems of the GEF has been the interpretation of the additional cost of protecting global goods as opposed to domestic public good benefits. Additionally, the focus of the GEF has been on conservation rather than on sustainable forest use, together with an over-scientific and non-participatory approach of GEF's portfolio as well as the failure to 'green donors' have been sources of major criticism to the fund (Richards 1999; 2000).

Environmental funds (or National Environmental Funds in Richards 1999; 2000) are raised through international (or private) transfers and are earmarked for conservation and/or environmental activities. They can as well be designed to compensate landowners no longer allowed to undertake particular activities in their properties (OECD 1999). Mismanagement and poor expenditure choices (e.g., following a few environmental goals rather than addressing national priorities like market and institutional failures) give rise to criticism to the use of such funds (OECD 1999: 95; Richards 1999).

Taxes on tropical timber trade (or redirecting existing timber taxes) target transfers from consuming to producing countries. Despite the attractiveness of this measure – high potential for revenue generation, resources for development are not diverted, contribution to reduce the problem of rent-capture by producing countries – importing countries object it mainly on the basis of the uncertainty that the money will be appropriately allocated (Richards and Moura Costa 1999; Richards 1999; 2000). Area-based payments (linked to timber trade taxation) have been proposed to compensate specific units for the costs stemming from sustainable forest management. The problems faced by this measure begin with the difficulty of defining what is sustainable forest management, followed by the difficulty of conducting reliable monitoring. Besides, a proper environmental legislation may be lacking (Richards and Moura Costa 1999; Richards 1999; 2000).

Market-based approaches

At the national level, this measure targets the commoditization of public goods through agreements between the government and private enterprises (for example for the protection of watersheds relevant to the production of electricity, or the benefits perceived by tourist industries through the protection of natural resources). The main problem faced by this measure is how to set accurately the value of such goods (Heindrichs 1997).

At the international level an instrument that has raised much controversy is the trade of forestry-carbon-offsets, an instrument ensuing the negotiations to the United Nations Framework Convention on Climate Change. The idea behind this instrument is that those (industrialized) countries compromised with a reduction of their carbon emissions can do so in places (developing countries) where capturing (sinking/fixing) of CO_2 is cheaper than if done at home. This environmental service implies that financial resources should flow from the polluting to the carbon-fixing country (Lindegaard and Segura 1998). Carbon fixation involves mainly forest plantations and logging in natural forests. Another variant (though not less controversial[51]) is the avoidance of emissions through the prevention of forest fires or deforestation. Despite the initial enthusiasm on this incentive measure, it appears that the market for carbon-fixation may be smaller than initially thought (Richards 2000). Transaction costs of carbon trading in the tropics appear to be large due to the need of information (and ensuring its transparency), payment protocols, monitoring, contract enforcement, etc. (Richards 1999). The main critique on this measure is that it may be just a gangway of polluting countries to "reduce" their emissions of greenhouse gases cheaper elsewhere to continue doing business as usual, while reducing the room for developing countries to target their own greenhouse gas emissions. Thus, CO_2 emission trading may not provide any incentive to buying countries to change their (polluting) technologies as long as they can reduce their bill cheaper elsewhere while developing countries will continue being the dump of developed nations (Richards 2000). In particular, it has been underscored that the countries responsible for the boycott of the negotiations on climate change are those promoting carbon-fixation trading, most particularly the USA and Japan.

Timber certification should contribute to enhance timber trade while enforcing sustainable forest management. The basic idea behind timber certification is that through time an environmentally discriminating market will drive those practicing unsustainable forestry towards an improvement of their forest management techniques. Otherwise they risk loosing this market segment (Richards 2000). Experiences from Central America and Mexico show that while certification enhances credibility and contributes to improve technical aspects of forest management, competitiveness, and social stability, it is also perceived to be expensive and forest owners are bound to be disappointed due to unrealistic expectations regarding economic benefits. Governments see in certification a good opportunity to improve forest management but this expectation is reduced by their lack of control over timber extraction and the uncertain role that they play in the process of certification (de Camino and Alfaro 1998). Likewise, governments have managed to establish but few links between forestry incentives and certification, hence failing to promote a wider engagement in certification (de Camino and Alfaro 1998; Mery et. al. 2001: 259). While certifiers see themselves as appropriate partners in making certification accessible they also underscore the weaknesses at the national level in establishing criteria and indicators on equity (benefit distribution) and protection of biodiversity. On the demand side, weaknesses are identified in the misuse of "green labels" and the fact that the demand for certified timber is limited (Panayotis et. al 1995; de Camino and Alfaro 1998; Becker 2000; Richards 2000: 1009; Keipi 2001: 299). While NGOs can play a role as promoters and guarantors of certification, their main shortcoming is the local perception that NGOs represent rather foreign interests (i.e., the conservationist scheme from developed countries) over national and local interests and traditional values (de Camino and Alfaro 1998).

[51] See Thiele and Wiebelt (1996) and Tipper (1998).

Bioprospecting relies on giving value to forests based on the potential of developing especially pharmaceutical products. Nonetheless this instrument faces several limitations. The first one is that the probability of success of developing commercial drugs from forest species is very small (OECD 1995: cited in Richards 2000). It is also likely that the benefits perceived by landowners from the development of drugs remains very modest, even assuming the best scenario. Another problem is that due to genetic engineering the need to obtain supplies from the sources are strongly reduced (Richards 2000). The future of bioprospecting depends strongly on the development and enforcement of international regulations, mechanisms and institutions that contribute to settle disputes over patent rights and licensing agreements (Barbier et al. 1994: cited in Richards 2000).

Similar to timber certification, fair trade draws on the development and expansion of a (discriminating) market where consumers recognize equity issues and are willing to pay a 'green or social premium' on prices. The main obstacle in the way of fair trade seems to be WTO regulations due to the fact that social standards can be seen as a limiting factor of economic decisions and likewise, environmental discrimination can be interpreted as a protectionist measure (Richards 1999).

Private/public investment flows

Because local forest users and communities have usually more difficult access to conventional state or private banking organizations, micro-finance initiatives are considered a possible alternative way to provide financial resources to these economic agents. Financing can be provided through revolving credits. To avoid the costs being transferred to the beneficiaries in the form of higher interest rates, it is recommended to finance the establishment of such funds (training, organizational building) through donations and/or grant aids (Fedora 1996: cited in Richards 1999). A potential problem with micro financing is that landowners may tend to use the credit to hire labor for labor-intensive land uses that deviate from forestry activities (Richards 1999).

Tradeable development rights (closely linked to the property rights enhancement approach) involve user rights to development in areas earmarked for conservation sold either to private or public organizations holding particular environmental interests. The sale of tradable development rights should provide financial means to compensate landowners for diminished use rights in 'restricted areas' affecting their properties. Since it is user rights that are being traded, landowners (or communities) performing forest-friendly activities (like ecotourism) should have no conflict with this measure (Richards 1999). The tradable development rights should reflect the buyer's willingness to pay for public good values. The ensuing question is: How much willingness to pay is enough to compensate for such values? This seems to be variable depending on the country-context (Panayotou 1994; Preston 1997: both cited in Richards 1999). In the revised literature it is not clear though how the amount of such payments is set. Theoretically, they should be the result of a market-analog negotiation process.

3.4.3 Enhancement of property rights approach

For economists a rule of thumb to realize the private benefits from the use of natural forests is to establish and enforce well defined property rights over clearly defined resources. Well defined property rights have the following characteristics (Sen and van Kooten 2001: 13):

1. *Comprehensive.* The ownership of a particular asset is assigned to a specific agent (private or public) as well as the right to use or dispose such assets at will according to the law. Comprehensiveness implies that the assets assigned to an agent cannot be arbitrarily seized or subject of encroachment by other agents.
2. *Exclusive.* This condition implies that all the costs and benefits derived from the use and/or disposal of the owned assets accrue to the agent possessing the assets in question.
3. *Transferable.* An agent owning an asset must be able to transfer its ownership to other agents.
4. *Enforceable.* This condition implies that the ownership of an asset must be guaranteed by a third party (usually the state). State enforcement of property rights actually provides comprehensiveness, exclusiveness and transferability of asset ownership. State enforcement of property rights contributes to strengthen the essence of such rights, which is the right to exclude others from their use and assure the appropriation of benefits by the owners (Nee 1998a: 3).

When considering forest resources, property rights in different countries can have several forms that go from the purely private ownership through concessions, communal and state ownership and where each of them specify different access and use possibilities. In this regard, incentives can be provided through property rights by clarifying existing property rights; determining community usufruct rights, overlapping property rights, service concessions and partial privatization (Richards 1999; Richards and Moura Costa 1999; Richards 2000; Sen and van Kooten 2001). The ensuing question is how to assign property rights over non-fungible goods.

Well defined property rights contribute to reduce uncertainty in transactions and promote efficiency by encouraging mid- to long-term planning of resource use. Insecure property rights are considered to increase the discount rates of users, who will try to obtain as much as possible in the short term before they loose access to forest resources (Richards 2000: 1010; Sen and van Kooten 2001: 16).

Supposing that the difficulties related to the allocation of property rights can be resolved, well defined property rights should induce the owners to maximize the net present value of all the benefits stemming from their resources within the framework of competitive markets (OECD 1999: 32). This rule of thumb supposes that within competitive markets economic agents will maximize an objective function (say absolute income). But, differently than assumed by many economists, human beings need not be natural born maximizers. Individuals may simply be –

culturally – accustomed to a way of life and pursue to live accordingly, or just follow a traditional rule, or may also seek social approval or prestige – which is a form of relative income (Olson 1968: 99; Zafirovski 2001; 71, 96). Hence defining property rights for forest resources may prove to be harder than just addressing the question of "who owns the land" because forests play a strategic role by providing society a wide array of collective goods – some of which are very diffuse like biodiversity – and because the relevance accruing to much of these goods (ecologic, life-supporting processes and genetic capital) is largely unknown and/or not thoroughly understood. This is not to play down the importance of property rights, but to show that the assignment of property rights is a necessary but not sufficient requisite to close the gap between public and private costs/benefits. Supposing that property rights are assigned, defined and enforced (i.e. the owners are known and property rights are comprehensive, exclusive, transferable and enforceable), in a market economy, if agents follow only their self interest there is no guarantee that they will not deplete their resources and move on to the next most profitable activity (Richards 2000: 1010). This holds true when the owners are the direct users of the resources and when particular – destructive – uses of natural resources cannot be hindered by society, which is actually the case in many developing countries. This means that very little can be achieved if property rights are clearly assigned, but norms of behavior and economic forces still support the depletion of resources (Sen and van Kooten 2001: 26-27).

This is why a combination of various incentive measures – together with regulations and covenants that restrict and control the use of forest resources – is necessary to protect and conserve intangible and natural goods and services associated to forests (OECD 1999: 32-33). Particularly, the role that governmental agencies play in building framework conditions is also an essential part of incentive measures. This means that the role of governmental agencies should not be understood exclusively as one of 'command and control', where the government has the main function of monitoring and punishing offenders. Rather, besides these functions, governmental agencies play a wider role where a partnership with other key agents – and most particularly landowners – is to be sought, and through which incentive measures should be complemented and their desired effect strengthened.

III. Results and discussion

4 Cash crops, cattle and chainsaws: The causes of deforestation and the forest sector in Central America

4.1 Chapter overview

Section 4.2 looks at how a particular style of development based on the specialization on the primary sector for export has favored the concentration of property and intensification of land use, which has broken traditional production systems and provoked the migration of farmers into mountainous areas underpinning so forest clearing. This process has been strengthened by existing property rights, migrations occurred in the wake of war, and cultural values anchored in agricultural activities. Section 4.3 depicts the forest sector in the region, its stakeholders and the significance of logging as well as of non-timber forest products activities for the economies and the livelihood of forest dwellers. Section 4.4 observes the existing instruments of forest policy used in the region and identifies some factors marginalizing less better-off groups (stakeholders) in the forest sector that further drives them to prefer other land uses than forestry. Also, innovative policy instruments used in the region are described and the factors encumbering a more straightforward development of the forest sector in the region are identified as well.

4.2 The underlying causes of deforestation

The economic, political and cultural factors underlying deforestation in Central America can be grouped in three broad categories.[52]

- Economic and infrastructure setting: development programs enforced in the region, the influence of multinational economic agencies on domestic and trade policy, external debts, missing environmental markets, perverse market incentives, skewed land distribution, and deficient communications;
- Legal and political framework: property rights, poor regulatory systems, ineffective agrarian and environmental policies, marginalization of civil society groups in the design and execution of policies, ambiguous forest policies, and war;
- Cultural framework: general perception of the forest and traditional livelihoods.

[52] For a more detailed list of the underlying causes of deforestation in Latin America, see IISD (1999). See also Adger and Brown (1994: 136-53). The order in which these categories are listed does not imply an order of importance.

Even though the different factors that have driven the process of land-use change in favor of primary sector activities in Central America present quite a complex picture, it can generally be said that the pattern of forest conversion reflects a specific *development model* based on the export of agricultural/primary products in which the intensified exploitation of natural resources has been emphasized. Thus, public policies have made agriculture and cattle ranching increasingly more attractive than forestry (CEPAL/FAO/OIT 1980: 21-22; Peuker 1991: 7-20; Kishor and Constantino 1993: 4-7; Stonich et al. 1994: 243; Cálix y Sossa 1997: 287; Elton et al. 1997: 67-68; Shión y Ambrogi 1997: 161; Segura et al. 1997a: 120-121; Simon et al. 1997: 322). Panama is somewhat an exception to the traditional agro-export model because its economy has specialized mainly on tertiary activities (Segura et al. 1997: 20).

The support of a country-wise product specialization has been based on the approach of comparative advantage as an efficient path to increase wealth. But comparative advantage may prove spurious when competitiveness is derived from the undervaluation of natural and human resources. This appears to be much the case of Central America (Stonich et al. 1994: 243; Hinkelammert 1998: 39, 41; Segura and Vargas 1999: 3).

Missing markets for forest environmental services are regarded as one of the underlying causes of deforestation. Society has traditionally determined the value of forests primarily through direct use values; and since forest owners do not perceive other economic rents that stem from indirect values, i.e., environmental services like watershed and soil protection, carbon fixation, genetic capital, etc., they prefer to convert it to other land uses. The argument goes, that if forest owners could receive the rents of those environmental services that their forests provide society with, they would be willing either to protect the forest or practice sustainable forest management. In this context, well-defined property rights are considered a key issue in creating payment mechanisms (Peuker 1991: 8; Adger and Brown 1994: 137, 146-148).

Public policies in Central America have promoted forest clearing as a pre-requisite for the access to property rights on land. As a result, the conversion of forests to agriculture and/or cattle ranching has been allowed in areas that should have never lost their forest cover – more than 70% of the Central American surface is on slope areas (Rodríguez 1997: 142). The effects of environmental degradation and declining wealth in such areas were either ignored or neglected by policy and decision makers who followed short-term policy goals (Peuker 1991: 7; CCT 1992: 9; Gillis 1992: 131, 135; Repetto 1993: 3-4; Stonich et al. 1994: 243; Barry et al. 1997: 203; Elton et al. 1997: 63, 66; Rodríguez 1997: 142; Segura et al. 1997a: 125-126; Suazo et al. 1997: 259).

Since the early nineteenth century, the Central American economies have gained increased access to international markets by means of cash crops like coffee, sugar, cotton, bananas and beef. Deforestation in the region is attributed primarily to the expansion of these activities. Deforestation sharpens in the second half of the twentieth century, when *international trade* creates favorable conditions for the increased export of agricultural products, of which beef is a prominent example (Adger and Brown 1994: 140-141; Segura et al. 1997a: 124). Since the late 1980s, as a result of agricultural product diversification (nontraditional exports) promoted by Structural Adjustment Programs, more forest has been cleared to produce export crops, like vegetables, fruits, nuts, ornamental plants, palm hearts, oil palm, etc. (Barry et al. 1997: 202; Segura et al. 1997a: 119; Suazo et al. 1997: 244; Gudynas 1998: 50).

Profit opportunities provided through increased international demand for beef between the 1950s and 1970s led to an expansion of pastures from 3.9 to 9.4 million ha, so that in the 1980s, about two-thirds of the agricultural land in the region was used for pastures (Utting 1993: 19). The conversion of forest to grasslands to produce export beef was accompanied by extensive credit programs financed to a great extent by international agencies like the World Bank and Interamerican Development Bank (Kishor and Constantino 1993: 6; Utting 1993: 38; Elton et al. 1997: 68; Shión y Ambrogi 1997: 161; Segura and Johnson 1998: 12). In Costa Rica, between the late 1960s and the 1980s, the largest proportion of credit was given for cattle under conditions of subsidized interest rates, thus pastures increased from 30% of the total land area in 1973 to 47% in 1988 (Segura et al. 1997a: 124). In the following years, as a result of the slump in the international demand for beef, many pastures were abandoned. In Costa Rica this led to an increased availability of secondary forests approximately amounting to 400 000 ha in 1991. The potential of these resources as a source of timber is considered relevant Müller and Solís (1997: 49). For example, it is estimated that approximately 50% of the tree species available in secondary forests distributed throughout Costa Rica have some commercial potential (ibid.: 149). Nonetheless, these assessments still say little about the market potential of these forest resources. Rather than being managed – due to unfavorable market conditions for secondary forest-timber and other related environmental goods and services – some secondary forest areas have been converted again to agricultural land in order to diversify export crops promoted under Structural Adjustment Programs (Finegan 1992: 295, 315-316; Rodríguez, 1997: 145; Segura et al, 1997: 120). The economic potential of secondary forests in Latin America is considered to be very variable and depends not only on their geographical location, but also on the resource endowments of the landowners, their land use strategies and the policies towards these resources like the marketing of products stemming from secondary forests, legislation and policies that allow the landowner to capture the value of forest environmental services (Smith et al. 1997).

Domestic *monetary policies* during the 1970s and the 1980s overvalued local currencies, distorting the terms of trade of agricultural products and disadvantaging export activities; as a result they generated unemployment in the agricultural sector and promoted even more extensive cattle ranching and agriculture, as more people were driven into forest areas (Rodríguez 1997: 145). Moreover, the increased service of the *external debt* reduced public long-term investment possibilities, particularly those related to sustainable development, and led to an augmented pressure on forests, because land was used more intensively to produce –

traditional and nontraditional – export crops that increased foreign currency stocks in the short-term (Stonich et al. 1994: 244; Rodríguez 1997: 146).

From the very beginning, *local oligarchies* have controlled the production and commercialization of agro-export products. They have had the necessary political and economic resources to take advantage of the profit opportunities that arise from the increased international demand of primary products; they were able to access land, credit programs, acquire information, technology, machinery and the labor necessary to grow crops on a commercial basis (Alvarado and Monge 1997: 7, 9-10; Cálix y Sossa 1997: 290; Elton et al. 1997: 68; Segura et al. 1997a: 123). The monopolization of income earning activities by oligarchic groups has consistently *marginalized* less wealthy producers from access to economic resources (particularly land), displacing them from fertile areas to places unsuitable for agriculture (Utting 1993: 16-17; Alvarado and Monge 1997: 7).

Highly *skewed distribution* of economic resources between oligarchic groups and large masses of population living in dispossession and poverty is maybe one of the most visible consequences of the agro-export model. While in many areas of Central America coercive systems of labor relations tied peasants and farmers to large landholdings, in countries like Panama and Costa Rica many small landowners, because of the lack of productive alternatives, decided to sell their properties due to higher land prices (Utting 1993: 36; Elton et al. 1997: 56).

The *intensification of land use* that followed the process of land concentration broke traditional productive systems (agroforestry systems and slash-and-burn agriculture that allowed for restoration of soil fertility during extended fallow periods) whose history in Central America goes back several hundred years (Utting 1993: 16; Muschler and Bonnemann 1997: 62; Shión y Ambrogi 1997: 161; Simon et al. 1997: 324). In many cases the migrating colonizers brought farming practices unsuitable for the new settlement areas (Barry et al. 1997: 207). At the same time, small producers became engaged in productive cycles of declining yields, forcing them to clear even more forest in order to maintain their income. Hence, while large landowners got a hold of the best agricultural lands, marginalized small producers saw no alternative but to further convert forest for agricultural use in order to secure their livelihood strategies, which combine subsistence production with cash crop production (Adger and Brown 1994: 139; Shión y Ambrogi 1997: 161). Another reason underlying farmers' clearing of forests was the urge to *demonstrate land possession* through so-called "land improvements" as stipulated by property rights laws. For example, before 1986, Costa Rican settlers did not have to prove their legal possession of land if 50% or more of the property was cleared from forest. By clearing at least half their land, possession could be assured and protection against squatters was attained (Peuker 1991: 8; Adger and Brown 1994: 139; Gottfried et al. 1994: 110; Mahar and Schneider 1994: 161-162; Elton et al. 1997: 65).

Such land improvements allowed people to access *property rights* and credit, an economic incentive for which forests have not been eligible (Kishor and Constantino 1993: 2; Elton et al. 1997: 63-64). In this context, extensive cattle ranching became rapidly a common way of land conversion, because it is less expensive than other agricultural activities; cattle unmistakably demonstrated land possession, enabling peasants to access credit as they could use their herds as collateral (Peuker 1991: 18; Schelhas 1996: 299; Cálix y Sossa 1997: 291). The policy and legal framework also generated a process of land speculation in which settlers – both those acting individually and those within organized bodies – increased the value of their properties through 'land improvements' before selling to either farmers or cattle ranchers (Peuker 1991: 9; Elton et al. 1997: 39; Suazo et al. 1997: 253). Still, many landholdings in Central America lack a land title or clear property rights[53] (Peuker 1991: 8; Cálix y Sossa 1997: 284, 290; Elton, et al. 1997: 65; Segura et al. 1997a: 126; Shión y Ambrogi 1997: 167). In Costa Rica, Rivera (1986) and Román and Rivera (1990) consider that the land distribution policy of the state had as its main objective the reduction of the social tensions that had arisen in the wake of the economic crisis of the 80s, and so instead of distributing abandoned lands suitable for agriculture – much of them in the hands of oligarchic groups – forest lands were expropriated and awarded in the same regions where the social conflicts were latent.

Cultural values have seen the forests in public lands as rightful areas to be colonized, and therefore suitable to be cleared from forest and dedicated to agriculture (Peuker 1991: 8; Kishor and Constantino 1993: 2). Secondary forests, if available on a property, are considered by farmers as a sign of mismanagement because the land is not used in the traditional way, i.e., for agriculture; landowners regard fallow areas as diminishing the value of their properties as such natural regeneration hampers agriculture (Müller and Solís 1997: 151; Rodríguez 1997: 147-148).

The expanding *road network* has been a decisive factor influencing deforestation because it has either enabled agricultural expansion and/or land speculation through increased land value. Roads created by logging activities also eased the encroachment of land-seeking peasants, or ranchers that followed the farmers or land speculators, in areas that otherwise would have remained untouched (Peuker 1991: 3; Utting 1993: 19; Mahar and Schneider 1994: 161, 164; Sader et al. 1994: 324-325; Chomitz and Gray 1996; Elton et al. 1997: 60-62; Segura et al. 1997a: 127).

War and political instability have also been important factors influencing deforestation in the region. While deforestation slowed down in the conflict areas, migrants pouring into neighboring countries or regions exacerbated deforestation in those places. Once the conflicts were over and the people came back to their homesteads, deforestation took off again (Utting 1993: 41; Cálix y Sossa 1997: 298; Simon et al. 1997: 309-310, 326).

---

[53] For example, in Panama 46% of the agricultural landholdings lack a title (Elton et al., 1997: 65) and in Costa Rica it has been estimated that – until the beginning of the 90s – 60% of farms lack a title (Peuker, 1991: 8).

4.3 The forest sector in Central America

The stakeholders in the Central American forest sector are mainly: state agencies, NGOs, private enterprises (investors, sawmills and loggers) and landowners.

State forest agencies are in charge of management and control of forestry activities in both public and private forests, but their performance is hampered by the lack of an articulate and coherent policy. Sector policies often lack coordination, and agriculture is still more promoted than forestry (Segura 1997a: 117). Likewise, despite many reforms in the governmental sector oriented to attain a more efficient management and control of forestry activities, this goal is daily encumbered by low-qualified personnel, low salaries, and insufficient material resources to perform an efficient control of logging activities (Cálix y Sossa 1997: 276-282; Elton et al. 1997: 51; Shión y Ambrogi 1997: 153, 159-160; Segura et al. 1997a: 116; Simon et al. 1997: 314, 320-322; Suazo et al. 1997: 247, 252-253). The excess of bureaucratic requirements needed to obtain permission to perform logging activities underpin illegal logging and corruption in several countries (Elton et al. 1997: 51; Cálix y Sossa 1997: 276; Segura et al. 1997a: 105, 116; Simon et al. 1997: 320). Moreover, the lack of reliable data on the state of forest resources in the different countries turns the efficient management and control of forestry activities into a largely unattainable task (Utting 1993: 6; Cálix y Sossa 1997: 279).

Characteristic of many loggers in the region is that they do not own forest lands, and, according to the regulations established by governmental agencies, operate either under contract or concession (license) to exploit forest areas. In Guatemala, Costa Rica, and Panama small landowners depend on larger loggers to use their forests commercially, as they possess neither the technical nor the financial capacity to carry out logging operations beyond small-scale timber extraction for household consumption needs; in other words, the fulfillment of legal and technical requirements implies costs that are prohibitive for most medium and small landowners to undertake (CCT 1992: 13; Cálix y Sossa 1997: 276; Elton et al. 1997: 52-53; Watson et al. 1998: 22; Segura and Vargas 1999: 7).[54] Survival strategies arising from the deteriorated socioeconomic condition of many landowners are closely linked to short-term land use decisions. Albeit low income is directly associated with slash and burn agriculture, forest fires, illegal hunting, squatting and illegal tree felling (Myers 1994, cited in Adger and Brown 1994: 139; Simon et al. 1997: 323), findings from Nicaragua suggest that improved income of households (on the agricultural frontier) facing labor and investment constraints, i.e., poorly functioning factor markets, will also lead to more extensive cattle ranching (Farris 1999).

There is a broad consensus on the fact that landowners base their land-use decisions on their resource endowments, i.e., the availability and quality of productive factors (land, labor, capital and technology) as well as on the availability of markets to sell their products, and that

[54] Reports on this subject were not found for the other Central American countries.

the political and institutional context has acted against any sustainable form of forest use (Farris 1999: 2; Scherr 1999: 164). However, Schelhas (1996: 305) argues that landowners may also have other criteria that might favor forest conservation, i.e., that while the intensity of forest use is likely to vary with the size of the landholding, landowners (proprietors with income generating activities) value forests not only on the basis of their potential – or actual – profitability but also on the production of subsistence products, environmental services (mainly watershed protection) and their potential as savings account. Jantzi et al. (1999) also provide evidence for some landowners' decision to conserve forest (patches) for practical reasons (e.g., watershed protection), basing their decision on personal experiences related to environmental degradation seen on other areas and even childhood exposure to environmental problems.

Economic approaches have repeatedly demonstrated that alternative land uses have been traditionally more profitable than forestry or any other forest-related activity and conclude that this is the main reason why landowners prefer them. For Costa Rica, Howard and Valerio (1996) – based on a study performed by Howard (1995) – argue that if the changes in timber stump prices between 1983 and 1993 are accounted for when discounting cash flows, the profitability of sustainable forest management is higher than that of other land uses; therefore, they conclude that landowners do not base their decisions only on economic criteria. They contend that information costs and technological constraints are important factors hindering the adoption of sustainable forest use. Nevertheless, while this may be partially true, Kishor and Constantino (1993: 1) argue that there is also a lack of private demand for this kind of land use.

As the economic importance of broadleaf, coniferous and mangrove forests in Central America has traditionally been assessed through their contribution to the GDP, their economic value has been reduced to that of timber. This means that the national accounting system has systematically considered the depletion of natural resources as an investment, when their loss should have been accounted for as a decrease of natural capital, hence the forest resources have been used (or in the worst case lost) sacrificing the future rents that otherwise they would have been able to provide (Solórzano et al. 1991; Repetto 1993: 3-12; Elton et al. 1997: 50; Segura et. al. 1997a: 99; Suazo et al. 1997: 259; Cálix y Sossa 1997: 276). Moreover, because of the strong emphasis of development based on the growth of the primary sector, forests have been regarded either as unused/abandoned land or as an obstacle for development (Utting 1993: 16; Suazo et al. 1997: 260; Segura and Vargas 1999: 6).

Forests play a pivotal role in the livelihood of many ethnic and peasant groups throughout Central America, since they provide not only game and fish but also fuelwood and timber for construction in addition to a host of non-timber forest products (NTFPs). Estimates of CATIE indicate that nearly 72% of all households in the region used fuelwood during the 1980s (Utting 1993: 30). Fuelwood gathering represents a serious threat to the existence of natural forests in some areas of Central America, particularly in the northern Pacific zone of Nicaragua, the western highlands in Guatemala and El Salvador (ibid.: 28). El Salvador is perhaps the most dramatic example of forest depletion due to fuelwood gathering. In this country, fuelwood supplies the urban household, commercial and industrial demand of energy. El Salvador is not only the Central American country with the smallest percentage of natural forest cover, but also the country with the highest population density and the highest per-capita fuelwood consumption (Utting 1993: 29; Barry et al. 1997: 186, 203-204).

The use of other NTFPs also plays an important economic role in the livelihood of many Central American forest dwellers, extracting ornamental and medicinal-plants, ferns, orchids, seeds, nuts, gums, dyes, etc. But despite the fact that the social and economic importance of NTFPs is acknowledged, it is feared that the lack of knowledge on these commodities may misguide the development of forest use strategies and lead to their overexploitation (Elton et al. 1997: 39-40; Segura et al. 1997a: 104; Simon et al. 1997: 313; Suazo et. al. 1997: 237, 240; Watson et al. 1998: 14).

Compared to the rest of Central America, logging is a relevant economic activity only in Honduras, where the lumber industry plays a major role as a sector and foreign currency earner. In this country, the logging of pine forests accounted for 94% of round wood between 1990 and 1994, and the value of forest products represented around 10% of the Gross Agricultural Product in 1994 (Utting 1993: 21). In Nicaragua, the export of wood products is dominated by foreign enterprises whose main contribution to the local economy is the provision of employment and the payment of taxes (Shión y Ambrogi 1997: 166).

Throughout Central America inefficiency and/or excess production capacity characterize the lumber industry that processes predominantly timber extracted from broadleaf forests (Utting 1993: 21; Elton et al. 1997: 41; Segura et al. 1997a: 106-107; Shión y Ambrogi 1997: 151-152; Suazo et al. 1997: 252; Cálix y Sossa 1997: 276). In Guatemala, illegal logging outweighs legal logging. Illegal logging produces mainly three commodities: roundwood, fuelwood and construction materials. It is estimated that by 1997 only 2% of the country's total value of industrial wood production was produced under legal terms (Cálix y Sossa 1997: 276).

The exploitation of broadleaf forests is known to be highly selective in most Central American countries. The fact that only a few tree species are commercially exploited implies that a good number of other timber species with potential commercial value is foregone during logging activities. Damage and waste is observable through the huge amount of felling debris left in the forest rather than through the volume extracted. The use of heavy machinery on poorly drained soils accounts for further damage throughout Central America (Solórzano, 1990: 3; Elton et al., 1997: 52; Shión y Ambrogi, 1997: 151; Cálix y Sossa, 1997: 280; Simon et al., 1997: 311, 319). In contrast, it has been documented that the environmental damage of artisanal felling and timber extraction is far less harmful than conventional logging practices (Utting 1993: 22). But in regard to conventional logging, standing trees are often undervalued by the buyers (usually loggers), and many landowners are often primarily interested in getting rid of them in order to prepare the area for agriculture or cattle (Peuker 1991: 2; Cálix y Sossa 1997: 276; Suazo et al. 1997: 252).

Efforts in Honduras and Costa Rica to reduce the intermediation costs arising through loggers have had significant price effects (and therefore increased the value of timber for the landowner). For example in Costa Rica, where all forest lands outside nature reserves are in private hands, the auctioning of timber has enabled landowners to obtain almost double the prices for their timber[55] (Segura et al. 1997a: 108). In Honduras, where the state owns most forest land, lumber prices have more than doubled between 1990 and 1996 since auctioning is practiced (Suazo et al. 1997: 238). Because of trade liberalization, Honduran loggers buy timber from Nicaragua. This has created discontent among Nicaraguan loggers, who claim they are disadvantaged due to unequal access to timber concessions (Shión y Ambrogi 1997: 165-166).

4.4 Forest policy issues in Central America: governmental strategies and private actors

A common goal of the Central American forest policy is the modernization of the forest sector so that the forests are valued for not only the provision of raw materials, but also for the provision of environmental goods and services to society. Concerning natural forests, the most immediate goals are their sustainable use and preservation (Segura et al. 1997: 13).

An important instrument used in all Central American countries to arrest deforestation and protect biodiversity has been the creation of a protected area network (national parks, wildlife and forest reserves). Non governmental organizations have played an important role in the creation and management of protected areas. But management is sometimes hampered by factors like scarce financial resources and lack of well trained and enough personnel. Also, local communities have been excluded from the decision process of establishment of such set-asides and from the benefits they are supposed to provide, leading to illegal hunting, squatting, mining and forest fires (Utting 1993: 105-112; Elton et al. 1997: 48-50, 54; Shión y Ambrogi 1997: 158-160; Barry et al. 1997: 186-188; Suazo et al. 1997: 237, 262-263; Simon et al. 1997: 316-318).

Characteristic of the Central American forest sector, especially during the last 30 years, is the lack of governmental continuity and enforcement of forest policy regulations. As a result, there is widespread insecurity among stakeholders who sometimes do not know what to expect. In other cases inefficient activities are encouraged, creating an adverse environment for both the forest-based industry and the conservation of forests (Solórzano 1990: 24-25; Current 1994; Cálix y Sossa 1997: 279-280; Elton et al. 1997: 44-46; Shión y Ambrogi 1997: 153, 159-160; Suazo et al. 1997: 252-254).

---

[55] Timber auctioning is however not a generalized practice in Costa Rica. Felipe Vega, personal communication.

Nevertheless, throughout Central America innovative forest policies are being pursued and related programs have been launched lately.[56] Efforts of governmental decentralization and the reduction of bureaucracy underpin the process of innovation. Traditional forest use paradigms viewing forest clearing as a way to improve or increase the value of land are being reviewed. New forest policy instruments are designed to foster the sustainable use and conservation of forests, curb illegal felling and enhance the development of forest plantations.

In Panama, Costa Rica, Nicaragua and Guatemala, fiscal and financial incentives shall foster natural forest exploitation and forest plantations.[57] However, the incentive and regulatory systems suffer from flaws and conflicts. While in Guatemala forest incentives have not necessarily made forest management a more attractive land-use option (Cálix y Sossa 1997: 284), in other cases it is evident that economic policy instruments have stimulated the stakeholders to opt for forest plantations at the expense of natural forests. For example, in Costa Rica the approval of management plans allowed for conversion of primary forest into forest plantations with the sole objective of capturing the incentives (Solórzano 1990: 15; Peuker 1991: 17), which are higher for forest plantations than for natural forest management, and much higher than for forest conservation.

Land-based groups – like small farmers and ethnic groups – have largely been marginalized from the process of design and implementation of forest policy instruments, instead, influential groups have traditionally obtained significant economic benefits from the different policy instruments used throughout the region, reducing therefore access of medium and small landowners to resources that could have had a positive influence on the way they use and perceive the forest (Elton et al. 1997: 51; Segura et al. 1997a: 116; Shión y Ambrogi 1997: 165, 166; Suazo et al. 1997: 252). In the case of fiscal incentives, these influential groups are often not even genuinely interested in forest-related activities but in the reduction of their tax liabilities (Cálix y Sossa 1997: 284; Elton et al. 1997: 51; Segura et al. 1997a: 116; Watson et al. 1998: 72).

In Belize, Guatemala, Honduras and Panama, licenses or permits as well as concessions for the extraction of timber are granted both in private and public forests. Subsistence is an important motive driving forest use in Panama, where 66% of the wood extracted from natural forests stems from so-called subsistence permits (Elton et al., 1997: 47). Elsewhere in the region, subsistence needs are also a prime motive of forest use and/or land-use change (Barry et al. 1997: 201; Cálix y Sossa 1997: 298; Segura et al. 1997a: 117; Shión y Ambrogi 1997: 152; Suazo et al. 1997: 236).

---

[56] For example the Plan de Acción Forestal Tropical de Centro América (PAFT-CA) launched between 1989-1990; Convenio para la Conservación de la Biodiversidad y Protección de Areas Silvestres Prioritarias en América Central (CCAP) agreed in June, 1992; Convenio Regional para el Manejo y Conservación de los Ecosistemas Naturales Forestales y el Desarrollo de Plantaciones Forestales, agreed in October 1993. (see, Segura et al., 1997: 13-14)

[57] Costa Rica, besides using forest funds to finance forestry activities, also uses marketable bonds.

Forest management plans are used as an operational policy instrument in Costa Rica, Nicaragua, Honduras and Guatemala. They shall promote sustainable forest management practices, but due to enforcement deficiencies and excessive bureaucratic requirements the monitoring of such plans is severely hampered and they are frequently approved within a context of corruption (Solórzano 1990: 14; Cálix y Sossa 1997: 297; Segura et al. 1997a: 105; Shión y Ambrogi 1997: 154, 159; Suazo et al. 1997: 246, 255).

According to Segura et al. (1997: 16-19), despite the efforts that the Central American countries have undertaken to reach a more effective protection and rational use of forest resources,[58] several factors hinder the achievement of these goals:

- Forest users still lack negotiation capacity in order to influence political processes. There is also scarce articulation between national development objectives and those related to forest management, leading to institutional weakness and incoherence toward the achievement of forest policy objectives.
- Structural conditions. National economies are strongly based on the export of agricultural products. On the one hand, such export policies have actively promoted deforestation; on the other hand, forestry activities have traditionally had a much lower profitability than agricultural land uses, since the markets for forest products (and services) are rather poorly developed. The colonization of forest areas has been induced by land tenure policies and the construction of roads. An agricultural culture predominates in the region.

Though the deforestation rate in Central America has diminished during the last decade, forest conversion continues unabated, particularly in tropical rain forest areas. Annual deforestation in the lowlands of Costa Rica, Honduras and Nicaragua is estimated to be around 3000 km^2 (Rodríguez 1997: 142; Segura et al. 1997: 16).

[58] Central American countries developed agreements and guidelines for the protection and use of natural resources within the framework of the "Alianza para el desarrollo sostenible". Among those agreements are: Plan de Acción Forestal Tropical de Centro América (PAFT-CA) launched between 1989-1990; Convenio para la conservación de la biodiversidad y protección de áreas silvestres prioritarias en América Central (CCAP) agreed during June, 1992; Convenio Regional para el Manejo y Conservación de los Ecosistemas Naturales Forestales y el Desarrollo de Plantaciones Forestales, agreed in October 1993.

5 Costa Rica: Institutional change in the forest sector and conflicts

5.1 Chapter overview

In this chapter the recent changes of the formal institutional framework in the Costa Rican forest sector are analyzed. It will be shown which groups contributed to the change of the formal framework as well as the advantage they are bound to obtain from such changes, and how the potential benefits from these changes contributes to the formation of coalitions. At the same time, the ensuing social conflict over the result of such changes is also considered. For this matter it is looked at the role and performance of not only the state, but also of the involved private actors that, together, form the surrounding environment with which landowners are confronted daily and within which they take forest use decisions. The changes of the system of forestry incentives actually used in Costa Rica is also analyzed, and an assessment is made of their potential to target environmental, economic and social policy goals, and thus their potential to address the provision of collective goods. The analysis undertaken in this chapter is inspired by Nee's and Ingram's (1998) model presented in Chapter 2.

Following, the analysis is based on the revision of laws, primary and secondary literature, data obtained from governmental agencies and NGOs, on my own field research including interviews, direct field observations and the attendance of several public activities, including meetings in the Osa, the press conference given by FECON on March 3rd 2001, the reunion of environmental organizations in the Legislative Assembly organized by congressman José Merino del Río on May 24th 2001 (attended by FECON, APREFLOFAS, ASCONA and Colegio de Biólogos), and the forum at the Legislative Assembly held on June 5th 2001, also organized by congressman José Merino del Río (attended by governmental representatives, academicians, farmers of the Osa, COVIRENA and representatives of the mentioned NGOs). The procedure I follow in this chapter is that the changes in the formal institutional framework are first introduced, then I let the results of the empirical research flow in the analysis to highlight conflicting issues.

5.2 Background

Private forest use embodies both formal and informal institutional arrangements, hence how much compliance there is to formal ends depends on how far the interests of private actors converge with the normative content of sustainable forestry and/or forest protection. The formal institutions ruling private – natural – forest use are mainly the laws that support sustainable forestry and forest protection. These institutions aim at the provision of private goods, for example timber for landowners and their business partners, and collective goods like biodiversity, air quality, recreation, landscape protection etc.[59] Both institutional ends (sustainable forestry and forest protection) aim at the permanence of the tree cover and hence at the availability over time of the collective goods and services that forests provide. The groups interested in promoting these institutional ends embody large portions of society and include landowners, citizens (in urban and rural areas), academicians, politicians and environmentalists. Please note I am not referring to 'pure' public goods but to collective goods. In the case of collective goods – like with public goods – exclusion is very difficult and the costs of exclusion are likely to be so high that preclude any attempt of exclusion. The main difference between public goods and collective goods is that the increased consumption of collective goods leads either to the crowding or to the decreased quality of the collective good. In the case of pure public goods, no matter how much the good is consumed, there is always enough available to everyone (Olson 1968: 63; Hardin 1982: 17-20).

5.2.1 The main actors

The actors on which this study concentrates are the following:[60]

- 'Ministerio del Ambiente y Energía', MINAE (Ministry of the Environment and Energy). MINAE has undergone a process of decentralization and has divided the country into a 'Sistema Nacional de Areas de Conservación', SINAC (National System of Conservation Areas), comprising 11 conservation areas. The field research was performed in the 'Area de Conservación Osa', ACOSA, specifically in the Osa peninsula.

- The Ministerio de Agricultura y Ganadería, MAG (Ministry of Agriculture) and the Instituto de Desarrollo Agrario, IDA (Institute of Agricultural Development) play a decisive role in the use of forest resources since they have – through agricultural and settlement programs – strongly influenced land conversion. This is also the case in the Osa, as will be shown below.

- Organizations of forest entrepreneurs undertake a wide range of activities at the national level from joint productive projects to lobbying their interests at the national policy level. The 'Cámara Costarricense Forestal' (CCF created in 1994) is the largest organization of private actors and comprises medium and large landowners and forest entrepreneurs (including the timber industry, producers of wood products, owners of forest plantations, proprietors of managed natural forests, loggers and forest engineers).

- Organizations of small producers. There are different types of organizations at the communal, regional and national levels. At the national level, the most important – and practically the only one mentioned by governmental authorities[61] – is the 'Junta Nacional

[59] Though a fraction of these collective goods is appropriated – for example – privately by the tourism industry.

[60] See also Watson et al. (1998: 18-28).

[61] See for example the 'Plan Nacional de Desarrollo Forestal'.

Forestal Campesina (JUNAFORCA)' which represents small and medium landowners. JUNAFORCA's main focus is reforestation; it has no associates from ACOSA.[62]

- Medium and large landowners dedicated to reforestation and logging with commercial purposes. Loggers are the main buyers of their timber.
- Small landowners, who engage mainly in low-risk/low-investment activities (cash crops, cattle) and obtain part of their income through subsistence agriculture. Their income is correspondingly low. The average annual salary of someone employed in agriculture ranges $3000 a year.[63] Many combine agriculture with forest activities, including logging, agroforestry and extraction of NTFP. Loggers are also the main buyers of their timber.
- Loggers perform timber extraction (from natural forests or forest plantations) and transport it to the sawmills. Landowners do not usually fell trees on their own but through loggers, who apparently pay low prices for standing timber (see Solórzano, 1990: 5; Segura and Vargas, 1999: 7). Traditionally loggers have maintained a direct relationship with sawmills, and some loggers own at the same time sawmills. Characteristic of loggers is that they do not perform this activity during the whole year, but only during the dry season. During the rainy season many engage in the construction branch (houses, roads, etc.) as the machinery they use for logging is rather appropriate for construction purposes.
- Indigenous communities. Actually indigenous communities are secluded in 10 reservations covering 278.839 ha, of which the larger ones are located in the 'Talamanca' mountain chain. The population is about 19000, and their livelihood depends heavily on fishing and hunting in forest areas. They also perform agriculture in small areas allowing fallow periods long enough for soil recuperation. Isolation and lack of social and economic attention from the government traditionally has put these groups at disadvantage.[64]
- Individual academic and political leaders have been very important in Costa Rica in the diffusion of ideas regarding forest management, conservation, and scientific research as well as in the creation of national parks and the support of initiatives like 'Debt-for-Nature Swaps' and the development of a market for carbon offsets within the framework of the UNFCCC.[65] Some of them have become important figures in the international conservation movement and have strong influence among environmental and donor groups.

---

[62] Felipe Vega, President of JUNAFORCA: Personal Communication.

[63] See 'Proyecto Estado de la Nación' at http://www.estadonacion.or.cr/Compendio/est-so3a.html. Though this is not necessarily the annual income of a private landowner, it can be assumed a reasonable approximation of the income of small landowners matching the above description.

[64] Even though the focus of my research is not on indigenous communities, I consider it important to mention them because in the ACOSA there are several indigenous reserves, and I will bring forward an example of the negotiation style (power) of the government and loggers involving these groups.

[65] See UN (1992b).

- National and international NGOs support and perform not only research activities, but also coordinate activities with academic organizations. These groups have acquired political relevance and play an important role in denouncing activities and policies that harm the environment.
- International donor groups (governmental and private) finance governmental and local projects and have reached political influence.

5.2.2 Land use conflicts and land use capacity

The process of land use change has led to a situation where inappropriate land uses (overuse) persist in several places of the country. The use of areas that should be devoted to forest cover includes mainly grazing and agriculture and accounts for approximately 11500 Km^2 distributed throughout the country. Of this area, approximately 2800 Km^2 are appropriate for forest plantations, 4600 Km^2 are considered suitable for natural forest management, and some 4100 Km^2 should be used only for forest protection.[66] An immediate goal of the Costa Rican forest policy is to bring these areas back to uses that match their potential.

Table 2. Conflicting land use in Costa Rica

Land uses	Ha	%
Appropriate land use (Agriculture, forest plantations, natural reserves and forest outside natural reserves)	3 914 244	76,7
Sub-use (mainly forest plantations in areas suitable for agriculture)	38 089	0,7
Overuse	1 148 191	22,5
Total area of the country	5 100 524	100%

Source: MINAE/PNUD/ONF (2001: 19)[67]

From the late 1960s onwards, different Costa Rican governments have made use of mainly two policy instruments to promote forest protection and curve deforestation – one of the highest in the world during the second half of the 20th century. These are the creation of a protected area system and the award of economic incentives. The Costa Rican state has also a history of a deficient command-and-control strategy and monitoring of logging activities.

To date, Costa Rica's system of protected areas includes 24 National Parks, 9 Biological Reserves, 31 Protecting Zones, 12 Forest Reserves, 39 National Wildlife Refuges and 14 Wetlands. Taken together, these protected areas sum up to approximately 25% of the

---

[66] See MINAE/PNUD/ONF (2001: 18).

[67] This gross estimation of land use does not include water areas, urban areas, streets, etc. It is therefore probably assumed that these areas, particularly streets and urban areas are "appropriate" land uses, which is not necessarily true.

country's area.[68] A formal mechanism largely used by the state to expand the system of protected areas has been the expropriation. An unintended consequence of this mechanism has been that it has failed to anticipate strategic (rent-seeking) behavior of private actors like squatting and speculation to profit from the buy-out (Peuker, 1991: 11), and/or – due to increased insecurity of land tenure – to the extraction of as much timber as possible before the expropriation takes place (CCT, 1992: 11). Through expropriations, the Costa Rican state has accumulated a debt that until 1999 represented approximately 4% of the 1999 GDP.[69]

Table 3. Expropriated (unpaid) protected areas and expropriation costs ($)

Status	**National Parks**	**Biological Reserves**	**Protecting Zones**	**Forest Reserves**	**Wildlife Refuges**	**Wetlands (including mangroves)**
ha	*522 778**	*40 242*	*184 496*	*286 185*	*181 693**	*50 465*
Paid	85%	54%	24%	26%	41%	88%
Unpaid	15%	46%	76%	74%	59%	12%

Natural Reserves, total area (ha)	**Total paid (ha)**	**%**	**Unpaid areas (ha)**	**%**	**Acquisition costs****
1 265 859	703 682	56	562 176	44	$ 620 146 904

Source: Own elaboration based on data from: Periódico La Nación, February 10, 2000: 4a, and Mena y Artavia (1998).
*Excluding marine areas.
**Acquisition costs were in 1999 equal to 177,300 million colones. Annual average exchange rate in 1999: 1 dollar = 285.9 Colones.

According to Watson et al. (1998: 81) one of the biggest difficulties regarding the management of the unpaid protected areas consists on the fact that the government cannot force private actors to refrain from logging in those areas. Furthermore, the creation of many natural reserves has raised resistance among local communities because they are neither consulted before the decision of creating a natural reserve is made nor they perceive any direct economic benefits from such natural reserves. Therefore, natural reserves are perceived by many as a direct threat to their livelihood.[70]

Outside protected areas, and in private properties, it is considered that an equivalent of approximately 8,7% of the country's area should be dedicated to total forest protection.[71] These areas fall mainly into the category of Protecting Zone, Wildlife Refuge, and Forest Reserve. The other areas (also in private hands, and representing approximately 20% of the

[68] See Castro and Arias (1998: 5).

[69] See BCCR at http://websiec.bccr.fi.cr/ for an estimation of Costa Rica's GDP.

[70] Such conflicts have been documented for the "Carara" Biological Reserve on the central Pacific (Utting, 1993: 109-111), for the Forest Reserve "El Bosque Eterno de los Niños" on the northern zone, the "Braulio Carrillo" National Park on the central mountain range (Watson et al. 1998: 82-83) and for the Forest Reserve "Golfo Dulce" on the Osa peninsula on the south Pacific of the country (Utting, 1993: 111; Barrantes et al., 1999: 6-14).

[71] See MINAE/PNUD/ONF (2001: 20).

country's area) suitable for forest management show signs of forest fragmentation (i.e. forest degradation) and are distributed in small patches throughout the country, but mainly in the Nicoya peninsula, the Tilarán mountain range, the buffer zones of the National Parks in the Central Mountain Range, the Osa Peninsula, Burica (in the south Pacific of the country near the border with Panama) and the foothills of the Talamanca mountain range. Several of these forest patches are also located inside indigenous reserves. Even though these areas are considered suitable for natural forest management, it is also considered that much of these areas should be dedicated to absolute protection.[72]

Until 1998 the country's forest cover was roughly estimated of 2 million ha., of which 820000 ha. are found inside protected areas and the rest (1180000 ha) belongs to private landowners (de Camino et al. 2000). If one takes the whole area under some kind of – economic[73] – incentive between 1979 and 1997, it turns that approximately 280000 ha. have received forestry incentives (Castro y Arias 1998: 6).[74] Assuming a scenario in which all of this area still remains under some kind of economic incentive, it turns that yet less than 25% of the forest areas owned privately have received or receive economic incentives. Interviews in FONAFIFO during the year 2000 revealed that the demand for the Payment for Environmental Services is more than double than what FONAFIFO can actually supply.[75]

During the 1990s onwards, a decline in the deforestation rate has been observed in Costa Rica, which is considered to be the combined result of forest policies and the following circumstances (Solórzano 1990; Watson et al. 1998; CCT/CIEDES 1998):

- the economic crisis during the 1980's, which made imported production factors and their maintenance very expensive
- abandonment of grasslands due to declining international meat prices
- the remaining forests are physically less accessible, which increases exploitation costs and risks.

Specifically in the Osa Peninsula, the government's 'Plan Nacional de Ordenamiento Ambiental, POA'[76] establishes that 60% of the peninsula (64 512 ha.) should be used only for forest protection. Logging is apparently not desired, since POA assigns no area for natural forest management. The plan also states that 7% of the total area is being overused, and that there is no data available for 30% of the peninsula's area, i.e., some 20000 ha. Following the

---

[72] See MINAE/PNUD/ONF (2001: 20).

[73] Including; financial, fiscal, credits and PES.

[74] It should be considered that the area under incentives can vary over time as the covenant (incentive) agreements fall due. The figure introduced above is 'optimistic' since the authors assume that the area under incentives has grown (accumulated) continually, which may not necessarily be true.

[75] Jorge Mario Rodríguez, personal communication.

[76] See Decreto Ejecutivo N° 29393 – MINAE (POA).

POA, in the areas for which there is no data available the government admits that it failed to determine conflict areas because the actual land uses, as well as the potential land use remains unknown, which is a large source of uncertainty about the existence and appropriateness of agricultural activities and logging operations in those areas.

The peninsula has a history of recent colonization, and governmental agencies have followed conflicting policy goals. Thus in 1979 the 'Reserva Forestal Golfo Dulce, RFGD' was created (61701 ha.)[77] while at the same time the 'Instituto de Desarrollo Agrario', IDA (Institute for Agricultural Development) established farmer settlements in the same area accounting for approximately 45% of the RFGD.[78]

5.3 The evolution of formal arrangements in the forest sector

5.3.1 The Forest Law and the concept of sustainability

The Costa Rican legislation is strongly engaged in the conservation and maintenance of a healthy environment. Articles 46 and 50 of the constitution state that 'every person has a right to a healthy environment and thus a right to the protection of their health and environment'. Additionally, several laws that regulate – directly or indirectly – the use of forest resources have been either approved or reformed during the second half of the 1990s. Hence, there is the Forest Law,[79] the Environmental Law,[80] the Biodiversity Law,[81] the Wildlife Law,[82] the Soils Law[83] and Water Law.[84] All of them have the basic common goal of achieving the protection and sustainable use of natural resources. The laws of forestry, environment and biodiversity are approved in the aftermath of the Rio Conference and the international negotiations on climate change and the prevention of loss of biodiversity. The term 'sustainability' is consequently widely adopted in the political discourse and in the mentioned legislation, and follows the definition of the Bruntland report where "*sustainability means meeting the needs of today without compromising the ability of future generations to meet their needs*".[85] Kishor and Constantino (1993: 1) define sustainable forest management as "*consistent with the continuity of important environmental functions from the forests. Although some biodiversity may be lost, many other environmental services such as carbon sequestration, hydro-ecological buffering and soil conservation will continue as long as there*

[77] Originally, the RFGD was larger (some 84000 ha), but it was reduced to allow agricultural activities in plain areas.

[78] See Decreto Ejecutivo N° 29393 – MINAE (POA).

[79] Ley 7575.

[80] Ley 7554.

[81] Ley 7788.

[82] Ley 7317.

[83] Ley 7779.

[84] Ley 276.

[85] See also Ley 7788: Artículo 11, Inciso 3.

is no major disruption of the forest cover." Putz (1994: 1) gives the following definition: "*Sustainable forest management is based on methods that jeopardize neither future harvests of forest products nor future benefits of environmental services*". Even though it is also widely acknowledged that sustainable forestry must also contribute to – or at least not worsen – the well being of the people depending directly or indirectly on forest resources, the question of how to approach social sustainability remains one of the most difficult to address due to the wide variety of interests involved in the use of forest resources and the varying perceptions of different actors of what is fair, which is determinant of local well-being (Pierce et al. 1995: 2).[86]

Goodland (2002: 490) contends that "*social sustainability means maintaining social capital. Social capital is investments and services that create the basic framework for society. It lowers the cost of working together and facilitates cooperation: trust lowers transaction costs. Only systematic community participation and strong civil society, including government can achieve this. Cohesion of community for mutual benefit, connectedness between groups of people, reciprocity, tolerance, compassion, patience, forbearance, fellowship, love, commonly accepted standards of honesty, discipline and ethics. Commonly shared rules, laws and information (libraries, film and diskettes) promote social sustainability*". Human sustainability is a related – but different – concept. In this regard, Goodland (ibid.) argues that "*human sustainability means maintaining human capital. Human capital is a private good of individuals, rather than between individuals or societies. The health, education, skills, knowledge, leadership and access to services constitute human capital. Investments in education, health, and nutrition of individuals have become accepted as part of economic development*". In view of these definitions it turns that human sustainability is a key element of social sustainability. The most widely accepted rule-of-thumb concerning social sustainability in forestry is that the sustainable management of forest resources requires the "*active involvement of stakeholders, in varying degrees, in forest management decisions*" (Pierce et al. 1995: 6; see also Ostrom 1999). Though 'active involvement' raises a key issue in the debate over social sustainability, it leaves open how this active involvement is to take place, and who shall be involved and in what degree. Evidently this will depend on the social setting and on what is considered socially desirable, but also on the bargaining power of the involved actors. Since institutional outputs are the result of an ongoing social conflict over the benefits stemming from such institutional arrangements, it follows that 'active involvement' can be influenced if the bargaining power of target groups can be influenced as well. Another element of sustainability, economic sustainability, is related to the maintenance of capital, of which natural resources are an essential part, namely, natural capital (Goodland 2002).

---

[86] Pakrash and Thompson (1994, cited in Pierce et al. 1995: 2) have "*identified four different ways to perceive fairness,..., proportionality (to each according to contribution), parity (equal distribution), priority (inherent rights, like rank/station), and potluck (equal chance, like a lottery).*

Albeit the general adoption of the term sustainability in the Costa Rican laws and in the governmental discourse, the question of what exactly is sustainable forest management, and how can sustainability be measured remains a fuzzy concept in the laws mentioned above, particularly in relation to social sustainability. Additionally, the Costa Rican state shows concern for the sustainability of biodiversity, a substantial element of Costa Rica's natural capital. Repeatedly, laws regulating the use of natural resources bring up and stress the issue of the importance of the correct (sustainable) use of natural resources to maintain biodiversity. The biodiversity law even declares biodiversity a 'merit good'.[87] In this regard, to assess the sustainability of natural forest management in tropical settings, several authors suggest a series of indicators of the maintenance of ecosystem functions and the maintenance of biodiversity – compatible with financial profits and socio-economic goals (Putz 1994; Stork et al. 1997). Nonetheless, these same authors underscore that overall – ecologic, social and economic – sustainability cannot be conclusively proven because unforeseen losses of non-target species due to forest management cannot be avoided, and because tropical settings vary widely.[88] The bylaw to the new Forest Law includes several guidelines for forest management that partially coincide with the criteria suggested by the authors mentioned above, and will be presented and discussed in detail below.

5.3.2 Governmental reorganization and prevailing lack of coordination

The Biodiversity Law introduces a significant change in the organization of the governmental organizations that manage the use of natural resources by creating the 'Sistema Nacional de Areas de Conservación' SINAC, (National System of Conservation Areas). The organization of SINAC is meant as a decentralized and participative system of management and institutional coordination that harbors the areas (formerly separated in different organizations) of forestry, wildlife and protected areas (Araya and Artavia 1998). The policy of SINAC is oriented to the definition and consolidation of several land use types; protected areas, private properties identified as buffer zones of natural reserves, and private properties dedicated to unrestricted production (Segura et al. 1997a: 110). The objective of SINAC is to dictate, organize and execute policies towards the achievement of the sustainable use of natural resources.[89] It corresponds to SINAC the implementation of all the legislation ruling the use of natural resources, including the environmental law, the biodiversity law and the Forest Law.

One of the basic ideas that inspired the creation of SINAC is that – before this reorganization – different governmental organizations tended to act separately hampering each other and/or performing the same activities, leading to an inefficient resource allocation. While this was true for the areas of wildlife, forestry and protected areas, it was – and still is – also a problem

---

[87] See Ley 7788, Artículo 9. A merit good is a good or service whose consumption or production is encouraged based upon non-market value judgments. As with 'public goods', of which merit goods are a subset, the private market cannot profitably provide the quantity or quality that a society considers satisfactory.

[88] See also World Bank (2000: 35).

[89] Ley 7788: Artículo 22.

between governmental organizations in charge of agriculture and land distribution. The organizations in charge of these two last areas are the 'Ministerio de Agricultura y Ganadería, MAG' (Ministry of Agriculture and Livestock) and the 'Instituto de Desarrollo Agrario, IDA' (Institute of Agricultural Development).[90]

The scant coordination between governmental organizations – now and then – is evident in the case of ACOSA. During the field research in the year 2000, I attended a meeting between an organized group of farmers of the settlement 'Los Planes', the IDA, the Ombudsman and SINAC. The main purpose of the reunion was to reach an agreement about the legal situation of the farms, since the IDA insists that these people can be granted property rights, while SINAC argues the opposite. The farmers have a primal interest in obtaining property rights because if they are definitely expropriated, they will be at least indemnified by the government. But their main interest is not to move, but to stay, since they were brought there by the government and as they say "our lives are here". Many farmers there said they were ready to make an agreement not to log the forest conventionally, instead they wanted to be able to take out fallen timber with oxen, and were open to negotiations. The meeting began two hours later than expected because everyone was waiting for the ACOSA officials to arrive, but they did not show up.

During 2001, I also interviewed a functionary of the MAG at Puerto Jiménez. This functionary said that the MAG in Puerto Jiménez has pursued several times to coordinate its agenda with ACOSA, but to no avail. Interviewed functionaries of ACOSA said not to be aware of such an initiative. Most striking is that in Puerto Jiménez the offices of ACOSA are scarcely 200 meters away from those of the MAG.

5.3.3 The Forest Law

Before the new Forest Law was approved in 1996, Richards et al. (1996: 23) contended "*that there are at least three lobbies campaigning for some degree of reform: from the environmentalists' call for a complete moratorium on logging for one or two years,...,; for reform of the DGF*[91] *but maintaining it as a public sector institution, favored by those with most interest in keeping things as they are; and for the creation of a new predominantly private sector or parastatal forestry authority, favored by the privatization/deregulation lobby.*" Actually it can be considered that the new Forest Law is the combined result of the second and third lobbies as will be seen below. The Forest Law prohibits explicitly any kind of logging inside protected areas.[92]

---

[90] See: Alcance N° 34 a La Gaceta. Decreto N° 29393 – MINAE. Plan de Ordenamiento Ambiental, Capítulo IV. Additional governmental organizations mentioned in the decree are the ICT (Instituto Costarricense de Turismo), the municipalities, MOPT (Ministerio de Obras Públicas y Transportes).

[91] DGF stands for 'Dirección General Forestal', the organization that formerly embodied the National Forestry Administration.

[92] See Ley 7575: Artículo 1.

The influence of the private sector in the development and formulation of the forest policy during the last years has been strong (Arias 1998). Watson et al. (1998: 69) state that the CCF was quite successful in assuring its representation in the organisms created by the new Forest Law, particularly in the 'Oficina Nacional Forestal (ONF)' and the 'Fondo Nacional de Financiamiento Forestal (FONAFIFO)'.

The expert interviews indicate that the new Forest Law is chiefly the result of the lobby of the CCF,[93] and that prior to the approval of the law consultation of several stakeholders was scant, especially of environmental NGOs, who constantly complain being marginalized of the process of policy design. The main interest of the CCF is to establish less cutting restrictions and increase the incentives for industrialized forestry (Watson et al. 1998; Robertson 2000). The CCF enhanced its bargaining power by engaging lawyers and professionals in forestry to promote the project law in the Legislative Assembly. Then, the government gave the draft to the representatives of other organizations for debate under time pressure, thus the debate was curtailed and the assistants were not really consulted, and they were not in a position to raise much objections because they had little time to study the document. Rather, the so consulted groups were more informed of how the new law was going to be than consulted.[94] JUNAFORCA apparently did not object the draft, presumably because the organization focuses on reforestation (forest plantations) and they may have an interest in obtaining the largest payments from the PES.[95] This points to a possible coalition between JUNAFORCA and the CCF.

The definition of forest: Of semantic and advantages for conventional logging

A strong debate ensued the approval of the new Forest Law and the definition of forest contained therein. The new Forest Law defines a forest as "a native ecosystem,..., of 2 or more hectares, characterized by the presence of mature trees of different ages and species with one or more canopies and a canopy closure of at least 70%, and where more than 60 trees/ha with a dbh. of 15cm or more are found".[96] The old Forest Law defined forest in a much broader way, namely, "forests are all plant-associations composed predominantly by trees and any other woody vegetation".[97] This last definition was much closer to that used by the FAO, where forests are lands "*with a tree canopy cover of more than 10 percent and area of more than 0.5 ha. Forests are determined both by the presence of trees and the absence of other predominant land uses. The trees should be able to reach a minimum height of 5m. Young stands that have not yet reached, but are expected to reach, a crown density of 10 percent and tree height of 5 m are included under forest, as are temporarily unstocked areas. The*

[93] The CCF represents mainly the interests of large landowners and industrials in the forest sector.

[94] Vicente Watson, personal communication. Guillermo Navarro, personal communication.

[95] The PES for reforestation are the largest and account for approximately $650/ha distributed over 5 years in 1996.

[96] See Ley 7575: Artículo 3.d.

[97] See: Ley 7174: Artículo 6.

term includes forests used for purposes of production, protection, multiple use or conservation (i.e. forest in national parks, nature reserves and other protected areas), as well as forest stands on agricultural lands (e.g. windbreaks and shelterbelts of trees with a width of more than 20m),...,. The term specifically excludes stands of trees established primarily for agricultural production, for example fruit tree plantations. It also excludes trees planted in agroforestry systems."[98]

Environmentalists and academicians have mainly two objections to the definition of forest contained in the new Forest Law. Many academicians think that primary forests should not be logged any more, because they produce highly complex ecological processes that mankind still does not fully understand and from which society benefits.[99] These two groups contend that attending the principle of prevention – endorsed by the Biodiversity Law[100] – conventional logging should be stopped in such areas. Instead, logging should focus on secondary forests and forest plantations.[101] The main objections of these two groups to the definition of forest in the new Forest Law are first, they do not find any logical explanation for the area limit of 2 ha. for a forest to be acknowledged as such, as this leaves many fragmented areas outside the definition even though the canopy closure can match it, and second, many intervened forests have a canopy closure of less than 70%, which leaves them out of the definition. In both cases, these areas are not considered forests. The main concern behind these objections is that forested areas that do not classify as forests can be logged without as much bureaucratic obstacles than otherwise.

The organization representing small landowners (JUNAFORCA) does not share the idea that logging in primary forests shall be stopped, and holds that those wanting to completely protect forests are those rich people who can afford not using them, and that is not the case of small landowners.[102] Another academician, Olman Segura,[103] shares partially this opinion, contending that forest use is the only way through which a forest culture and innovative uses of the forest can be developed. Nonetheless, the definition of forest in the new Forest Law raises much doubts among environmentalists and academicians about how can it be possible to develop a forest culture when the law itself declares as non-forest many intervened and fragmented forested areas. Their main concern is that through such a conception of forest it will be very difficult to make landowners perceive intervened areas as 'real' forests, and not just fallows or useless lands that they can convert at will.

---

[98] See FAO State of World Forests 2001, Annex 1.

[99] This is the position – for example – of MSc. Quírico Jiménez.

[100] See Ley 7788: Artículo 11.

[101] Dr. Gerardo Budowsky: Declarations given for the video "Osa, la última frontera", produced by the Universidad Estatal a Distancia (UNED).

[102] Felipe Vega, personal communication.

[103] Interview performed on the January 12, 2000.

Government officials have admitted lately that the definition of forests should be revised.[104] But to the best of my knowledge, this has not yet happened.

The change of advising organizations to forestry government authorities, or, the positioning of the private sector

Most noticeable in the new Forest Law is that the private sector receives increased importance in its role as governmental advisor. In the old Forest Law, the Ministry of the Environment was permanently advised by the 'Consejo Nacional Forestal, CNF' (National Forestry Council) in matters related to the protection and management of forest resources. Half of the members of this Council belonged or were directly related to the public sector. The council had voice but no vote in the decisions of the State Forestry Administration.[105] The new Forest Law (# 7575) abolishes the National Forest Council and establishes the 'Oficina Nacional Forestal, ONF' (National Forestry Office), a public – but not a governmental – organization composed mainly by private actors close to the CCF, environmentalists are a minority in the ONF.

The functions accruing to the ONF include basically to propose to SINAC policies related to forestry activities, and additionally, to promote investments and obtain financial resources to support the forest sector. The definition of the functions of the ONF make evident a transference of tasks from the public to the private sector. This reflects that the private sector – represented mainly by the CCF – has gained a much higher partake than before in the design and implementation of policy measures.

While the government admits today that one of its ongoing problems is the lack of coordinated work between governmental organizations – and even though this was already a problem of the late CNF, where several ministries and other public and private organizations met – the chances that this can be improved with the ONF appear today narrower than before. But this way, the private sector can come out to the government with a clearer voice that represents its interests, instead of investing time and resources in negotiating with other organizations with diverging – and even opposing – goals.

In both – old and new – Forest Laws the government is represented in the forest sector by the 'Administración Forestal del Estado, AFE' (State Forest Administration).[106] New to the responsibilities of the AFE is its entitlement to establish – via decree – the minimum prices of

---

[104] Fax-interview with Elisabeth Odio (answered by Guido Chávez Chávez), former Minister of the Environment. November 15th 2001. SINAC-DGF-CF-218

[105] See: Ley 7174: Artículo 30.

[106] Under the new Forest Law, the State Forestry Administration is under the guardianship of SINAC.

roundwood.[107] Today, the CCF is the only organization in the country that regularly publishes prices of standing timber for the different regions of the country.[108]

Table 4. Advising organizations to the National Forestry Administration and their composition

CNF (old Forest Law)	ONF (new Forest Law)
– Minister of the Environment (Ministerio de Recursos Naturales Energía y Minas) – Forestry Department (Dirección General Forestal) – Minister of National Planning and Economic Policy (Ministerio de Planificación Nacional y Política Económica) – Agriculture Development Institute (Instituto de Desarrollo Agrario) – Costa Rican Institute of Aqueducts and Drains (Instituto Costarricense de Acueductos y Alcantarillados) – National Chamber of Forest Entrepreneurs (Cámara Nacional de Empresarios Forestales) – Forest Corporations – Forest Cooperatives – Universities – The organization representing the professionals of forest sciences	– Two representatives of small forest producers – Two representatives of 'other' (larger) forest producers – One representative of the organizations of timber merchants (wholesalers) – One representative of the organizations of handworkers and furniture producers – One representative of the ecologist groups of the country

Source: Own elaboration based on the Laws 7174; Art 30, and 7575; Art. 7-10.

5.3.4 Forestry incentives foreseen in the law

Framework incentives

A common characteristic of the laws of forestry, environment and biodiversity is that they pursue to establish framework incentives by the declared public interest of creating and distributing information among stakeholders as well as the active involvement of local communities and related actors in decision making processes and the monitoring of the correct use of resources.

Whereas the old Forest Law assigned to the AFE the technical assistance of forest owners and those performing silvicultural activities in their properties, it was also obliged to promote the

[107] See: Ley 7575: Artículo 44.

[108] Manuel Gómez (CATIE), personal communication.

formation of organized groups to encourage and develop forestry activities and to maintain relations and communicate with the representatives of those organized groups.[109] The new Forest Law redistributes the responsibilities between the AFE and the ONF. For example, both organizations are in charge of distributing information, but while the ONF appears to be specialized on market information, the AFE undertakes aspects related to forest resources, training and education (presumably of forest owners and officials/functionaries).[110] It is also a responsibility of the ONF to organize landowner groups towards forestry activities, which was formerly a responsibility of the AFE.[111] But this group organization is rather oriented towards forest plantations, and no mention is made of resources like secondary or intervened natural forests.

According to the new Forest Law it is a task of the AFE to collect, analyze and divulge information about forests and their sustainable use and define – together with other governmental organizations – suitable land uses in the different regions defined by SINAC. It is also a task of the AFE to promote the acquisition of financial resources for the forest sector. Meanwhile, it is the task of the ONF to distribute information among all producers[112] about markets, costs, prices, tendencies, buyers, stocks, etc, as well as to undertake information campaigns at the national level about the benefits of proper natural forest management, forest conservation and the area increase of forest plantations. The field research in the Osa revealed that very few landowners actually were aware of the market prices of standing timber.[113] It is also notorious that even though the law refers in several clauses to 'development', the concept is not defined and delimited, and even an approximation of what is meant is missing, i.e., is it meant the development of commercial activities, of educational activities, protection activities or a combination of those? The term can thus be freely interpreted.

The focus of the work of the ONF with small landowners is on forest plantations, not on intervened or secondary forests. The creation of a forest culture thus seems to be mainly oriented to forest plantations – which is the activity receiving the highest financial incentives per hectare (as will be shown below) – and not to natural forests. The ensuing question is then: Why is this focus so narrow? The answer is likely to be twofold. First, forest plantations are likely to be more lucrative than the commercial use of secondary forests and than small forest patches usually owned by small landowners. While sometimes it may be desirable not to perform logging in patches of natural forest to meet environmental goals, secondary forests seem to be left at disadvantage, even though some researchers maintain that their productive

---

[109] See: Ley 7174: Artículos 43-5.

[110] I say presumably because it is not specified in the law.

[111] See: Ley 7174: Artículo 44.

[112] The use of the word 'producers' in the law is generic. Thus the reader does not know who is exactly meant: Are producers the landowners? Or are they the loggers and the sawmills?

[113] See Chapter 6 on transaction costs of conventional logging in the Osa.

potential is comparable to forest plantations,[114] though their commercial potential is still not clear. On the other hand, if secondary forests are left out of focus, it is probable that the natural regeneration will be hindered to establish forest plantations, in a situation similar to that depicted in Chapter 4 on the effect of market conditions and Structural Adjustment Programs on secondary forests,[115] which can actually hinder governmental goals of preservation and enhancement of biodiversity. Second, the focus on forest plantations can be due to the fact that forest plantations are carbon sinks, an environmental service for which an international market is being developed and strongly supported by industrialized countries like the USA and Norway. But secondary forests also fix carbon, and would also meet this goal. Therefore, it is not so clear why the narrow focus on forest plantations, except for the assumption that they are more profitable, their management is easier and the private sector is interested mainly in maximizing profits, and not necessarily in managing and/or conserving natural forests.

An important change of the assignment of framework incentives is that the technical assistance is transferred to a third private actor, i.e. accredited forest engineers, who are endowed with 'public faith'. But as the field research and the forest engineer and the logger interviews showed, the landowner is not always technically assisted by the forest engineer because this depends heavily on for whom the forest engineer works. As a private actor, the forest engineer can work in three fashions. First he can be contracted by the landowner. Second, he can work directly for the logger. Most of the interviewed loggers said to 'have their own' forest engineer. Third, the forest engineer can work for himself, and act as an intermediary, i.e., he looks for the landowner and buys the standing timber from him and then he brings a logger to perform the management plan and works with him on a partnership basis. During the field research I was informed of several forest engineers who worked in this fashion.[116] The immediate result of the second and third working fashions is that the landowner is bound to receive partial information, and not everything he needs to know to successfully engage in logging. In this regard, not only technical information – on tree species, volume measuring etc. – but also basic market information is bound to be strategically held back from the landowner. This issues will be deepened in Chapter 6.

[114] See Müller and Solís (1997: 49) for some arguments on this issue.

[115] On this issue see Finegan (1992: 295, 315-6); Rodríguez (1997: 145); Segura et al. (1997a: 120)

[116] I also contacted one of those forest engineers and asked him about his activities in the Osa during 1999. First he denied having performed any work during that year in the Osa. Then he became somewhat angry when I told him that he appeared in the listings of ACOSA as the forest engineer of several management plans approved in 1999 and broke the interview. I had his number from a landowner for whom he had written a forest management plan.

Table 5. Distribution of responsibilities between the AFE and the ONF

Administración Forestal del Estado (AFE)	Oficina Nacional Forestal (ONF)
a) Conserve the forest resources of the country in public and private lands. b) Approve forest management plans following the guidelines stated in the Bylaw to the Forest Law. This responsibility cannot be delegated onto any other organism. c) Dictate the guidelines for forest management plans. d) Administer the Forest Fund (explained below). e) Establish bans on logging of endangered forest species, or on the logging of tree species that may jeopardize other plants, animals, etc. f) Coordinate logging- and fiscal control with the police, municipalities and the Treasury (Ministerio de Hacienda). g) Prevent logging activities that do not comply to the law. For that matter it must perform field inspections, exercise control on roads, log landings etc. to detect and denounce illegal logging. h) Perform a forest inventory and evaluation of the forest resources of the country together with other involved organizations. i) Maintain an inventory of forest research together with involved organizations. j) Promote the systematization of information on forests as well as the divulging of such information, and forest education and training. k) Prevent and combat plagues, diseases and forest fires in state and private properties. l) Develop and execute information programs that contribute to the sustainable development of forest resources in coordination with other competent organizations. m) Participate with the other governmental organizations in the definition of the land use capacity following technical studies. n) Promote the acquisition of financial resources for the development of forest resources.	a) Propose to the Minister of the Environment and Energy policies and strategies for the appropriate development of forestry activities. b) Execute and support programs of technical training and research applied to the forest resources of the country for their improved development and use. c) Launch programs to protect forest resources from fires, plagues, diseases, erosion, soil degradation etc. d) Launch programs to support investments in the forest sector and promote the attraction of financial resources to develop the forest sector. e) Divulge among all producers information – national and international – about markets, costs, prices, tendencies, buyers, stocks, etc. for the optimal commercialization of the sector's products. Also, direct – within and outside the country – the necessary promotion to present the Costa Rican forest products. f) Promote the constitution and strengthening of associations and organized groups for the development of the forest sector, with an emphasis on the participation of small producers of the benefits of the use, the commercialization and industrialization of forest plantations. g) Support programs directed at rural communities to incorporate small landowners in reforestation programs. h) Perform campaigns of information and training for the national community about the benefits that may stem from the appropriate management, conservation and increase of forest plantations. ... l) Advice the 'Regional Environmental Councils' (Consejos Regionales Ambientales) and coordinate with them their functions.

Source: Ley 7575, Artículos 6, 10.

The new Forest Law also assigns to the ONF the counseling of the 'Consejos Regionales Ambientales', CRA (Regional Environmental Councils). The CRA are created by the Law of the Environment.[117] The counseling that they may receive from the Oficina Nacional Forestal (ONF) is determinant of their role as proponents of regional policies and their performance in the management of forest resources (see Table 6). That is, appropriate counseling can improve not only the bargaining power of local groups, but can also influence collective action towards environmental goals. But an outspoken weakness of the CRA is that despite the role assigned to them by the law, their actual input concerning the conception and formulation

[117] See: Ley 7174: Artículo 7

of forest policies remains markedly limited.[118] This was observed repeatedly during the field research in the Osa. For example, the members of the Council were not present at meetings attended in ACOSA, where affairs related to the creation of the Mesoamerican Biological Corridor in the region were discussed. Also, the interviewed landowners did not know of the existence of such a Council, and interviewed members of the Comité de Vigilantes de los Recursos Naturales (COVIRENA) considered it barely relevant.

Table 6. Members and tasks of the Regional Environmental Councils

Members	Tasks
a) One of the provincial governors in the region.	a) To know of, and analyze forest issues in their region and assist in the control and protection of forests.
b) One representative of the Municipalities.	b) Participate actively in the conception and formulation of the regional policies of incentives for reforestation (natural forests are not mentioned)
c) One representative of ecologic organizations.	c) Prevent and combat plagues, diseases and forest fires in state and private properties.
d) One representative of the other Environmental Councils operating in the region.	d) Give follow-up to the advance and compliance of the regional policies of forest development and pronounce themselves about them (again, forest development is not defined)
e) One representative of the 'Student Governments' of the regional high-schools.	e) Recommend to the State Forestry Administration the priority areas to be incentivized.
f) One representative of the entrepreneurial chambers of the region/or present in the region.	f) Authorize the felling of trees in areas that do not qualify as forests.
	g) Any other function that the State Forest Administration assigns to them.

Source: Ley 7554, Artículos 7, 8.

Municipalities (a member of the council) are empowered by law to grant logging permits in areas that do not classify as forests according to the law. Municipalities can approve timber extraction if the number of trees to be extracted yearly per hectare in such areas is less than 3. If the trees to be felled in the property are more than 10, a permit of the AFE is needed.[119] But according to Watson et al. (1998: 65) these organisms lack the human, material and technical resources to effectively perform this type of function. A key informer in the Osa peninsula (who wished to remain anonymous) declared that the years previous to 2001 the municipality of Golfito sold the logging permits for ¢40000 each, and that there was no technical advice to

[118] See also the MINAE/PNUD/ONF (2001: 68, 70).

[119] See: Ley 7575: Artículo 27.

the landowner or even an inspection of the property to determine if the area classified or not as forest.

While the ONF has its focus on market information, the state has to do with education and training, two areas that can promote social sustainability, enhance the bargaining power of local actors and influence collective action. Another example of the Osa will help illustrate the governmental performance in this region of the country.[120] Since the 1990s ACOSA has had to its disposition a trust (some ¢194 million) donated by the Swedish government. Of these funds the half was to be allocated in community extension work and the other half was intended to finance the operations of ACOSA. Even though ACOSA has a department dedicated to community extension (see MINAE 1999), during the last years these funds were not used for community extension but to pay for additional personnel for other areas, including monitoring. The contracting of additional functionaries through these funds was done following a weak personnel management approach because these persons were dismissed and re-contracted every year, this way ACOSA/SINAC/MINAE saved on the unemployment benefits foreseen by law for employees.[121] In this fashion some of these functionaries had been working for ACOSA for almost ten years, which means that probably several of them had already acquired knowledge that only work experience provides. During 2002 the government emitted a decree by which all of these functionaries could not be paid from these funds anymore because their purpose is communal extension, so they were finally dismissed. This way, during this time ACOSA failed in focusing on two goals, first, to motivate its personnel to perform their duties to their best, and second, it missed the chance to enhance the contact and work more closely with local communities as foreseen in its environmental education plan of 1999.[122] The kind of relationship that ACOSA maintains with local communities is basically of mutual mistrust. A functionary of ACOSA of the program of environmental education said during an interview that the environmental education program has its focus on youngsters, as the older people already have their own way of looking and using natural resources, that is, ACOSA has given up on reaching them, specially those logging illegally. This functionary said that many landowners are not willing to go through all the bureaucracy to take out one or two trees, so they decide to log illegally, or end up making a management plan, financed by the logger, who fells more trees than originally wished by the landowner. The point here is that through the work with communities and landowners, ACOSA could have identified their needs and negotiated a way out with them, but that did not happen. Now, it is but an exercise of imagination to think what would have been more effective in the long-term, to work closer with the local communities following a long term plan and develop trust, a partnership relationship, and flexible rules concerning the use of

---

[120] On a more general critique of the governmental performance at the national level by the establishment of framework incentives see Torres (1998: 6).

[121] Merly González, former attorney of ACOSA, personal communication.

[122] See MINAE/ACOSA (1999), Programa de Educación Ambiental.

timber, or to hire personnel to monitor them. Framework conditions remain thus quite poor in the Osa.

Another incentive that the Forest Law provides to landowners is protection against encroachment (squatting, etc.) in properties under forest protection and/or dedicated to forestry activities. The old Forest Law guaranteed protection against squatting only in properties dedicated to forest protection.

Economic incentives

Following Segura et al. (1997a: 110-111), Castro and Arias (1998: 13), and Watson et al. (1998) the use of economic incentives for forestry in Costa Rica can be divided in three phases:

1. Between 1979 and 1987 income tax exemptions for reforestation (i.e. forest plantations) are introduced favoring mainly large enterprises.

2. Between 1988 and 1995, marketable certificates (for forest plantations, natural forest management and forest protection) are introduced. Such certificates could be used to pay either taxes or sold. Between 1988 and 1992 only forest-plantations received certificates. After 1992 certificates were granted for forest management (Certificado de Abono Forestal para Manejo del Bosque, CAFMA) and after 1995 for forest protection (Certificado de Protección de Bosque, CPB) as well. The certificates for forest-plantations paid the highest amounts, while those for forest-protection paid the lowest. Other financial incentives were soft-credits, and forestry funds. During this period small and medium landowners were incorporated to the perception of incentives through local organizations. Incentives were also given for the export of timber products (except for roundwood, on which an export ban persists). Export of forest products were classified as non-traditional and received all the incentives foreseen for such activities like tradable certificates, tax exemptions (from income, import of inputs) and accelerated depreciation.

3. From 1996 onwards, the new Forest Law (Ley Forestal #7575) changed the 'spirit' of the existing incentives by establishing the 'Payment of Forest Environmental Services' (PES). Allegedly, the PES represent an effort to move away from the concept of subsidies towards the payment for collective environmental goods – services – provided by forests to society. Following the expert interviews, the PES were created in a moment when the World Bank was demanding from the Costa Rican state the removal of all subsidies in the economy, including those for forestry. It is at this moment that the Costa Rican policy makers decided to introduce the PES,[123] moved partially by the lobby of private actors within the forest sector (e.g. the CCF).

Besides the PES, the new Forest Law also includes credits and a forest fund.

[123] Vicente Watson, Felipe Vega, Olman Segura, personal communication.

Landowners can obtain credits through the 'Fondo Nacional de Financiamiento Forestal', FONAFIFO (National Forest Financial Fund). Also, forest areas can be used as collateral. An important difference here is that the old Forest Law specified that the land as well as the standing trees could be used as collateral. Instead, the new Forest Law states that even though forested areas can be used as collateral, creditors do not acquire any rights over timber extraction. Therefore, it remains an unclear issue how creditors are to be moved to grant loans on forested lands when – should the debtor fail to pay back – they do not acquire any particular use-rights over the resources supposedly used as collateral.

The Forestry Fund is a financial instrument administered by the AFE. The purpose of the Fund is to finance programs to promote products from forest plantations, reforestation of areas suitable for forests and agroforestry, prevent and combat plagues, modernize the forest industry, support activities of research and training, perform actions and projects oriented to curve the deterioration of natural resources. The Fund is financed partly through a forest tax equivalent to 3% of the value of roundwood.[124] This tax was of 10% of the value of standing timber in the old Forest Law. While the original tax (10% of the value of standing timber) was collected before any logging took place, the new tax (3%) is collected at the sawmills. Thus, while under the old law it was not possible to log until the tax had been paid due, now, some sawmills can even hold back the tax payment.[125] This is another advantage reached by the private sector under the new Forest Law.

The PES are framed in an oligopsonic market, as the state remains the main buyer and/or intermediary of environmental services. The state establishes each year – via decree – the values of the PES. In the case of carbon fixation the landowners receiving PES cede automatically the rights over the marketing of carbon fixation services to the state.[126] Likewise, the state arranges covenant agreements between landowners protecting watersheds and hydroelectric plants. According to Chomitz et al. (1998: 18), the PES target several goals:

- Carbon sequestration and hydrological services
- Conservation of biodiversity and genetic assets
- Conservation of soils
- Increase the income of small landowners

The PES are awarded – in national currency – during a five year period, and the currency devaluation provokes a loss of value of the PES in terms of current dollars. This is important because in the country it is usual that people convert/think Colones into Dollars, so the effect

[124] The law defines roundwood as the section of the tree shaft without branches and with a diameter equal or larger than 29cm on its thinnest end.

[125] Guillermo Navarro, personal communication.

[126] See FONAFIFO (1996; 1997).

of the devaluation on income is perceived by most Costa Ricans this way. Thus, in a hysteresis related way, it is likely that the larger the area, the more a landowner will perceive he becomes less for the PES he is being paid. For example, if a landowner receives PES for forest protection on 10 ha., instead of receiving $2090 at the end of the period he receives $1840 ($250 less). If the same landowner receives PES over 100 ha. he will receive $2500 less at the end of the period. The devaluation effect is not so strong in the case of forest management and forest plantations because the largest payments are made the first year.

Table 7. PES and the effect of devaluation

Modality		Yearly (%) distribution of PES					
		1	2	3	4	5	
Forest plantations		50%	20%	15%	10%	5%	
Forest management		50%	20%	10%	10%	10%	
Forest protection		20%	20%	20%	20%	20%	
		Year					
Total PES ¢/ha (1999)		**1999**	**2000**	**2001**	**2002**	**2003**	
Forest plantations	*154.000*	77.000	30.800	23.100	15.400	7.700	Current value at the end of the period
Forest management	*94.000*	47.000	18.800	9.400	9.400	9.400	
Forest protection	*60.000*	12.000	12.000	12.000	12.000	12.000	
Total PES $/ha (1999)							
Forest plantations	*538*	269	100	70	44	21	504
Forest management	*328*	164	61	29	27	26	306
Forest protection	*209*	42	39	36	34	33	184

Source: Own elaboration based on data provided by FONAFIFO. Exchange rate 1999: BCCR; 'tipo de cambio usado en las cuentas monetarias': ¢/$=286,46.

Whereas the old legislation provided different incentives for different forestry activities (forest protection, forest management and forest plantations), the PES support the same activities using the same structure of payments. Even though the incentivized activities are the same in both laws, the spirit of the new Forest Law is clearly different, because it directly addresses the issue of environmental services, absent in the Costa Rican legislation hitherto. Thus, while the old incentives were subsidies, the PES are conceived as a payment for the services forests provide. Nonetheless, the similarity of the structure of the PES to the old incentives is remarkable – though the PES started off with lower values than the former incentives. In both laws the payments are distributed over five years. The maintenance of the structure of the PES equal to the former incentives is bound to several difficulties, as will be explained below.

The requisites that a landowner must fulfill in order to receive any form of PES are also the same as those required for the incentives given under the old Forest Law. These begin with a written application to the respective Conservation Area including:

- The name of the proprietor, identity card (personal or entrepreneurial), type of PES, area to be incentivized, data of property registry and location of the property.

- Copy of the property title inscribed in the land registry, where the area to be incentivized is marked.
- Certification of the public registry of property.
- Management plan elaborated by an accredited forest engineer according to the criteria emitted by the AFE related to the forest activity to be undertaken.
- Proof of no tax liabilities emitted by the National Treasury (Tributación Directa)
- Proof of up-to-date payment of municipal and territorial taxes, given by the corresponding municipality

Table 8. Forestry incentives and distribution of payments before and after 1996, ($)/ha

	Old Forest Law*	New Forest Law (PES)**					
Incentivized forestry activities	*1995*	*1996****	*1997*	*1998*	*1999*	*2000*	*2001*
Forest protection	270		214	233	209	214	220
Forest management	520		344	364	328	305	344
Forest plantations	650		514	597	538	548	564
	Example: Distribution of PES awarded in 1997		*Yearly distribution of payments (%)*				
			1	*2*	*3*	*4*	*5*
Forest protection	214		*20*	*20*	*20*	*20*	*20*
Forest management	344		*50*	*20*	*10*	*10*	*10*
Forest plantations	514		*50*	*20*	*15*	*10*	*5*

Source: *Watson et al. (1998). **Own elaboration based on data provided by FONAFIFO. *** Though the new Forest Law was approved in April 1996, the first Payments for Environmental Services (PES) succeeded in 1997.

Landowners and private enterprises can receive PES in areas of up to 300 ha., while cooperatives and other social organizations can be awarded PES over larger tracts due to the fact that they can group many landowners. The current values (in Colones) of the PES are to be actualized yearly by the government, who also decides on the allocation of PES. Whereas one of the intentions behind the decentralization pursued by SINAC is that landowners can apply for the PES directly in the regional offices of SINAC, similar decentralization efforts have not been undertaken in other governmental organizations. Consequently, certifications from the Land Registry and from the Treasury can only be obtained in the capital city, San José, which contributes to increase transaction costs.

The PES for – voluntary – forest protection are awarded under the 'Certificado de Protección de Bosque, CPB' (Certificate of Forest Protection), which already existed in the old law, and they can also be either sold or used to pay taxes. The CPB will only be awarded in forest areas where there has been no forest felling the previous two years to the award of the incentive. The landowner must sign a covenant agreement with the state in which the landowner acquires the compromise not to perform any kind of forest felling during the next 20 years in the incentivized area. This covenant is to be annotated in the property registry, as well as the perception of CPB. Under the 'old' CPB no compromise was required from the landowner not to perform logging over a certain period of time. According to an interviewed expert, the CPB alone is weak to induce landowners to protect the forest (in those areas where this is wished) because they represent the lowest payments of all the PES. Therefore, a landowner will probably try to log first as much as he can before he goes for the CPB.[127]

To further compensate landowners for the environmental services stemming from forest protection, those awarded with CFPs are also exempted from taxes on property and assets (today repealed). The same is foreseen for natural forest management and forest plantations. The government charges 5% over the value of CFPs. The awardee must deposit this sum in the account of the Forestry Fund to cover the costs of control and monitoring.

The Costa Rican state, through the introduction of the PES, continues to set its focus on the use of financial instruments to guide the private use of forest resources. The Forest Law lumps together forest environmental services and fails to distinguish which environmental services can be obtained from different forestry activities.

To group indiscriminately different forest environmental services has the advantage that the PES are easy to administer, but include also the disadvantage that they make it difficult to target specific environmental services. This means that a shortcoming of the PES is that they embody in a single payment different environmental services that may actually tend to exclude each other, i.e., there may be tradeoffs between environmental services depending on what forestry activity is undertaken. For example, a primary forest will produce a series of environmental services, but will not fix carbon actively. A tropical primary forest, having reached a climax stage, is rather a deposit of carbon and may even tend to release carbon.[128] On the other hand, a logged forest will actively fix carbon, though the quality of other environmental services may be diminished through logging itself, for example biodiversity and soil protection.[129] Hurtado (1996, cited in Barrantes et al. 1999: 56) found that conventional logging in the Osa peninsula – in parcels subject to extraction during 30 years – caused the reduction of the availability of 5 tree species common in the peninsula, and lead to the extinction of 2 tree species in those parcels. Robertson (2000) points out that conventional logging in the northern lowlands of the country of the tree specie 'Almendro' (*Dipteryx panamensis*) degrades the habitat of the green macaw (*Ara ambigua*) and other species. Bertie (2000) demonstrates that logging roads in slopes steeper than 15% in the Osa peninsula significantly increase runoff and reduce the quality of the studied watershed (Río Riyito). These authors show that conventional logging reduces the quality and availability of biodiversity, soil and watershed services. Newspapers report that – due to selective logging –

[127] Guillermo Arias, personal communication. See also Aylward, cited in Watson et al. (1998: 78)

[128] Guillermo Navarro, personal communication.

[129] See for example Kishor and Constantino (1993).

some 40 tree species in Costa Rica are jeopardized or in danger of becoming extinct.[130] The performed interviews confirm that – due to the use of heavy machinery not designed for logging, scarce training of forest workers, limited monitoring of the forest engineer of the logging site,[131] scant monitoring of the authorities of the AFE, etc. – the contribution of conventional logging to the maintenance of the quality of several forest environmental services like biodiversity and watershed protection is rather poor. Therefore, it is questionable that PES – for the protection of soils, biodiversity, watershed, etc. – are given to operations where conventional logging takes place, and where probably the only environmental service that can be convincingly argued is carbon fixation.

But since carbon fixation is apparently the most relevant environmental service enhanced by logging, one could hypothesize that PES are – despite their generic treatment in the law – paid indeed for different environmental services, and that the less valuable are those produced by forest protection (e.g. biodiversity and soil protection) and for which there are no efforts being made to develop a market. In contrast, the most valuable are those that stem from logging and forest plantations, and for which markets instruments are being developed, namely, carbon fixation. Industrialized countries like the USA have been eager to develop a carbon market to offset their own emissions since the UNFCCC was negotiated, and Costa Rica has been quick to react to the signal launched by industrialized countries. The CCF has recognized this opportunity and JUNAFORCA has allied itself to these efforts by making forest plantations its priority. This way, the alliance between these two organizations can be explained, which is evident in the document of the 'Plan Nacional de Desarrollo Forestal'. These two organizations show few conflicts with the government, except that they complain that the government fails to transfer timely the financial resources from the tax on fossil fuels to FONAFIFO.

Taken at face value – from the point of view of the state – logging and forest plantations deliver more valuable environmental services (carbon fixation) than forest protection (biodiversity protection, soil protection, etc.). The development of markets for carbon fixation is probably the most straightforward explanation. Apart from this observation, it is difficult to explain why the most lucrative forestry activities – that tend to deliver carbon fixation more than other environmental services – receive the largest PES when forest protection actually delivers a larger variety of these goods and services, but not carbon fixation.

Considering that the use of forest resources by private actors is influenced by the profitability rendered by different uses, a first question that arises when the award of financial incentives for forest protection and natural forest management is considered is, how do these incentives

[130] See La Nación, Revista Dominical, p. 3: "Agonizantes". Inerview to Quírico Jiménez, INBIO.

[131] As revealed by the logger and forest engineer interviews, scarce monitoring of the logger engineer of the logging site can be due to either one of the following situations: First, the logger wishes to lower operation costs and reduces the monitoring of the forest engineer. Second, the forest engineer has many management plans to monitor, so he cannot supervise them all as he should.

influence the profitability of different forest uses and which policy goals are likely to be achieved? To answer these questions, the following exercise was prepared based on the data obtained during the field research performed in the Osa.

PES and the profitability of competing forest uses

Based on the data provided by ACOSA on the volume of approved timber for logging during 1999 and the corresponding area, the average felled volume per hectare was estimated for the visited farms (n=44). To reduce the effect of extreme values on the average volume/ha, the six highest and lowest values of the figures (m^3/ha) were eliminated (this way the standard deviation was reduced from 16m^3 to 7m^3) and an average volume of timber of 27m^3/ha was obtained (n=32). The distribution of commercial timber was estimated following the model of composition of commercial timber species in Osa found in Jiménez (1996) and Barrantes et al. (1999).[132] Timber extraction was assumed in different scenarios (i.e. in areas of 10, 50, 100, 150, 200, 250 and 300ha). The profitability of different forestry activities was calculated as a function of the area size subject to incentives. For comparison purposes, it is assumed that these areas are all equally suitable for logging. In this sense, the landowner chooses between logging and forest protection.

The profitability of forest protection and natural forest management was estimated according to the net present value (NPV) of the investment the landowner must make to receive the PES. In the case of forest protection – because no felling activities take place – it is assumed that the landowner pays cash for the management plan and paperwork. A forest management plan is different, and cheaper, when made for forest protection than when done for natural forest management. The cost of both management plans is also derived from the area.[133]

The profitability of natural forest management is assessed by making the following assumptions:

1. The landowner confers a legal empowerment to the logger to undertake all of the paperwork (from property certifications to the contracting of the forest engineer to elaborate the forest management plan).
2. The service provided by the logger is paid by the landowner in timber.
3. All the transaction costs (equivalent to the 37% of the value of standing timber according to the prices of soft, semi-hard and hard timber available at the 'Cámara Costarricense Forestal')[134] are added to the value that the logger charges for paperwork.
4. The transaction costs are considered part of the investment and occur in period t_0. Even though the period t_0 to t_1 describes a year, I consider it relevant to discount this value

[132] See Chapter 6.

[133] See logger and forest engineer interviews.

[134] See Chapter 6.

because the amount is not negligible in terms of the forgone income, i.e., in terms of the costs that the landowner is willing to incur to perform logging.

Another case of the profitability of natural forest management was calculated for logging within forest reserves, in this case the 'Reserva Forestal Golfo Dulce (RFGD)'. An additional condition (requisite) in this case is that an environmental impact study must be presented. Though the cost of an environmental impact study is bound to vary with the area, I am assuming a one-cost-fits-all because the same figure was mentioned repeatedly by landowners, forest engineers and loggers with reference to small areas (50-100 ha). The reader should be aware that – in this exercise – this may make logging in larger properties inside a forest reserve appear more profitable than it really may be.

Opportunity costs of alternative land uses are not included. The reason is that if the law forbids land use change in forestlands, then opportunity costs cannot arise in terms of agriculture or cattle ranching, because these land use changes are not allowed. Moreover, land use change being banned by law, the potential gains that a landowner may obtain from cutting down the forest for agriculture or cattle ranching may be offset if he is discovered and punished by the state, which would make the election of opportunity costs rather arbitrary.[135]

The discount rate used is an average of the real discount rates of the Costa Rican economy for the years between 1997 and 2000. The real discount rate was estimated by subtracting the annual inflation rate from the passive interest rate of the national banking system. This way an average real discount rate of 10% was assessed.

The calculated NPV of the investment needed to receive the PES for forest protection is equal to zero at a forest size of 20 ha. Below this area the current investment required renders a negative profitability. Above this area, the returns on the investment are positive. Natural forest management is already profitable in properties with 10 ha. forest upwards (see Graphic 1).

When the profitability of forest protection is compared to that of natural forest management, it can be seen that in all cases – except two – the profitability of natural forest management is higher than that of forest protection. When logging takes place within a forest reserve, logging is profitable in areas slightly smaller than 50 ha. upwards, and should the logging operation become PES, profitability is positive in areas equal or larger than 25 ha. From the point of view of the landowner, should he/she have the choice between forest protection and logging, he/she will choose logging, that is, unless the landowner has an income source that makes logging unnecessary and wishes to engage in forest protection. Should the landowner have pressing economic needs, and the chance to log, logging should be preferred. On the other hand, a wealthy landowner may just wish to log for money's sake, not because he needs it. In

[135] For an argument on the PES as a rough approximation of the land use opportunity cost see Chomitz et al. (1998: 7-8).

the terms the PES are structured, forest protection does not represent a serious financial competition to conventional logging in areas where forest protection might be desirable. To become a competitive financial alternative, the PES for forest protection should be at least $750/ha.

The ensuing question is then, why should landowners in the Osa be brought to protect the forest? Forest protection is a policy objective in buffer zones of national parks and other protected areas, and in locations that are sensible and strategic for the maintenance of the quality of forest environmental services like watershed, soil and biodiversity protection.[136] As Bertie (2000) and Barrantes et al. (1999) show, much of the problem of conventional logging in the Osa is that the area has many such locations but logging still takes place in many of them as well. In areas like the Osa – that show a lack of local economic dynamism (unemployment, slacking agricultural markets, etc.)[137] – conventional logging is for many one of the few income sources available, so why should a landowner with pressing economic needs choose forest protection? From a landowner's point of view, and given the structure of PES, the answer is he/she should not.

Considering that the PES target the increase of the income of the smaller landowners, it turns that – in the case of forest protection – the smaller landowners have the less advantage from the PES, in comparison to those having 100 ha. or more of natural forest in their properties. This is most evident in the case of conventional logging in stands equal or larger than 50 ha (see Graphic 1). Taking into account that the average income of a small farmer in Costa Rica rounds $3000 a year,[138] the additional income derived from PES for forest protection distributed over 5 years does not appear very impressive in stands of up to 100 ha. But in the case of landowners logging conventionally in stands of 50 ha – for example – the award of PES distributed over 5 years is almost as high as the yearly income. That is, the award of PES for conventional logging does boost the income of landowners with forest stands of 50 ha. or more in their properties. But paradoxically, conventional logging is already a lucrative activity in any stand equal or larger than 50 ha., i.e., provided the stand is outside a forest reserve. Conventional logging is on the spot of criticism of many academicians and environmentalists on the grounds that it does not do improve, but reduces the quality of several environmental services (like biodiversity and watershed protection), except for carbon fixation. The paradox is that PES are given to an activity that already is lucrative, and rather tends to reduce or even worsens specific environmental services except one.

As a function of the forest area, the PES tend to be socially inefficient (i.e. have a social-selective effect), since landowners with larger forest tracts are evidently more benefited, and

[136] See for example: Ley 7788, Artículo 37. Also, in its POA (Plan de Ordenamiento Ambiental), SINAC assigns no area in the Osa for natural forest management.

[137] Personal communication of a MAG agricultural engineer in Puerto Jiménez. This assertion is also based on direct field observations.

[138] See Proyecto Estado de la Nación at http://www.estadonacion.or.cr/Compendio/est-so3a.html.

this is a main shortcoming of this instrument to boost the income of small landowners. Landowners with larger properties may tend to be the wealthier members of the community, hence the ones with the power to access the PES. Also, the investment needed to engage in conventional logging does not necessarily represent an entrance barrier to conventional logging for the landowner, because the logger can – and usually does – pay for all the paperwork and obtains that cost back in kind, i.e. timber. But – as several loggers and landowners commented – loggers are not much interested in logging in small tracts unless these harbor valuable timber. Landowners with less than 20 ha. of natural forest in their properties will definitely remain excluded from any potential benefits of the PES for forest protection, no matter how strategically relevant their properties might be in achieving policy goals, and will definitely wish to engage in logging. The PES for forest protection fail consequently to effectively boost the income of smaller landowners, while logging, even if no PES are awarded, has a much larger potential to increase the landowner's income in the short term. But still one must consider that the figures related to the PES in Graphic 1 are discounted over a time horizon of 5 years, and the socioeconomic effect of increased income flows will depend on the landowner's managerial capacity to administer these financial resources.

Graphic 1. NPV of forest protection and natural forest management, with and without the award of PES in 1999 as a function of the area (ha, USD)

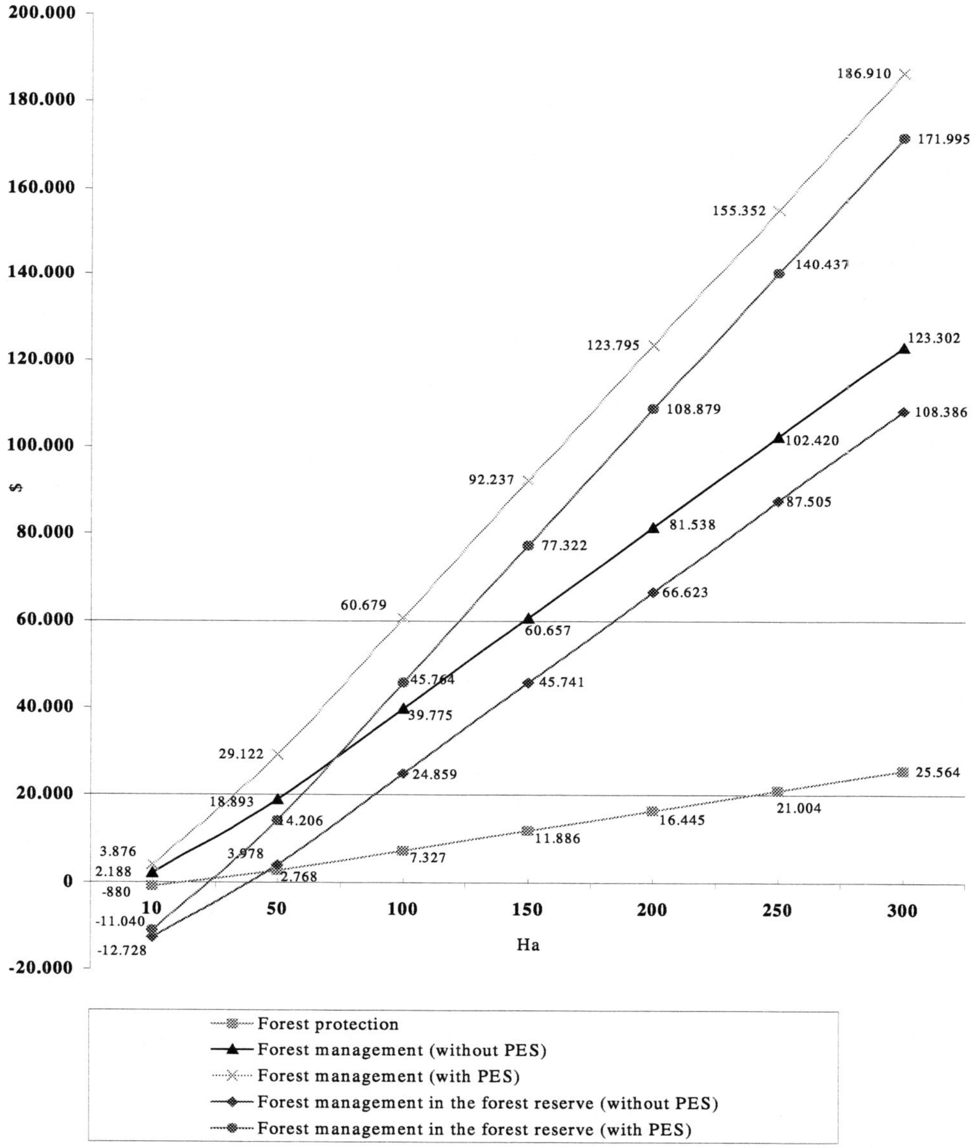

Source: Own elaboration

The PES and the rules that grant access to forest resources fail not only to effectively target smaller landowners and move landowners in general towards forest protection – or at least make them consider it a viable option – in areas where this is desired, but they also preclude alternative forestry activities (e.g., small-scale logging) that can actually bring the landowner closer to the development of a 'forest culture'. This is so, because under the 'new rules' the landowner is bound to remain a client of conventional loggers, and no space for 'innovation' is left open in this regard. I mean 'innovation' not because small-scale logging might be new, but because many small landowners do saw and take out timber from the forest, but illegally, and an official acknowledgement of this activity would be an innovation. The absence of the AFE as a counseling agent and partner of the landowner worsens the situation even more. The interviewed landowners tend to see ACOSA as anything but as an organization to which they can turn to – in a constructive sense – regarding forestry issues. They feel the requisites for logging are much too complicated and out of their reach. In general, the perception they have from the whole bureaucratic apparatus is 'they want to keep us out'.[139] While more flexibility of the formal framework to allow for differentiated forestry activities could effectively reach those landowners willing to engage in small-scale logging, it remains unclear if this would also catch the interest of those landowners who wish to continue engaged in conventional logging and/or wish to cut down the forest for cattle and agriculture.

One should be aware that, in the governmental political discourse, small-scale logging is associated with illegal logging, an activity that the government and the CCF repeatedly condemn.[140] The position of the CCF against small-scale logging can be rapidly understood if one considers that this organization represents mainly loggers and owners of sawmills. Therefore they do not have an interest in the allowance of any small-scale logging, as this would represent a loss of 'clientele'. The CCF contends that conventional logging is not a source of trouble because through the forest management plans, principles, criteria and indicators of sustainability are introduced. But this position should be taken with some skepticism.

---

[139] This is, for example, one of the main arguments that SIPRAICO (Sindicato de Productores Agrícolas Independientes del Cantón de Osa) holds against ACOSA and the government. Regarding the conflict between SIPRAICO and the government see: Sala Constitucional de la Corte Suprema de Justicia: Recurso de Amparo No. 3605-V-92.

[140] The 'Plan Nacional de Desarrollo Forestal' contains a whole chapter on this issue, and it implicitly assumes that forest management (i.e., conventional logging) tends to fall out of the category of 'illegal', even though Campos et al. (2001) define illegal logging as any activity that does not comply to the law, which means that conventional logging can also incur in illegal acts. Campos et al (2001) elaborate the document by charge of the 'Comisión de Implementación del Plan Nacional de Desarrollo Forestal'.

5.3.5 The perceptions of landowners, PES and fuzzy targets

In the landowner interviews two questions addressed were:

1. 'What environmental services does your forest provide?' This question was stated – as far as possible – without reaching to introductory explanations, so as to not bias the answers toward what the landowner might think the researcher wants to hear. When the landowner did not understand the question a brief explanation was given without listing 'typical' environmental services like watershed protection etc.

2. Contingent forest use. 'If you could do anything with your forest at this moment, what would you do?'

These two questions were stated during the first and second visit to the Osa. Because of this, the two sets of interviews were used. From the first set of interviews (n=33), four landowners were excluded because they were interviewed again during the second field research (n=44). The group size in this case is of 73 interviewees.

When asked about environmental services provided by their forests, several interviewed landowners mentioned up to three different environmental services, and few (5) mentioned up to five different environmental services. Of these five landowners, three are farmers with good relationships to the COVIRENA, the fourth is a school teacher, and the fifth is a USA citizen with university studies in forestry. The following table depicts their answers.

Table 9. Landowners' perception of forest environmental services

Environmental services	First answer	Total mentions
Watershed protection	47	53
None	10	10
Construction materials	4	11
Micro climate	2	11
Biodiversity	2	28
Landscape	2	16
Firewood	1	12
Air	1	14
Medicines	1	1
Food	1	2
Life	1	1
Soil protection		2
Recreation		2
Seeds		1
Carbon fixation		3

Source: own elaboration

These results coincide with research performed by Schelhas (1996) and Jantzi et al. (1999), and suggest that landowners perceive environmental services mainly through practical (business) criteria. Consequently, watershed protection is for them the most important environmental service providing drinking water and farm irrigation. Still, a relatively large group failed to perceive any environmental service from forests. These results signal that the landowners have a limited perception of what is – in general – being meant by the state regarding the maintenance of forest environmental services, and show that they are not being accurately targeted as key actors since they fail to recognize that the governmental policy targets several environmental services at the same time and not just one.

Table 10. Landowners' contingent forest use

		Occupation		
Contingent forest use	Number of respondents	Low income	Professional/–entrepreneur	Unemployed
Protection (if incentives were available)	22	21	1	
Forest protection (unconditional)	14	7	7	
Sell it	11	9	1	1
Regular logging	9	1	5	3
Cut it (for cattle and agriculture)	7	6		1
Small scale logging	7	5	2	
Cut it and cash the money	1	1		
Protection (hillsides)	1		1	
Stable income (from incentives)	1		1	
Total	**73**	**50**	**18**	**5**

Source: Own elaboration

When asked about contingent forest use, the largest group of landowners (22) answered they would be willing to protect their forests if PES were available. Despite this 'willingness to protect', most landowners complained 'the PES for protection are too low', and that the amounts foreseen by the PES would not be enough to increase their income significantly even in combination with their actual occupation. They are either engaged in low-income activities (farmers, labor on other farms, policemen, small retail) or unemployed. Only one of them is dedicated to small-scale tourism. The property size in this group ranges between 50 and 300 ha, and only one farm reaches 500 ha.

The second largest group (14 landowners) is already engaged in forest protection, and answered 'I would continue doing with it what I have done until now, protect it'. Relevant to these landowners is that they did not demand (or mention) any particular condition – like receiving PES – to continue protecting the forest. The income source of half of them stems from either professional, commercial or tourism activities. The other half is engaged in low income activities. In this group, 10 farms are smaller than 100 ha while one is larger than 100 ha, two others are larger than 200 ha and one is 600 ha. This last property belongs to a USA citizen.

Eleven landowners contended they would like to sell their property and move elsewhere. The majority (9) are engaged in low income activities (farming, laboring on other farms etc.), one is unemployed and the last one is a small retailer. Eight properties are smaller than 100 ha, and only one is larger than 250 ha. Common to the members of this group was their frustration derived from not being able to use the forest at their will.

Nine landowners said they would wish to continue engaged in regular – conventional – logging. In this group 4 landowners are loggers (of which none lives permanently in their farms), one is a small retailer, one is dedicated to farming and the rest is either unable to work or unemployed. Loggers have also the largest properties (200-900 ha), while the rest are around 100 ha or smaller in size.

Eight landowners expressed their wish to 'cut the forest for cattle and agriculture', or just 'cut it and cash the money'. All except one (unemployed) are engaged in low income activities. Half of the properties are equal or slightly larger than 50 ha, the rest is smaller than 40 ha. Among this group (and several landowners in the other groups), it was usual to hear the comment that 'the forest is indeed nice and I like it, but cattle,..., that is something you carry in your blood'.

Seven landowners expressed their wish to perform small scale logging, e.g., saw timber in the forest and take it out with oxen, horses and/or light trucks for either their own consumption or to sell it. Five of them are engaged in agriculture, one owns a small sawmill and one is a preacher. Three properties are smaller than 100 ha., the rest is equal or smaller than 200 ha.

Only one landowner contended he would protect the hillsides, he being an agricultural entrepreneur, and his property is approximately 120 ha large. Another landowner said he would like to maintain a stable income from the PES for forest protection. He is a tourism entrepreneur, and his property has an area of 180 ha.

Landowners interest themselves in small-scale logging because, first, it increases the aggregate value of the timber (and makes access to it cheaper if they wish to use it in their household), and second, it does not cause as much damage to the property as when the loggers come in. Actually, several interviewed landowners did not have the intention of engaging in conventional logging in the first place, originally, they wanted to extract fallen trees in their properties, but due to the bulk and cost of the required paperwork, they ended up engaging in conventional logging. The reason is that to take out a fallen tree the landowner is compelled to present a management plan to the AFE, and an environmental impact study if the tree is inside a forest reserve, which many landowners find – with a sort of tragic humor – ludicrous. In view of this, many decide themselves for conventional logging, since under such requirements, loggers are the second-best choice they have.

The government argues that the award of PES is done according to priority areas,[141] i.e., specific places where the maintenance of forest environmental services is desired like river basins or places that harbor rare species relevant for the maintenance of biodiversity. But it remains unclear how consequent is this principle being followed, and it is also unclear how – under the principle of priority areas – the government wishes to attend social issues that can threaten the conservation, production and enhancement of forest environmental services. That is, are priority areas really being incentivized, or are the payments being awarded on a first-come first-served basis? In other words, are the PES being awarded to those who have the power to access them instead of those in areas strategically relevant for policy objectives? The reason for this doubt arises from the fact that under the former set of incentives, it was generally acknowledged that the existing economic incentives tended to benefit the middle and the upper classes involved in forestry – i.e. the larger and more economically powerful agents – and not necessarily those representing an immediate source of pressure on forest resources relevant for policy objectives. Today – though under a different spirit – the PES maintain the very same structure of payments, and incentive the same forestry activities. In view of this, can one reasonably assume that the previous situation has changed regarding priority areas? Or even for the benefit of the smaller landowners? The reasons why I come back to small landowners are, first, many small landowners live in the Osa peninsula which is by far a priority area in ACOSA, hence the state has an interest in effectively managing the forest resources therein, second, it is a declared interest of the government to support this group. I will try to obtain some insights on these issues by looking at the data for ACOSA on the award of PES between the years 1998 and 2001.[142] The listing of ACOSA does not provide information on the location of the areas and the priority these may have regarding policy goals, thus this is a matter pending further clarification. But the data do provide some information on what groups may be obtaining the largest benefits from the PES for the different forest uses.

It can be seen that private landowners accrue the largest proportion of the incentivized area for forest management (almost 900 ha, which is relatively small compared to the area under forest protection, 15000 ha, see Graphic 2).[143] Nonetheless, it is reasonable to assume that the landowners engaged in this activity are attracted by the higher profitability of logging together with the award of PES for logging, and the fact that they have the means to access the PES. Groups representing small landowners are absent in this category. The only recipients of PES involved in natural forest management for this period are indeed private landowners (14) and private enterprises (4), to whom some 1160 ha of forests accrue (see Graphic 3 for the total number of recipients of PES according to the category).

---

[141] See MINAE, Decreto N° 29393.

[142] See MINAE/ACOSA (2000).

[143] It is worthwhile to have in mind that the total area approved for logging was of 3846 ha. for the year 1999.

Concerning the interviewed landowners, two of them are receiving PES for forest management because one engaged the logger in the application, and the other the forest engineer, and both are charged a fee. The rest of the interviewed landowners did not perceive PES either because of incomplete property rights or because they did not know how and/or were reluctant to engage the logger or the forest engineer for that matter. Many landowners showed themselves reluctant to engage either loggers or forest engineers in the application of PES because they fear being ripped-off. This reflects a low level of trust between these actors. The landowners who engaged a forest engineer (the same one) in the application of PES gave some insights on these issues.[144] The forest engineer demanded a legal empowerment from them to cash the money himself, so that the landowners would not be forced to travel far to cash the payments and the forest engineer would bring the payments to them. In this fashion, the forest engineer let FONAFIFO transfer the payments to his own account and paid the landowners with a personal check amounts inferior to the original PES. Apparently, this forest engineer is facing trial but not because of these deeds, but because of the 'incorrect execution' of forest management plans.

Regarding forest protection, it can be seen that all the associations taken together (13) accrue the smallest area under PES (see Graphic 2). This stands even if the only NGO receiving PES for forest protection is included.[145] The listing provided by ACOSA for this period does not show how many landowners are represented by each organization, except for three. One is a 'Cantonal Agricultural Center' and represents 28 small landowners whose incentivized areas are not larger than 50 ha, and together they add up to 600 ha. The other two are cooperatives that together represent 6 landowners, but in the case of cooperatives, I am not sure if one can call these landowners small, because some of them appear under the name of an enterprise. The point that I want to make is, that in comparison to 35 private enterprises receiving PES for forest protection (see Graphic 3) for some 4000 ha, small landowners hardly reach together 3600 ha, and their number is likely to be larger than that of private enterprises, and due to the fact that one cannot know how many are really represented, no comparison can be made with the group of 'independent' landowners.

[144] One during the first field research in the year 2000, and the other one during 2001.

[145] Though NGOs are non-profit organizations, they do not necessarily group small landowners.

Graphic 2. ACOSA, distribution of PES (ha) according to type of activity and recipients between 1998 and 2001

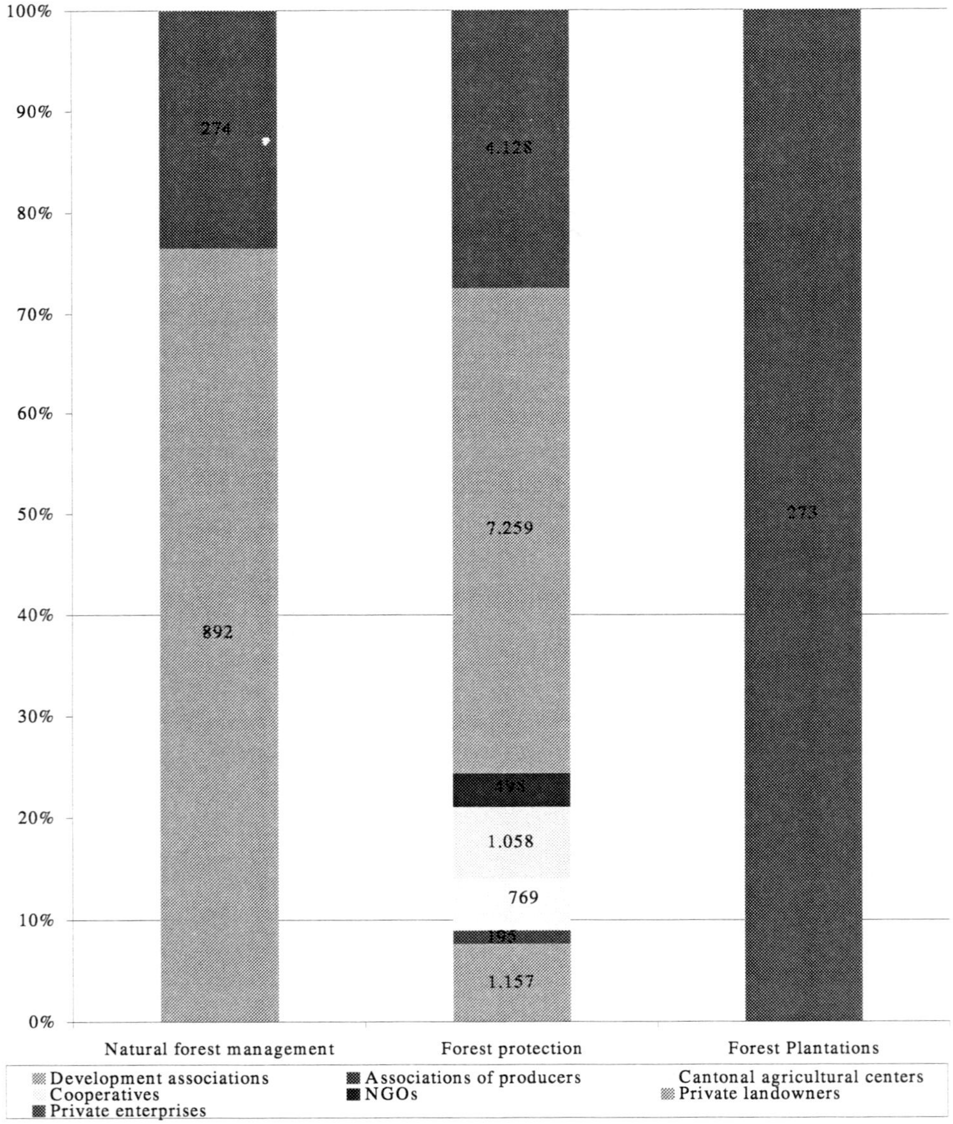

Source: Own elaboration

Graphic 3. ACOSA, recipients of PES between 1998-2001

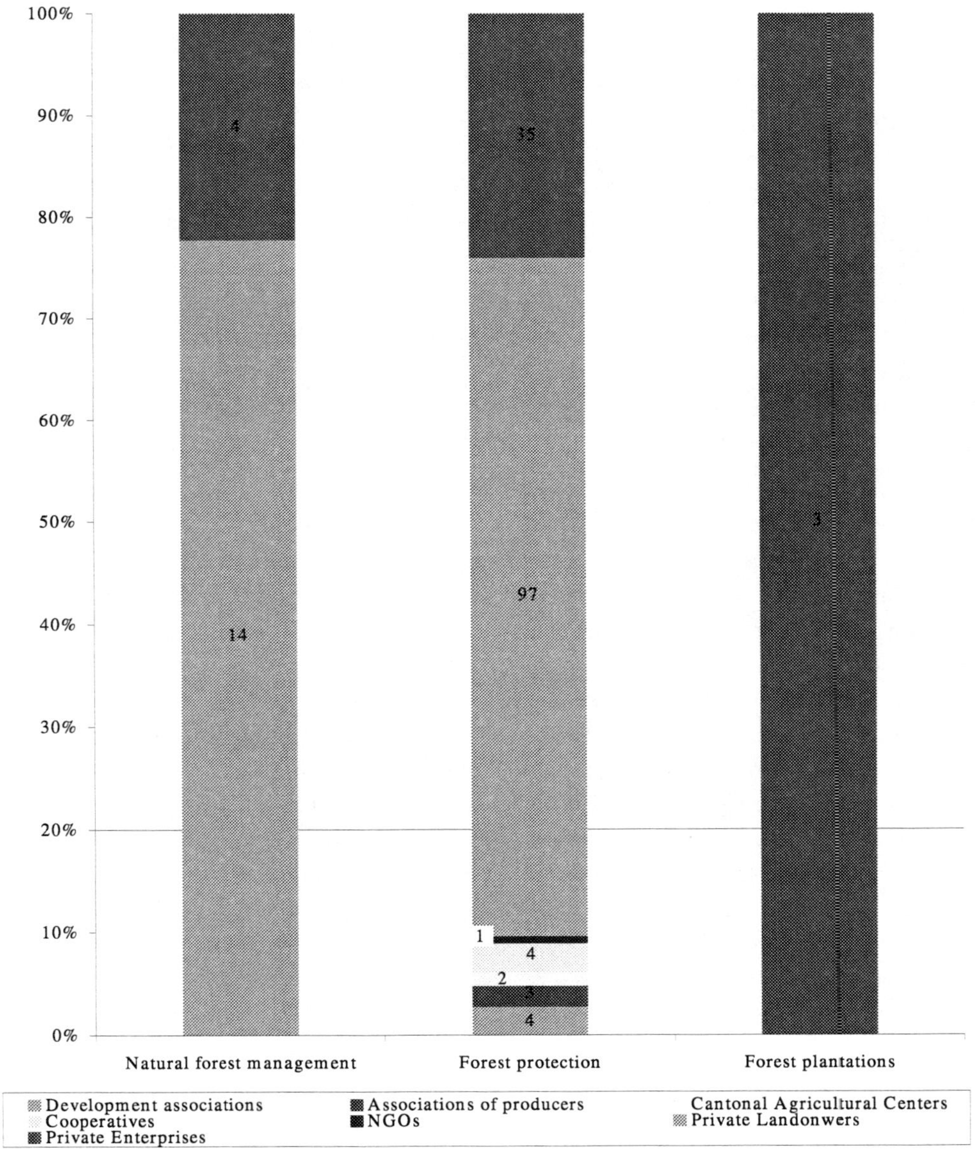

Source: Own elaboration

When one looks at the private enterprises receiving PES for forest protection, it is most noticeable that many are dedicated to tourism, that is, these are enterprises already obtaining a profit from forest protection and pose no threat to the forest. Other enterprises are cattle ranches or agricultural enterprises. Other enterprises in the listing belong to loggers who live in Cartago (the capital city of the province Cartago). Of the private landowners receiving PES for forest protection, some of them are also loggers, some of Pérez Zeledón, some others of Cartago. I know this because their names were mentioned repeatedly during the interviews. Others are timber intermediaries whom I met during the field research. Hence while one cannot rule out the fact that some of those private landowners are probably locals to the area and may be renouncing to alternative land uses, one cannot exclude the possibility that others are absent owners as well, and receive PES additionally to an already existing source of income.

Large landowners can act opportunistically to cash more PES than the maximum allowed (300 ha) when they divide their property among their kin in the land registry. This way they can maximize the income from PES.[146] Indeed, if one looks at the listing provided by ACOSA, it is obvious that several recipients of PES are members of the same family, so this last possibility should also be considered.

A question that arises when considering forest protection is: Why would an enterprise (or a small, medium or large landowner)[147] dedicate land to forest protection when the profitability of forest protection is so low and it actually precludes their main productive activities? One can assume several scenarios. The first one is that they were caught by the new Forest Law and they are refraining from changing the land use (a strong assumption in the case of farmers), hence they claim PES as a form of compensation for forgone income. The second one is that they have already changed the land use as much as they could, and the areas they are devoting to forest protection are rather inaccessible and/or protect vital resources for the farm – like water springs – and consequently they are in no peril of being logged. I mean they are in no peril of being logged and not something else because the new Forest Law forbids land use change, therefore, logging would be the first-best alternative of maximizing profits in a forested area, but they apparently refrain from this alternative. A third scenario would be that they have already logged the accessible forested areas, and now (e.g. two years later) the best alternative is to apply for PES for forest protection. A final scenario is that the private actor protects the forest voluntarily and cashes the PES as a form of retribution. But it is hard to believe that someone would want to protect a forest if this would lead to a relative household impoverishment.

The question on the effective targeting of policy objectives remains unclear for several reasons. For example, in the provision of watershed protection, the properties in a river basin

[146] Guillermo Arias personal communiation.

[147] For obvious reasons, tourism enterprises are not meant.

are more relevant to the award of PES than others outside the basin, independent if these are small or large. Similarly, the maintenance of biodiversity is difficult to target not only because such goods are difficult to value, but because their preservation requires the representation of different species and habitats. Chomitz et al. (1998: 22) posit that large properties might prove to be more cost-effective than small properties to protect biodiversity because they can ensure minimum habitat sizes and contiguity. But cost-effectiveness criteria alone would oversee the fact that many small neighboring properties can build a considerable forest mass, and/or connect large properties, which is also the case of the Osa. Therefore, in a situation where the government has a tight budget, rent-seeking behavior and power of some groups to access the PES might tend to produce a crowding-out of those with less power to access the PES independently of how relevant their forest resources are for forest policy objectives. Consequently, the normative framework might hamper the achievements of its own goals.

If the rule to award the PES is thought after priority areas, it is rather unimportant if these areas belong to large, medium, or small landowners, as long as the targeted areas are brought under the desired – appropriate – land uses, which would tend to overrule social goals allegedly linked to the PES. But if a target of the PES is indeed to boost the income of small landowners, the data obtained from ACOSA suggest that small landowners are probably a majority of beneficiaries, but taken together they receive the smallest proportion of PES in the only activity in which they are being paid for, forest protection. Consequently, the potential of this financial instrument to boost the income of small landowners is – under the actual conditions – questionable. The landowner interviews also show that the governmental policy has limited success in improving local awareness towards forest environmental services, or in inducing more forest friendly activities.

5.3.6 Formal norms and conventional logging

Formal norms for natural forest management

In both Forest Laws (the old and new) the technical instrument through which natural forests are to be managed (i.e. either logging or forest protection) is the forest management plan. It is conceived as the technical instrument through which – compellingly – logging is to take place and through which sustainable forest use is to be achieved. New in the recent Forest Law is that the technical assistance to forest owners – formerly accruing to the AFE[148] – is transferred to a private agent, namely the forest engineer, who is in charge of the elaboration and supervision of the forest management plan, and is in charge of assisting the landowner in matters related to the sustainable use of forest resources. The new Forest Law also endows private forest engineers with public faith (i.e., management plans and reports on logging activities elaborated by accredited forest engineers are recognized as valid and credible by governmental authorities, as are protocols elaborated by lawyers).

[148] See: Ley 7174: Artículos 10, 43

The Bylaw[149] to the new Forest Law creates the 'Comisión Nacional de Certificación Forestal' (National Commission of Forest Certification) whose main obligation concerning the sustainable use of forests is to recommend to the AFE the principles, criteria and indicators of sustainable forest management to be required from management plans in natural forests.

According to the law, the correct execution of a management plan implies compliance to the guidelines recommended by this commission and approved by the National Forestry Administration. The guidelines (criteria) related to sustainable natural forest management require:[150]

1. Forest management must comply to the laws of the country. Logging in natural forests can be either certified or not. In the case of certified logging, a contract must exist between the owner and the certifying agency for a period of at least five years, where the compromise of adherence to the principles listed herein is established. In the case of not-certified logging, a declaration – under oath – of those responsible is required to assure compliance to these principles.
2. The ownership of the land as well as of the forest resources under management should be clearly defined and documented.
3. Natural forest management must contribute to maintain or increase social welfare of forest workers and respect communities' rights. It is desirable that local persons are benefited (directly or indirectly) from logging activities. There shall be effective communication between community representatives and those in charge of logging operations; legal mechanisms for the solution of conflicts must be available.
4. The rights of indigenous communities to possess, use, and manage their lands, territories and resources is recognized.[151]
5. Forest management shall promote the efficient use of forest resources and services to assure economic viability and a wide array of social and environmental services.
6. Natural forest management must promote the conservation of biodiversity, water (hydric) and edaphic resources. With the compliance to this guideline, forest ecological functions (forest integrity and environmental services) shall be maintained. Rare (scarce, threatened) forest species, as well as their habitats should be protected.

---

149 See: Reglamento a la Ley Forestal: Artículo 26.

150 For the details to these guidelines see: La Gaceta N°212. Lunes 2 de noviembre de 1998, p. 5-9. Decreto N° 27388-MINAE.

151 It is not clear though who is responsible for the regulation of this principle. Of course, the state is the main responsible for the upright attendance of the law, but who is to work together with it is not clear. There is the "Comisión de Asuntos Indígenas", but it is mentioned neither in the law, bylaw nor the "Plan Nacional de Desarrollo Forestal (PNDF)". The "Mesa Nacional Indígena" is vaguely mentioned in the PNDF, but apparently it accrues no significant role.

7. The design of roads in the forest shall be explained to the forest workers on the field, as well as to which trees are to be felled and which are seed trees. The forest workers shall receive a theoretical course and training, and after this they should be awarded a certificate to demonstrate that they are able to perform forest labor. Also, they shall be supervised on the field to assure that the management plan is performed accordingly. The planning of natural forest management shall be found in a written forest management plan. The criteria that a management plan must fulfill is distinguished at two levels. The first one is a general plan and the second one is an operational plan.

8. According to the size of the managed area, the condition of the forest, the chain of custody and the social and environmental impacts are to be monitored and evaluated. In the case of a – state defined – certified chain of custody, the responsible actors must maintain (available) a registry of the origin of raw materials.

9. Natural forests shall be managed sustainably to assure their permanence. These areas cannot be replaced by forest plantations nor by any other land use.

Concerning the conservation and management of forests in the old Forest Law, the National Forestry Administration was also entitled to ban the use of heavy machinery if its use could negatively affect forest regeneration.[152] Instead, the new Forest Law prohibits explicitly land use change in any area covered by natural forests. Furthermore, neither the new Forest Law nor its bylaw make any mention of secondary forests, a resource considered to have much potential as a timber source (see above).

[152] See: Ley 7174: Artículo 49.

Table 11. Criteria required from forest management plans

General plan	Operational plan
a) An executive summary of the management plan b) The purpose of the forest management c) Access roads, land use and a general description of the adjacent areas d) Description of the forest resources to be managed based on the results of a preliminary inventory (that includes trees with bhd.>30cm), the bio-physical limitations and the management risks according to the structure and composition of the forest. The sample error of the preliminary inventory should be less or equal to 20% of the basal area for all species e) Description of the silvicultural management system, based on the characteristics of the forest and the information obtained in the preliminary inventory. Additionally, the felling cycle is indicated and justified, as well as the list of species and the intensity of use per specie f) Monitoring plan g) An evaluation of the possible impacts of felling on the residual mass, on the hydric and edaphic resources and the corresponding mitigation measures h) Identification of rare forest species, threatened or in danger of extinction and the protection measures i) Maps that describe the forest resources, the felling areas, conservation areas, hydric resources, buffer zones and existing roads. The maps should include the corresponding information from the land register (cartographic location). The conservation areas include fragile zones and of ecological and/or cultural importance j) Description of the measures to control hunting, fishing, capture and collection of flora and fauna k) If the management affects communal goods (common pool resources), the mechanisms for their protection should be included	a) A topographical map (levantamiento topografico) that shall be elaborated by means of specialized software[153] b) Regarding the felling activities, the topographic map includes (besides topographic characteristics) hydrological resources, primary and secondary roads, log landings, trees to be felled and seed trees. A copy of the map shall be used in the field as a guide for the forest workers c) The description and justification of the used silvicultural and felling techniques as well as of the used machinery d) Based on the topographic map, infrastructure is included to guarantee that neither the natural drainage system nor any water system will be obstructed due to felling activities e) Market prices of timber as well as the alternative commercialization channels are depicted f) List of the felled trees and the seed trees g) Technical justification of the extraction of dry (dead) trees and already fallen trees

Source: Own elaboration based on Decreto Ejecutivo No. 27388-MINAE, Principio No. 7.

[153] The bylaw does not specify which.

Conventional logging and the performance of governmental organizations

While the Costa Rican state assumes that forest management plans and the PES for forest management allow a more efficient control over the execution of management plans and the activities derived from them,[154] different governments, and different SINAC administrations are repeatedly confronted with criticism from several actors due to the poor execution of forest management plans and the deficient monitoring of these logging activities.

Several factors affect the performance of governmental organizations. First, it is widely known that ever since SINAC (Sistema Nacional de Areas de Conservación) was created (and before), the system has lacked qualified personnel, equipment and financial resources. According to the minister of the environment (Elisabeth Odio), the reason why citizen participation is fostered by the government is for citizens to directly control logging activities.[155] But while the state expects local communities to participate in the monitoring of logging activities, the same local communities are poorly supported by the state in the monitoring of these activities, as will be shown below in the case of the 'Comité de Vigilantes de los Recursos Naturales, COVIRENA', and other individual community members in the OSA.

The governmental failures in monitoring can be looked at in several stages, which weakens its performance regarding the sustainability criteria described above. Lack of personnel and equipment is always mentioned, but what does this mean in practical everyday terms? In the Osa, between 1997 and 1999 some 164 forest management plans were approved in the peninsular area accounting for approximately 3.486 ha.[156] This task had to be fully supervised by two functionaries (one forest engineer and one agronomist) and two or three assistants. This meant that these functionaries were in charge of the office work (bureaucratic evaluation of the applications for logging permits) and the field work (technical inspections of what was evaluated in the office) corresponding to those 3.486 ha. The lack of equipment meant that these personnel could only seldom perform field inspections (*ex ante* and *ex post*). Recharged tasks lead inevitably to a situation in which the same functionaries responsible of approving a logging permit bureaucratically and evaluating the approval of the permit on the field (*ex ante*), are responsible of certifying that the logging operations were concluded according to the permit or not (*ex post*). If the logging permit (management plan) is performed irregularly, the functionary must proceed to file denounce. But it is unlikely that a functionary will denounce an irregular logging operation – for example, if trees are cut in a protection area, say a riverside – when he approved the felling of those trees, inasmuch this would put his reputation, and probably position, at stake.[157] According to an ACOSA functionary – and key informer – the scarcity of personnel has lead to a situation where inspections of ongoing

[154] See 'La Gaceta, Diario Oficial. Miércoles 28 de abril del 2001. Decreto N° 29394-MINAE, Considerando # 7.

[155] See Periódico La Nación, martes 6 de marzo del 2001, p. 11A.

[156] See Barrantes et.al (1999: 15). According to Barrantes et al. (ibid: p. 13) the peninsula has some 160.000 ha, of which 108.000 ha were still forested in 1995.

[157] Interview with Merly González Mayorga, former attorney of ACOSA in Chacarita.

logging activities of approved management plans are rather undertaken when a denounce is filed. This assertion was confirmed by interviewed loggers and forest engineers.

But overcharged responsibilities are not only seen at the level described above but also at the highest governmental levels. One of the first actions of the second government in office (1998-2002) since the approval of the new Forest Law was to recharge the position of Minister of the Environment to the position of the Vice-President.

According to an ACOSA functionary at a transport checkpoint, monitoring deficiencies in the transport of timber are manifold. Among them is the fact that timber transport is mostly controlled following the loaded volume, while the control of timber species being transported is often left aside. This creates an incentive for loggers to cheat on ACOSA by trying to transport timber that was not approved in the management plan. This functionary said that he has become aware that this way, loggers try to smuggle more precious timber than allowed in the management plan. Another deficiency in monitoring includes improperly archived files, thus sometimes another file is created for the same management plan. The consequence of this is that the logger can eventually use his permit to transport timber twice.

Though lack of personnel and 'culture in the management of information' is one of the admitted weaknesses of SINAC, other circumstances also hamper its efficient operation at rather basic levels of communication even among its own personnel.

During several years of the 90's (mostly the second half) the government of the United States supported – together with the Costa Rican government and universities – the establishment of the project REFORMA in the Osa to improve the capacity of ACOSA in monitoring logging activities. For this matter infrastructure was donated to be used at timber transport checkpoints, together with equipment including computers and software to create a data base that would allow improvements in the monitoring of forest management plans and thus of timber extraction. Despite large donations and the availability of material resources, the project was quit and the donated equipment was scantly used to monitor logging due to – allegedly – lack of qualified personnel.[158]

During the fieldwork it was seen that ACOSA actually has a geographical information system through which monitoring of logging sites can be performed. But only one functionary has access to the system (namely, the sub-regional director of ACOSA for the peninsula). Initial information from ACOSA suggested that only this functionary had enough training (knowledge) to use the system properly, but paradoxically he was not directly involved in monitoring of logging in ACOSA. When I asked ACOSA's forest engineer in charge of monitoring logging activities why he did not have access to the system he said 'to avoid problems with my immediate superior'. This functionary did not say he did not know how to use the system, rather, he implied he was not allowed to. Thus through one single functionary,

[158] Eric Rusmann, ex-executive director of Cecropia, personal communication.

and due to deficient communication between supposedly working mates, stalling of monitoring occurs.

Personnel is not only scarce but also unstable, particularly at leadership positions. For example, ACOSA had 7 different directors between 1996 and 1997. Positions like these are given according to political interests.[159]

Additional to the lack of qualified personnel, signs of corruption are also recurrent. They are recurrent because it is not the first time this issue is raised long before the creation of SINAC. Nonetheless SINAC still has trouble in coming to grips with this problem. While ACOSA officials deny this, the logger interviews provided some evidence in this regard. Even though almost none of the loggers admitted to have ever paid a bribe to a state official to obtain a permit to log or transport timber, they did not deny this either. They said they knew it happened. One logger openly admitted to have bribed ACOSA officials, but he also said 'if you quote me saying this, I will deny everything'. The forest engineer interviews provided more insights on this. Even though they were also very careful in what they said, they also contended that corruption in SINAC is an everyday fact. One forest engineer who dared to talk openly about ACOSA, said that bribes are a two way street. For example, when the officials/functionaries try to control timber transport, they are offered bribes, and the other way around, some officials control timber transport expecting to be offered a bribe, and when they are, they not only expect to be paid but they also say how much is it that they want. An interviewed ACOSA functionary provided further information. This functionary confirmed that almost every time he inspected a timber transport he has been offered money. When he rejected the bribe, the price (bribe) went higher, and when he rejected the bribe again he was threatened by the trucker (and/or the logger) he would get killed. When he was new at the transport check-point and the truckers came along with the loaded timber, they asked for 'the other functionary', and asked further, at what time the 'other' functionary came in, and on what days.

It is imaginable that a combination of lack of – qualified – personnel, recharged functions, scarce material resources and corruption – among other factors – is what led to the deficient approval of many forest management plans in the Osa between 1997 and 1999. The evidence for this period is anything but encouraging. Of the 43 forest management plans evaluated by Barrantes et al. (1999) for this period, only about 50% had a forest inventory of the logging site, around 40% presented deficient maps of the logging areas and more than 50% did not have any reports of the forest engineer of the logging operations (this to mention some of the deficiencies found by this group of researchers). Likewise, an evaluation commission of SINAC[160] found that many logging permits were awarded without the fulfillment of priority

---

[159] COVIRENA, personal communication. Several ACOSA officials confirmed this thesis, but asked to remain anonymous.

[160] See SINAC(1999).

requisites like a preliminary forest inventory, location of the trees in the inventory map, forecast of logging impact and mitigation measures in the logging stand, establishment of protection measures for 'rare' and banned tree species, lists of trees – that should be left standing for reproduction and trees to be felled – by scientific name, map of the logging site, reports of forest engineers of logging operations, etc.

The lack of material resources has probably its roots in – what can be called – fiscal indiscipline recurrent in different governments. With fiscal indiscipline I mean that the financial resources raised for a particular end are not allocated for the purpose they were raised for, contributing to a sort of domino effect augmenting SINAC's inefficiency – less money means less personnel and less equipment, hence poor performance. Since the approval of the new Forest Law, FONAFIFO complains that it can only attend about half of the demand for the PES (for all forestry activities).[161] While the government attends past – forest related – liabilities through the tax on fossil fuels, the transfers to FONAFIFO for PES remain irregular. The same way, several forestry organizations have repeatedly complained about the state not honoring its obligations with FONAFIFO, and question therefore its seriousness concerning forest affairs.[162]

The Law 7575, in its article 69, states that one third of the financial resources raised by a tax on the consumption of fossil fuels is to be transferred to FONAFIFO to provide the financial background for the PES. This raised positive expectations about the potential of such measures – following 'the polluter pays principle' – to finance sustainable forestry and contribute to the creation of missing markets for forest environmental services.[163] Nonetheless, in the year 1998 – for example – the amount stemming from this tax that should have been allocated for the PES, was approximately \$33 million. In this same year the government destined some \$4.9 million for the PES and approximately \$9.2 million to the payment of pending liabilities (mainly CAFs). An additional source of financing of the PES is also a Forestry Fund, but the General Director of SINAC himself complained that the resources of this fund were reduced in 1998.[164]

---

161 Jorge Mario Rodríguez, Executive Director of FONAFIFO, personal communication.

162 See La Nación, domingo 16 de enero del 2000. Campo pagado por: Cámara Costarricense Forestal, JUNAFORCA, Oficina Nacional Forestal, and UPA-Nacional.

163 See for example Heindrichs (1997).

164 See Bolaños (1998). Opening statement of the General Director of SINAC, Lic. Luis Alberto Bolaños for the conference "Foro Nacional sobre Análisis de las políticas Forestales y Recursos Naturales de CR.

Table 12. The tax on fossil fuels and transferences to FONAFIFO ($*)

Year	Levy on the consumption of fossil fuels	Sum to be transferred to FONAFIFO	Pending liabilities		TOTAL transfers to FONAFIFO	Payment difference
			CAF	PES		
1995	8.964.074	2.988.025	8.954.768	0	8.954.768	5.966.744
1996	73.303.352	24.434.451	7.937.913	0	7.937.913	-16.496.537
1997	115.452.119	38.484.040	7.684.048	0	7.684.048	-30.799.992
1998	101.393.361	33.797.787	9.249.446	4.929.671	14.179.117	-19.618.671
1999	49.705.068	16.568.356	5.560.850	8.414.721	13.975.571	-2.592.785
2000	348.817.975	116.272.658	39.387.025	13.344.391	52.731.417	-63.541.241

Source: Own elaboration based on data provided by FONAFIFO. *Current USD

The creation of a system of national protected areas, better known as SINAC, aimed at the decentralization of the management of the conservation areas, its personnel, natural resources, and the relationships with the local communities to provide a holistic management of resources. Nonetheless, the government publicly admits that all relevant decisions still depend from what is said in San José. That is, there is not a real break-through regarding this so-called decentralization process.[165]

Landowners in between loggers, academicians, NGOs, and the government: Sparks fly over forest management plans

The interviewed loggers show rather homogenous arguments concerning the execution and monitoring of forest management plans. When asked about the guidelines for sustainable forest management they mentioned the elaboration of a forest inventory prior to logging, the use of maps and the planning of roads but repeatedly contended that the forest engineer is the one in charge of that. The personnel contracted by the loggers is rarely formally trained in 'low impact logging techniques', since the costs of such training are high and logging is only seasonal.

The forest engineer interviews revealed that these professionals rarely supervise constantly a logging site. Instead, they inspect the logging sites every two or three weeks, because this way the operation costs of logging can be reduced. The reduction of the operations costs is mainly in the interest of the landowner, because in the – contractual – negotiation with the logger, it is usually stated that the landowner has to pay not only the management plan, but also the inspections of the forest engineers, while the logger limits himself to finance the operation.

[165] Luis Barquero, regional director of ACOSA in Puerto Jiménez, personal communication. See also MINAE/PNUD/ONF (2001: 70).

Loggers hold that their business is definitely environmentally sustainable, because when one returns to a logging site some 5 years after logging has taken place, everything is green again. A similar argument is upheld by the ONF,[166] who even contends that one year after logging has taken place, the stands look as 'pristine' again and sometimes not even an expert can tell the difference. Loggers consider that a logging site in a primary forest – in the Osa – can be logged again 5-10 years after the first logging and fell 25-50% of what was taken out the first time, thereafter it can be logged again in 15-20 years. Loggers contend that their activities are forest friendly because they follow the forest management plan, and in this regard they insist in that the criticism of the environmental sector is unfair and intentionally exaggerated.

Academicians (on the fields of ecology, botany, forestry and ornithology) argue that conventional logging causes extended damage to primary forests, and that the conception of sustainability on the side of loggers is wrong, because the forest is seen only as a logging site and not as the ecosystem it actually is. They contend that conventional logging in primary forests contributes to an impoverishment of forests' biodiversity by removing individuals that are exposed to very strong competition to reach an 'adult' age. Therefore this artificial change of the forest dynamics introduces irreversible alterations of these processes jeopardizing the species themselves and other ecological processes on which very little is known. For this reason they insist that all primary forests in private hands outside protected areas should be preserved and landowners compensated with fair PES.[167]

The Ing. Msc. Quírico Jiménez (Congressman elected for the period 2002-2006 and former taxonomist of INBIO[168]) summarized the points of view of several interviewed academicians concerning conventional logging:

- Conventional logging is contributing to the fragmentation of the remaining areas with primary forest, which jeopardizes biodiversity.
- The assumption that conventional logging is an ecologically sustainable activity is wrong on several grounds:
    1. The felling of one single tree mostly implies the felling of several others at the same time, which creates larger clearings than when low impact techniques are really used.
    2. Many of the logged areas are mountainous with slopes larger than 20%, therefore runoff is increased in areas with poor soils.
    3. The conventional tractors used – that weigh between 20 and 50 tons – hinder regeneration by compacting and destroying the soil and the undergrowth.

---

166 Ing. Alfonso Barrantes Rodríguez, executive president.

167 Dr. Jorge Lobo (UCR), Dr. Mauricio Quesada (UNAM), personal communication.

168 INBIO: Instituto Nacional de Biodiversidad.

4. Despite the fact that land use is not being changed, the opening of roads in the forest favors illegal logging years after 'legal' logging has taken place.

5. Selective logging drives the extinction of commercial species.

6. Forest management plans are based on a series of statistics and procedures with no biological basis that can guarantee the survival of the exploited populations. Instead, they have become a sheer bureaucratic requisite to perform logging.

7. Neither forest engineers nor SINAC officials can guarantee the sustainability of conventional logging because neither perform proper monitoring of the logging stands. In the specific case of the Osa loggers manage to take out protected tree species by filling the forms for the transport checkpoints with – vulgar – names of other species. Some of these names are even made up.

– Many forest engineers incur negligence because they:

  - allow the felling of trees in protection areas (riversides and water springs)
  - allow the felling of trees that should be kept for reproduction or are banned to exploitation
  - allow the felling of more trees than foreseen in the management plans
  - trace skidding roads over streams[169]
  - make flaw identifications of tree species
  - elaborate deficient maps of forest standings, as well as deficient location of trees to be felled

– The new Forest Law does not meet appropriate guidelines for forest protection. On the contrary, the definition of forest adopted in the law favors its loss.

– The PES do not incentivize landowners to protect the forest.

Loggers, as well as forest engineers, get angry at the fact that they are constantly accused of destroying the forest because there is no such thing as a 'perfect execution of a forest management plan', because human beings are bound to commit mistakes and forest management has 'per se' an impact on forest resources.[170] They say that in comparison to the way logging was performed in the past, the way it is performed today is much more forest friendly than ever. Even though logging will always have an impact on natural forests, and that *errare humanum est,* the forest engineer interviews showed that one of the problems faced in the execution of forest management plans is that often the management plan is not

[169] On the effect of logging roads on tropical wet forests see also Bertie 2000.

[170] For a similar argument see Putz (1994: 2).

followed. For example the roads planned and traced by the forest engineer (access, and skidding roads) are not always followed because the logger (or the tractor driver) fancy the roads are better the way they figure during the execution of the management plan. Likewise, heavy vines connecting tree crowns are seldom cut to avoid that other trees are unnecessarily fallen because that makes the operation too time-intensive. Consequently in their closing reports, the forest engineers must often figure out a way of justifying the changes in the plan to make it look good before the AFE.

The law foresees sanctions for those not complying to the law, including jail. But the interviews revealed that sanctions are apparently not applied equally to everyone. Loggers are also faced with the seizure of their machinery and the timber, but loggers are apparently seldom arrested and machinery confiscations occur seldom due to an efficient informal information network (as will be seen below). This is perceived as unfair by landowners and heavily criticized by NGOs, who claim that until now, not one single logger has faced strong sanctions despite the repeated demonstration of negligent logging practices, i.e., non compliance to the Forest Law. Landowners feel that the law is not applied equally to everyone, and that – contrary to them – those with 'influences' can get away with anything.[171] On the other hand some loggers commented that they are being persecuted by environmentalists, who fail to see that they are performing logging according to the forest management plans. Some loggers even said 'why should anyone go to jail for cutting down the wrong tree? It is not as if one killed someone'. Examples of the conflict between consequent enforcement of formal norms and impunity are not rare.

For example, during the field research in march 2001, a denounce was filed against a logging operation of COOPEMADEREROS – in a property they own – due to excessive tree felling.[172] The AFE inspected the stand and closed it because of irregularities in the execution of the management plan and confiscated the timber. In this case, the loggers also knew in advance that a complaint had been filed, so they rushed to take all of their machinery out of the logging site before the AFE arrived. The information on which the denounce was based came from a small – illegal – logger neighbor of the location (Cañaza, some 14 Km NW of Puerto Jiménez). Some said that despite the complain and the big fuss around the case, nothing much would happen to these people (i.e., the loggers members of COOPEMADEREROS). This assertion was hard to believe because the case caught the attention of the media and the AFE had already confiscated the timber. Some two months later – and by sheer coincidence – I was performing an interview with a logger of Cartago who is a founding member of COOPEMADEREROS. During the interview he became a telephone call

[171] On the lax enforcement of the Forest Law prior to 1996 see Porras y Villareal (1993: 49-62).

[172] COOPEMADEREROS is a powerful organization grouping mainly loggers from Pérez Zeledón and Cartago, and though it owns the property in the peninsula where logging was taking place, it cannot be considered a 'local' organization to the Osa.

about the confiscated timber, when he finished talking, he said he was to take off the next day to Golfito to get back that timber. Indeed, some days later, the timber was given back.

Loggers try to make a strong argument against small (scale) loggers. Their concern is that – allegedly – small loggers cause more damage to the forest than they do since they are almost impossible to control and besides, they do not pay taxes like conventional loggers do. They said repeatedly that there is much fuss being made about logging in the Osa, but in other provinces/areas of the country – where they are also into business like the province of Limón, which comprises the conservation areas Tortuguero and Amistad Caribe – logging operations are much more chaotic. They attribute their difficulties to the massive presence of environmentalists in the Osa on the one hand, and the 'foreign interests' in the peninsula on the other. Concerning the last explanation, some loggers argued that wealthy foreigners are looking to buy out the peninsula for themselves. This argument was also raised by some landowners. I did not find any strong evidence for this last argument. Foreigners have indeed bought land in the peninsula and many of them are dedicated to tourism, especially in the neighboring areas to the Parque Nacional Corvocado. But I do not see this as an evidence of a buy-out on the side of foreigners.

Loggers themselves question partially the social sustainability of conventional logging. Though they say they represent the best access to timber resources for landowners, they do not feel responsible if the landowner ends up wasting the resources obtained through logging and fails in achieving any long term socioeconomic improvements. They distance themselves from the social impact of logging by pointing out that the market is not a charity institution, and they are only doing their business following the guidelines of the AFE. Nonetheless, loggers consider themselves as the 'real' friends of the landowners because it is through them that landowners have access to cash flows in the short term. In this regard they repeatedly attack NGOs that receive donations to perform community projects, and argue that the communities do not really perceive any long term benefits from such projects while the members of NGOs become rich. They contend that NGOs' mainly use landowners as a means to have access to financial resources from which landowners do not benefit. They say that NGOs are the only ones benefited from the donations they become, and in this spirit they are not really interested in improving the social standards of landowners, because as long as there are poor landowners and social-environmental problems, the NGOs will be receiving donations for their projects. Thus, the moment that such problems are resolved, NGOs would be out of business, so they have an interest in that the poor remain poor. This view is partially shared by many interviewed landowners, and it is strongly upheld by SIPRAICO. It is partially shared because landowners do not say loggers are their 'real' friends, but they agree that loggers do ease them access to short term cash. Landowners also see NGOs with some mistrust, and many do have the feeling of being used instead of helped. Both landowners and loggers mention repeatedly as an example the 'pejibayes'[173] project of Fundación Neotrópica during the 90s as an example of the failure of NGOs to attend socioeconomic issues. In this project many landowners participated cultivating pejibayes, but the project failed because the production of the fruit could not be marketed, and the landowners were left alone with the whole production. Several interviewed landowners manifested strong resentments against NGOs (and specially against Neotrópica). Likewise, some landowners also said the government uses them as an excuse to sell carbon fixation to developed countries and is making money on their account, but they do not receive anything for that.

In the Osa (specifically in Puerto Jiménez) there are two local NGOs, Cecropia and TUVA. Further northwest in the peninsula (some 40 Km from Puerto Jiménez) in the town of Rincón, Fundación Neotrópica has its local headquarters, but Neotrópica's main headquarters are in San José, and it performs activities in other regions of the country. The main focus of all these NGOs is towards the rational use of natural resources to attend social, economic and environmental needs at the community level. Cecropia has its focus on community based conservation strategies, and supports the transfer of conservation and production technologies and strategies to local communities. In this regard it offers technical and administrative support to promote sustainable forestry activities and primary rainforest protection as well as diversified organic agricultural production. Cecropia also supports financially the work of some members of the COVIRENA in the area to monitor logging activities. Fundación TUVA (Tierras Unidas Vecinales por el Ambiente) supports communal self-organization to bring forward the knowledge of local communities regarding the use of natural resources to attend social and economic needs. Thus TUVA has pursued over several years together with the inhabitants of the community of 'Piro' the extraction of fallen timber by means of oxen, now its focus has moved towards indigenous communities. Neotrópica has moved back from the support of productive activities in the Osa and works more focused on environmental education. A fourth NGO observed during the field research is APREFLOFAS (Asociación Preservacionista de Flora y Fauna Silvestre). This last NGO is based in San José and has its focus on combating deforestation through environmental education and the denouncing of environmental offenses.

While much of the information that NGOs use against conventional logging (especially local NGOs) stems from local neighbors, I observed that the same local neighbors (and even COVIRENAS) refrain from filing complaints themselves, mostly because they fear social control mechanisms (more insights on social control mechanisms are found in Chapter 6). As a result, when they have notice of 'irregular logging', they rush to inform local NGOs so that they will file the complain for them because they do not want to get into trouble. But on the side of local NGOs this is done rather unwillingly on two grounds. First, because by filing the complaint the NGO makes itself unwanted among the members of local communities, which

[173] The pejibaye is a palm (*Bactris gasipaes*), that produces fruits and palm hearts. Additionally, wood can be obtained from the palm and used for siding houses, veneer and tool handles (Morton 1987: 12-14).

hampers possible future work with them. Second, they contend that it is unfair that they are the ones who get into trouble for others since they are 'outsiders' and local actors should engage in the defense of what is theirs instead of fearing themselves from the threats of one or two loggers – or anyone else.

Non governmental organizations active in the Osa can be – in principle – distinguished by where they have their headquarters. During the fieldwork I observed that depending on where a particular NGO has its headquarters, so will be its role in a particular local situation.

NGOs active in the Osa are partially united by a common goal, which is to curtail conventional logging. The focus of their attacks is mainly the 'forest management plan', which has come to be the generic concept of conventional logging among its opponents in Costa Rica. At the technical level, they all use the same discourse, which can be basically resumed to the negative effects that logging has on primary forests (including forest degradation, forest fragmentation, destruction of ecosystems, loss of soil, etc.). It is a very technical argumentation shared by practically every NGO involved in environmental issues, and draws heavily on the work of academicians. The 'halo' effect of each is different depending on the audience they aim at.[174] Local NGOs are much more careful in the way they charge against conventional logging than San José based NGOs, basically because depending on how aggressive they may charge against logging, they can create either a negative or a positive image within their communities of influence. San José based NGOs are not as cautious when they argue against conventional logging, probably because they aim at a much wider audience than the local communities. Let me draw further on the example of COOPEMADEREROS mentioned above.

Because the denounce against COOPEMADEREROS was intensively followed by the media,[175] Cecropia tried to maintain a low profile, trying to stick to the case and not to demonize logging 'per se', as this would turn the locals against itself. At the same time, and after announcing the start of a new campaign against conventional logging (in San José at a press conference held by FECON), APREFLOFAS came to the Osa and started distributing stickers with the message "logging prohibited".[176] This campaign caused the rejection of many landowners who claimed during the interviews 'if it not were for logging, we would starve to death'. At the same time – and still drawing on my own experience – this campaign caused much confusion among landowners who tended to identify every NGO (and environmentalist) with this campaign, which was initiated by one single organization.

---

[174] The "halo-effect" is used by Volz (1997: 297) in reference to political discussions carried out for the public opinion, and where the "halo-effect" refers to the credibility of an organization (e.g. and NGO) that profits from its past successes to influence its audience in favor of its goals. That is, the credibility of an organization is like a halo that can influence the opinion of third parties that come in contact with its "light".

[175] See for example Periódico la Nación, martes 6 de marzo del 2001, p. 11A; The Tico Times, Friday, March 16, 2001, p. 1, 14-15; El Sol de Osa, abril, 2001 p. 1, 5.

[176] In this sticker, a falling tree can be seen encircled in red and crossed by a red line on a white background.

The argument of Cecropia is that one should not close one of the few and last sources of income to landowners in the peninsula (which is logging) because this would only lead to more social turmoil in the area, and that logging need not take place the way it has always done, that is by means of conventional loggers. Rather, logging should be allowed to take place in a small-scale fashion, so that landowners are able to appropriate a larger added value of their timber. Hence, Cecropia takes clear distance from – and basically rejects – conventional logging on the grounds of missing ecological and social sustainability. Rather, this organization contends that timber resources should be made available to the local communities to satisfy mainly local needs and the local demand for timber. While this position does not contradict the opinion of the members of APREFLOFAS, such statements were absent during their campaign at that time.

The main argument of APREFLOFAS (and several other San José based NGOs) during its campaign was that conventional logging only increased forest loss and for that reason all forest management plans – in the Osa and the whole country – should be stopped at once. It can be seen that in the end the goal of both organizations is quite alike, but while the locally based NGO takes a more conciliatory role while trying to provide a productive alternative to conventional logging, i.e. small-scale logging, the San José based NGO fails to bring concrete alternative proposals into its discourse. During the research performed in San José, it was seen that this is much the case of several other San José based NGOs.

It was observed that despite the fact that these organizations share largely the same discourse and objectives, they tend to act separately. They do not share a common/coordinate agenda, they do not consult each other, partly because the competition between them is very strong. Competition between NGOs, aroused partly by the need of donors, is a factor driving the lack of common work, resulting in a rather colorful array of isolated actions. Intrigues for power and to stand out before the public opinion are not seldom among NGOs. Such intrigues are stronger – and most evident – when NGOs compete against each other for financial resources, i.e., to gain the goodwill of donors. And even when different NGOs are together in the same proposal (for example 'Corredor Biológico Mesoamericano'[177]), I observed that two or more groups make coalitions against a third to throw it out of the race, presumably to get a larger slice of the cake.

At a national level NGOs show more group cohesion in their criticism of the actual forest policy. For example, this is reflected by their critique of the 'Plan Nacional de Desarrollo Forestal' (PNDF). This document is basically elaborated by MINAE and the ONF with the support of the PNUD and resumes guidelines of the national forest policy for the next ten years in six different areas:

---

[177] NGOs involved in the 'Corredor Biológico Centroamericano' in the Osa are –among others– Fundación Neotrópica, CEDARENA (Centro de Derecho Ambiental y de los Recursos Naturales) and Cecropia. Donor organizations are Fundación CR-USA (that undertakes the support activities of the late AID in CR), and the Nature Conservancy.

1. Planning of forest lands
2. Competitiveness and positioning of the forest sector
3. Follow-up, control and assessment of sustainability
4. Financial instruments and mechanisms
5. Information systems
6. Inter-institutional strengthening and coordination.

The critique of the environmental organizations (and some academicians) to the plan is that despite the fact that the document argues on the grounds of sustainability (ecological, social, productive), the conception of forest use remains that of a timber source, which plays down the importance of ecological and social sustainability. A specific criticism to the PNDF is that through this plan the government will receive credits – from the World Bank among other organizations – of approximately $60 million to finance the forest sector under the name of 'Proyecto Ecomercados'.[178] Their critique is that the PNDF makes conventional logging appear as environmentally friendly to the world, which in their opinion is not the case at all. Therefore, they see a large risk that through this plan conventional logging might be finally locked-in. They point out that – like in the approval of the new Forest Law – the plan is not the result of a negotiation and a consensus between all the interested parts, but reflects mainly the interests of the logging industry. In this regard they point out that the observations they brought forward about the 'draft' of the PNDF were largely not taken into account. The environmental sector also contends that the social sustainability of conventional logging is being taken for granted in the document.

For example, the PNDF has a detailed matrix of activities for each focus point of the plan that includes what is the pursued goal, what must be done to achieve it and who is to participate. Thus, while the PNDF states the need of creating a 'forest culture'(point 2 above), it fails to mention which organizations are to be included in the creation of such a forest culture, like for example, the Ministry of Education, the Ministry of Culture, NGOs with experience in the field of environmental education, etc. Instead, it only mentions JUNAFORCA and 'other organizations' which – they say – can be everyone, but it can also be nobody. In comparison, in issues directly related with the creation of financial mechanisms for the forest industry and market positioning (points 2 and 4 above), the matrixes are very detailed, and the CCF – and the private sector in general – appear as a participant in almost every activity, while other organizations like cooperatives, associations of producers, syndicates etc. are barely mentioned. Again, JUNAFORCA and 'other organizations' are brought forward.[179]

---

[178] According to the Minister of the Environment Elisabeth Odio Benito in the presentation of the 'Plan Nacional de Desarrollo Forestal'.

[179] See MINAE/PNUD/ONF (2001: 36-9, 57-8)

Characteristic of the negotiation style of the government is precisely its reluctance to negotiation. That is, when it wishes something to be approved, instead of consulting third parties for their opinion and real participation in the design and implementation of policy measures, it presents rather 'finished' drafts. That is why several NGOs and other actors (like indigenous communities) complain that they are not consulted, but only informed. For example the indigenous community of Rey Curré (in the south of Costa Rica and also inside ACOSA) reports confrontation with governmental agencies, namely with the Costa Rican Institute of Electricity (ICE) since their reserve is located in the river basin of an area that is to be flooded to construct a hydroelectric dam.[180] This area is included in the RAMSAR Convention on Wetlands. Also, a part of the area to be flooded has religious meaning for this community. Their main complaint against the government is its lack of willingness to dialog and consider the interests of the communities. In their opinion, what the government calls "dialogue" is rather the announcement of what is going to be done with their homeland, independent of their opinion. So far, ACOSA has failed to take a part in the conflict. A reluctance to negotiation is also observable between governmental organizations, for example between SINAC and IDA, where the ones say no property rights can be granted in the RFGD and the others say the contrary.

[180] CNN reported on this conflict on 17-03-2002.

6 Informal norms of behavior, transaction costs and conventional logging

6.1 Chapter overview

This chapter takes a look at the informal norms that rule conventional logging. The chapter begins by presenting the enforcement mechanisms of conventional logging at the local level and then introduces some complementary – semi-informal – mechanisms observed at the governmental level.

The following sections observe the transaction costs that arise through the existence of asymmetric information between private actors in conventional logging. The reason why transaction costs are presented as a part of the informal norms of behavior is that through them the role that the different private actors play in the process of conventional logging can be understood within the frame of informal behavior, as the transaction costs that are evaluated here arise from information deficiencies and asymmetries that give rise to strategic/opportunistic behavior.

6.2 Informal norms and enforcement mechanisms at the local level

In Costa Rica, it is acknowledged that group relationships – in general – are characterized by moderation and conflict negotiation, trying to avoid extremes and violence (Láscaris 1977: 112-115; Biesanz et al. 1979: 33). Nonetheless, conflict avoidance has been also acknowledged as a form to evade confrontation (Biesanz et al. 1979: 32). Concerning individual liberty, Naranjo (1977: 70) arguments that individualism can easily turn into egoism and even anarchism leading to a failure to comply to rules and resistance to law.[181] Resistance to law is reinforced by the expectation of impunity, that is, the belief that one can get away with anything as long as one knows the 'right persons' or knows how to 'properly' address the authorities (Biesanz et al. 1979: 34, 38). Despite this 'individualism' Costa Ricans usually fear social control, the strongest probably being the opinion of others. In this regard they are fearful of being exposed to gossip, ridicule or being laughed at. Biesanz et al. (1979: 33) say that these mechanisms appear to be very effective means of social control.

Biesanz et al. (1979: 35) also point out that the Costa Rican society is known to be conservative and reluctant to change, and that despite the 'openness' towards foreigners, Costa Ricans are very distrustful of new ideas, particularly when they believe they come from 'outside'. Regarding the resistance to change, Barahona (1975: 54-56) and Naranjo (1977: 41-42) observe that this problem is also underpinned by a sort of fatalism, that is, a feeling that it

[181] The most prominent example of this is the lack of compliance to the transit regulations.

is impossible to change anything. This is more or less reflected in a large number of popular sayings[182] that contribute to ameliorate failure.

Biesanz et al. (1979) make the observation that these values are profoundly internalized by the Costa Rican society and constitute an important factor hindering the acceptance of norms of efficiency, punctuality and competition. In this regard they are part of the country's business culture.

Following the example of the Osa, opportunistic behavior is one of the most salient characteristics of the business culture I observed, which is driven by the goals of maximizing benefits from timber trade, and is grounded on information asymmetries and information deficiencies. The following sections focus with more detail on these subjects. Concerning individual liberty, or individualism, the conception of property at the local level is a good example of how informal institutions are embedded in formal arrangements. I am not saying that private property is an informal institution – since it is anchored in the constitution – but the local conception of property, namely, 'what is mine is mine and I can do what I want with it' attach a series of informal norms of behavior to the formal concept enforced by the state. This conception of private property arises mainly from the fact that landowners have much trouble in identifying and recognizing what is meant with 'collective goods', namely, the forest environmental services envisaged in the new Forest Law. This problem on the side of landowners arises probably from the nonfungibility of forest environmental services. From the point of view of the landowner, the acknowledgement through the law of forest environmental services seems to affect little the characteristics of 'well defined property rights'.

Regarding the *comprehensiveness* and *exclusiveness* of property rights, landowners often hold against the government to fail to meet its obligations to pay for the environmental services inside their properties. Thus, they are not allowed to dispose of the resources inside their properties, and at the same time they do not perceive the –monetary – benefits that supposedly should stem from such forest environmental services.

Regarding *enforceability of property rights*, the landowner interviews revealed extended incomprehension in regard of what is allowed in forest use and what is not. Landowners perceive the monitoring performed by the COVIRENA and ACOSA officials as unfair and tend to see these agents as intruders. Landowners say that it is unfair that they are the ones carrying the whole responsibility before the law, when the ones performing logging is not them, but a logger with whom they – often – have a written contract that makes the logger the virtual owner of the timber. Therefore, when a third party files a denounce against irregular practices, they are the ones with a problem, and not the logger. Additionally, they consider it an intrusion that third parties can constrain their right of doing what they consider legitimate in their properties, most particularly when the logging permit is approved *ex ante* by the AFE.

[182] For example: "si Dios quiere", "qué le vamos a hacer", "el que nació para maseta de la ventana no pasa", "el que nació para martillo del cielo le caen los clavos", etc.

As a consequence, when a logging activity is denounced, inspected and stopped by ACOSA officials/functionaries, retaliation measures are undertaken against those who the landowner considers responsible for the denounce. Besides the landowner, retaliation measures are undertaken also by other members of the community – like timber intermediaries who are mostly neighbors to the area – and sometimes by loggers. When the informer turns out to be a forest worker, the immediate consequence is the loss of his job. In the other cases, the informer is usually either a neighbor or a COVIRENA.[183] Interviews with local NGOs, and a key informer (ACOSA functionary) revealed that the landowner and/or the logger find out 'who the informer is' from ACOSA. This assertion was confirmed by several landowners, and members of the COVIRENA. Loggers refrained from commenting the issue. These mechanisms contribute significantly to discourage third parties from filing denounces against – irregular – conventional logging.

The field research in the Osa revealed the following social enforcement mechanisms:[184]

- Local neighbors[185] enforce conventional logging against those monitoring conventional logging by means of threats (sometimes death threats) and physical violence. The ones most often threatened are members of the COVIRENA, because they are most usually involved in denouncing irregular logging. Local neighbors (who are not COVIRENAS) are less targeted by threats because they do not get as involved as COVIRENAS in monitoring. I witnessed during a SIPRAICO meeting (in February 2000) how the board of directors threatened their members – or anyone else – if they filed denounce against logging in members' farms. The syndicate's president directly threatened the members with the exclusion from SIPRAICO and – indirectly – even with violence in case they collaborate with any environmentalists (including COVIRENAS). At the same time he called for direct violence against environmentalists monitoring logging in their properties.
- Loggers also use similar ways (threats and physical violence) against COVIRENAS and others whom they consider to stand in their way. This was informed by an ACOSA functionary who has repeatedly received death threats several times from loggers at the transport checkpoints.
- Spreading rumors (gossip) about the actors monitoring management plans is another informal mechanism that leads to a loss of confidence of neighbors in those persons. The effect of this is the relative isolation (ostracism) of these persons in the community. This way, local forest workers (for example) will find it very difficult to find another job in the community and/or area. The main rumors about COVIRENAS are, first, it is believed that

[183] In the year 2000 there were more than 100 members of the COVIRENA in the peninsula. Many members of the COVIRENA are also locals. Eric Rusmann (former Director of Fundación Cecropia), personal communication.

[184] During visits to Sarapiquí (Cordillera Volcánica Central) in 2000 it was seen that the same informal enforcement mechanisms of conventional logging exist there.

[185] Intermediaries are mostly local neighbors.

COVIRENAS receive large donations to 'spy' on landowners. But actually COVIRENAS work on a voluntary basis and do not usually receive any additional income for their engagement. COVIRENAS even hold against the government not providing them any financial or material support to perform monitoring.[186] The second rumor is that COVIRENAS are after ruining everyone and they do not care about the fate of small landowners. Rumors like these appear to land in fertile soil when landowners have pressing needs of cash flows, thus any action against conventional logging is seen as something against their very own interests. To landowners' uneasiness contributes the fact that they do not fully understand why should someone tell them what or what not to do in their properties.

- Another informal mechanism supporting conventional logging is an information network that allows loggers to know not only when a complaint has been filed against their activities, but also tells them when the inspection of the complaint is to take place. This way loggers should have enough time to pull out of the area, so that their machinery will not be seized, only the timber. This information is supposed to leak out of ACOSA. This is not an isolated mechanism acting in ACOSA, similar examples have been documented for other parts of the country like in San Carlos in the northern lowlands.[187] The information of 'who called the AFE' can also stem from the community itself, because telephones are public and it is very difficult to keep such calls private. Nonetheless, it is unlikely that the community can also know when the inspection is to take place.

6.3 Semi-informal and informal norms in governmental organizations

The data available points towards the existence of what I would call semi-informal norms in governmental organizations. Semi-informal norms cannot be attributed to the formal framework and, at the same time, they cannot be assumed to be carried on independently by actors inside governmental organizations as part of social norms. Though these norms have an influence on the performance of some of ACOSA's functionaries, so far I have found no evidence that such norms are established per-decree or some specific guideline, and – despite their unorthodox character – they seem usual practices inside SINAC/ACOSA. The observed norms are;

- The government still has trouble in maintaining stable norms, for example, one year partial property rights are required for logging, and the next year partial property rights are accepted

---

[186] During the field research, the only organization I know supported COVIRENAS financially is Cecropia.

[187] See for example: Periódico La Nación. Lunes 11 de febrero , 2002: "Indagan tala y venta de madera". Internet WWW page at URL: <http://www.nacion.com/ln_ee/2002/febrero/11/pais8.html>

- SINAC has followed a discouraging employment policy of one-year employment contracts (firing and re-hiring) with functionaries in key positions of ACOSA – like approval and monitoring of forest management plans. Though practice is typical of the private sector – and through it the employer saves on the social costs, or social security that he should pay to the state for his employees – it appears inadequate for a governmental agency. Interviews with some of these functionaries revealed that this employment policy falls short in moving them to engage actively in the efficient performance of their responsibilities. Nonetheless, not all of the functionaries at ACOSA are in such a labor situation. Some of them enjoy a position of 'governmental officials', which means that their position is practically assured for life, but,
- governmental circles show tolerance for inefficient and even irregular performance of its officials, specially in the case of leadership positions. For example, a director and sub-director of ACOSA who supposedly acted negligently between 1997 and 1999 – because under their mandate many management plans were incorrectly approved – were not sanctioned, but only transferred from ACOSA to other Conservation Areas. This is likely to be a result of the situation described above, where the government is aware that it cannot demand a better performance of its employees under such conditions.

The most salient informal norms of behavior that the field research revealed in SINAC/ACOSA are that

- irregular approval of logging permits is not brought to light by SINAC/ACOSA itself but by third actors,[188] which allows the thought that those inside governmental organizations tend to 'cover up' their tracks when errors (and maybe even negligent performance) are incurred. That is, that information tends to be hidden from the public opinion, and it is only brought up and discussed when third parties have already filed denounce,[189] also
- information leaks from SINAC towards loggers. That means that some of ACOSA's personnel (governmental officials and functionaries) participate in the information network that prevents loggers involved in irregular logging from denounces and inspections by providing them with information of not only 'when' denounces are filed, but also when inspections are to take place and even who filed denounce. This form of behavior can be understood as 'tit-for-tat', i.e., you help me and I'll help you.

---

[188] For example Cecropia in the Osa, in the case of the forest management plans approved between 1997 and 1999.

[189] This can be observed in practically any governmental organization in any part of the world. But it does not pertain exclusively to governmental organizations. For example, the catholic church apparently reaches to similar ways when its clergymen are accused of improper behavior. See for example 'Badische Zeitung, Mittwoch, 10. April 2002, Seite 3.

6.4 Conventional logging and strategic behavior: Transaction costs and the role of information

6.4.1 Analysis framework: Transaction costs

Conventional logging is the product of a voluntary – contractual – agreement between private actors that expect economic benefits from timber trade, and this agreement has either written or verbal form, and it is an activity that embodies both formal and informal institutions. Conventional logging embodies formal norms such as demonstrating property rights over the stands to be logged, presenting a forest management plan to the AFE, and it is ruled by the legislation that guarantees the validity of private contracts. It includes informal institutions because it is carried on and enforced by private actors as described above, in this regard social values come strongly into play. Conventional logging is a task oriented institution because it has a specific goal, logging, and through the interaction between formal and informal arrangements transaction costs arise.

Landowners take forest-use decisions on the basis of incomplete information (bound rationality), and institutions contribute to the process of individual decision making by providing landowners with information about conventional logging. This process of information transfer is influenced by customs and habits, as well as by opportunistic behavior (Sen and van Kooten 2001: 62). The reputation of the members of the different groups participating in an institution actively influences the building of information assets within the members of different groups – and contribute therefore to the formation of expectations. Reputational information has public good characteristics and is available within the group through different sources such as direct communication with other group members, eavesdropping and gossip. Expectations are also based on experience and, in the case of newcomers, expectations are build more on a subjective basis (Casson 1991: 170-172).

There is actually more than one way of structuring institutions to produce gains from cooperation, coordination and trade, and the ensuing distributional outcomes are a major characteristic of different institutional forms. Why institutions are designed in one way – and not in another – is explained by the interests of those actors obtaining the larger payoffs from trade and who will try to influence institutional arrangements to maximize their individual benefits (Knight 1992: 25-27, 38, 126; North 1998: 249). It follows that self motivated actors will not comply to an institution if it does not give them larger benefits than non compliance. As already explained, shared rules (information) between the trading actors is determinant of institutional stability because when actors know the rules of the game, they are also able to build expectations, provided that the other actors will stick to the rules. When the less benefited actors lack the ability to coordinate the actions of others towards a new equilibrium, they have no other choice than to continue complying to the established rules (Knight 1992: 177).

Transaction costs arise because information is costly and asymmetrically held by partners in any form of exchange (North 1990: 108; Greenhill 1995: 186). Of course, the larger the transaction costs, the lower the overall benefits perceived by – some of – the actors. Nonetheless, self motivated actors may prefer rules that involve larger costs provided that these rules give them larger benefits than those involving lower costs. On the other hand, when facing uncertainty, actors may also fail to produce less costly rules due to either their lack of capacity or knowledge (Knight 1992: 110-112).

Information plays a key role in the way institutions achieve ends and guide individuals to fulfill their own. It plays also an important role in determining transaction costs, and thus benefit distribution. Economic activities are related to different types of information, and the availability – or not – of information in certain activities can be a part of the activity itself, hence specific transaction costs will belong to those activities as well. Information problems arise either due to deficient information or asymmetric information. Information deficiency ensues from incomplete information (in any case, one has never complete information) and the difficulty of improving information's quality. On the other hand, there is a cost of collecting, verifying, transmitting, processing and updating information available in various sources. While the effect of obtaining information can be positive for the productive process, it involves costs. Information asymmetry follows a behavioral process, where an agent has an incentive and the opportunity to hide information from his trading partner to obtain larger payoffs acting in his/her own self interest (Sen and van Kooten 2001: 62-63). In this regard, information asymmetry can be a product of opportunistic behavior.

Despite the fact that contracts are agreed (verbal or written) on a voluntary basis, it will always be in the interest of the principal (the one demanding) and the agent (the one supplying) to monitor the compliance of each other to avoid default behavior that might reduce benefits. In this case, the landowner is the principal, who contracts with the logger (the agent) the service of logging. The principal will try to maximize an objective function (income from the sale of timber to the logger) subject to the agent's objective function (maximize benefits from timber merchandizing) (Sen and Van Kooten 2001: 24, 55).

The income that the principal can derive from conventional logging depends heavily on the productivity of the forest he owns and factors like life zone, access, and the general information he/she has about the activity itself, including the price distribution of the different timber classes. Because I am referring to natural forests, and because the landowner plays a passive role in conventional logging, I will assume that the principal's income function is independent from labor and capital inputs on the side of the landowner. The principal's production function will have therefore the form

$$Q * P = f(l_z, a, i) * P$$

Where, Q is the productivity of the forest, P the timber price, *f( )* is the production function subject to the variables l_z the life zone, a the access to the forest, and i the information.

Likewise, because the landowner cannot influence variables like l_z and a, they can be assumed constant as well. Therefore, the income function of the principal (landowner) can be assumed to be mainly a function of information so that[190]

$$Q * P = f(i) * P$$

The agent's objective function is the optimization of his own production function, which is subject to the input of capital and labor in logging activities, and will be called 'effort' (e), the gross benefit he derives from the merchandizing of the timber bought from the principal (Q), and some exogenous factor that can be called weather (ϑ). Assuming the factor 'ϑ' constant, his production function will therefore have the form:

$$Max_Q F(Q,e) - C(e)$$

Thus, the first order conditions of the agent's objective function are:

$$\frac{\partial F}{\partial Q}\frac{\partial Q}{\partial e} = \frac{\partial C}{\partial e}$$

That is, the agent will optimize his production function when the marginal value of the last unit of effort is equal to its marginal cost. Because of bound rationality, the maximization of both objective functions will depend heavily on the availability of information to each partner. This means that even though both the principal and the agent will try to maximize their objective function, nothing guarantees that an absolute maximum will be reached. Instead, a – local – maximum can be reached depending on the information available to each.

"*Transaction costs arise when economic agents exchange ownership rights to assets and when exclusive property rights need to be enforced*" (Eggertsson 1990, cited in Sen and Van Kooten 2001: 69). Again, the appropriation of property rights is a function of the institutional framework, e.g. the formal framework, organizational forms, enforcement and norms of behavior (North 1990: 33). Following Kerr and Maré (1996; 1998), transaction costs will be assumed to stem from the following sources:

1. The *cost of optimizing*, which is related to the cost of learning the rules of the market. Not knowing these rules places stakeholders in serious disadvantages against those who know how the market functions. Lack of knowledge of market rules can be a particular problem of smaller stakeholders.

2. The *cost of using the price mechanism* is related to the data that the trader must find about the distribution of market prices and to the finding of a trading partner. Price distribution can be learned either through experience gained by trading or by word of mouth. The quality of this information depends on how the stakeholder is related to the

[190] I will elaborate more on this function below.

trading community, therefore, traders integrated to the trading community will have better information and it is also likely that larger stakeholders will be better linked than smaller ones, whereas organized bodies can make the process less costly providing contacts on a continuous basis.

3. The *cost of negotiation* arises from the negotiating styles of the different commercial partners. Similar negotiating styles can exist because of past negotiations or because of similar backgrounds. The cost of negotiation is also influenced by the liquidity of the market. Market liquidity can be recognized by how low the uncertainties about the execution prices are. This means that the existence of tranding costs like taxes, fees and information asymmetries affect market liquidity, as they prevent market participants from obtaining the information they need from the market price (Muranaga and Shimizu 1999; Muranaga, no date). Asymmetric information about the distribution of market prices leads to illiquid markets, hence bargaining turns important for the outcomes obtained by individual stakeholders, thus in this case experience plays an important role.

4. The *release of confidential information* is relevant when the traders are competing in a given product or geographical market. Here information acquires market value.

5. The trading of a good may involve the *loss of option values* due to market illiquidity. This is the case for many small economic agents.

To characterize the negotiation between a logger and a landowner in the conventional logging trade, the price negotiation that precedes the exchange of property rights of standing timber can be characterized as an example of the game of chicken, where "*each party would prefer the other to take a soft line in the negotiations, so they can they take a hard line and extract the major concession over price. Both would rather concede, however, than have the trade fall through. Mutual concession – such as a 'split the difference' compromise – is mutually advantageous compared to no trade at all*" (Casson 1991: 56).

6.4.2 Background conditions

The origins of conventional logging

Data on logging activities in Costa Rica go back as far as the 18th century, when cattle farm owners apparently financed partly their landholdings through the commerce of precious woods (Gudmunson 1983). During the 19th century, the Costa Rican government offered land and tax exemptions to encourage agriculture and the colonization of the territory (Seligson 1984; Quirós 1993).

Méndez (no date: 3-4) defines conventional logging as a highly selective, forest degrading activity. Its most visible characteristic is the use of heavy machinery. An additional characteristic is that loggers, besides performing logging activities, also undertake the bureaucratic paperwork for landowners to obtain logging permits.

Conventional logging has its roots in the period of intensive land conversion for agriculture and cattle ranching triggered in the second half of the 20th century (CCT 1992; 3, 8; Gottfried et al. 1994: 111). During this process the use of timber was extremely wasteful. Biesanz et al. (1979: 185-186) report that only 10% of the fallen timber from the conversion of forests to grasslands was further used, i.e. transformed into other goods. Indeed several of the interviewed loggers explained that before they became loggers they used to work as agricultural intermediaries (i.e. buy and sell). They said that it was very usual that farmers and private enterprises in general fell the trees and left them on the ground, or simply burn them. Thus their begin as loggers was eased by the fact that timber was very easy – and cheap – to acquire since people were apparently not interested in it, which allowed loggers to accumulate enough capital to buy machinery that could be used in several activities besides logging. This way – and excepting chainsaws – loggers locked-in technology that is mainly designed for activities other than forestry (e.g., road building and construction in general), but appropriate for land clearing, which is how logging was understood in those days.

Socioeconomic characteristics of the interviewed landowners

The socioeconomic profile of the interviewed landowners in the Osa peninsula matches the definition given in 5.2.1 for small landowners, where low investment and low-risk activities predominate in small farms and low income is characteristic.[191] For this exercise, 44 landowners were interviewed in 26 different locations. The visited locations are depicted in Map 2, and these were approximated with the help of co-workers of the 'Fundación Cecropia' (mainly COVIRENAS), as well as of ACOSA functionaries. Low production of cash crops due to weak local markets predominates in the peninsula. The production of agricultural crops is destined mainly to household consumption.[192] Cattle ranching is the most usual and extensive activity. The total area of the properties of the interviewed landowners accounts for approximately 5012 ha. The land use allocation of this area is shown in Graphic 4.

[191] See also Watson et al. (1998) for a general characterization of small landowners in Costa Rica.

[192] For a similar appreciation on the Osa see van den Homberg (1999).

Graphic 4. Land allocation of the interviewed landowners

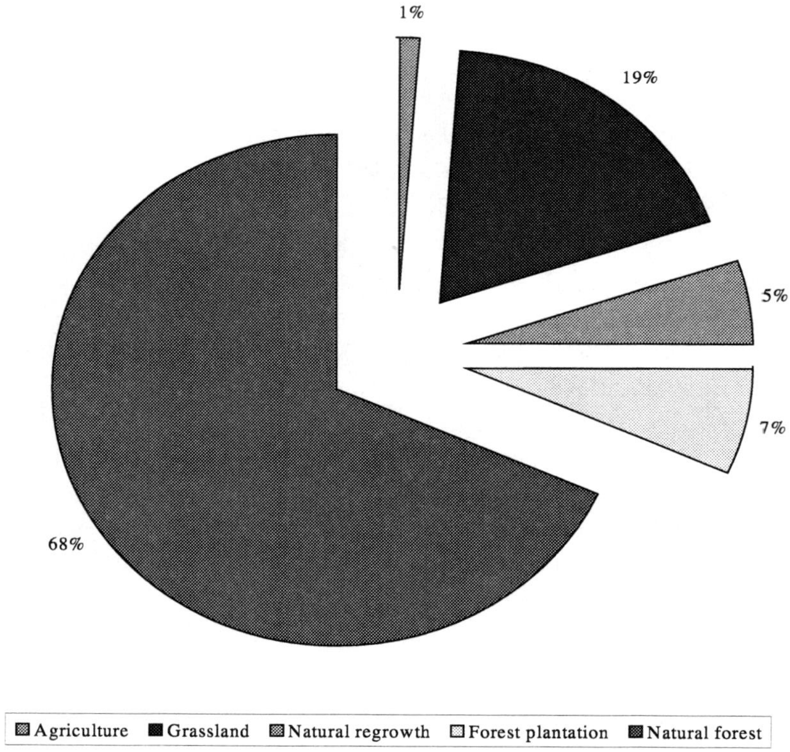

Source: own elaboration

The interviewed landowners (like most inhabitants of the Osa) are recent colonizers. Most interviewees (35) came to the Osa looking for land to perform agriculture and cattle ranching. The longest time of residence is 50 years, while the most recent settler came to the peninsula 5 years ago. The average years of residence in the farm is 20,9 years. The mode of years of possession is 20 years.

Many of these landowners came to the Osa after 1978, in the wake of the expropriation of the landholdings of the 'Osa Productos Forestales', a branch of United Fruit Company (Jenkins 2001). At this time, the governmental organization in charge of land distribution (ITCO) was trying to re-settle landowners from other parts of the country and develop the peninsula for agriculture. But in 1979, the government created the 'Reserva Forestal Golfo Dulce (RFGD)', which includes areas where the ITCO was trying to settle farmers. This aroused not only long discussions between these governmental agencies, but also created extended insecurity among farmers about the likelihood of settling and acquiring property rights. During the field work it was not possible to determine precisely which of these farms are within the RFGD and which not (sometimes the landowners did not know that themselves). Of the total interviewed landowners, 19 contended to have complete property rights, 22 had only partial property rights[193] while 3 said to have no property rights at all.

Characteristic of the interviewed landowners is their lack of formal education. Of the whole group, 8 do not know how to read or write, 17 did not finish primary school while 15 did, 3 went to secondary school but only one finished it, and only one said to have professional education. The main income sources of this group are cattle ranching (15) and labor on other farms (9). Only two planted cash crops on their own farms, while two others planted cash crops on rented tracts, and the rest is dedicated to activities that do not directly involve labor on the field. The following most important income sources are subsistence agriculture (16) and cattle ranching (8). Only three of the interviewed landowners are regularly engaged in logging activities, while several others have experience as forest workers and know how to use a chainsaw. Forty landowners said it was the first time logging was performed in their own farms.

An important background condition for the interviewed landowners is that as the new Forest Law was approved in 1996, only those landowners with complete property rights qualified for the award of logging permits. Later in 1997, the government authorized – by means of a decree – the award of logging permits to landowners with incomplete property rights. A fax-interview was sent to the minister of the environment (MINAE) – Lcda. Elisabeth Odio Benito – to ask her about the reasons behind this decision. A co-worker of the minister, Mr. Guido Cháves,[194] answered that the reason was to give those with scarce economic opportunities an option to improve their economic situation through sustainable forest management.

---

[193] That is, a letter of purchase or a "declaraciòn posesoria",e.g., the partial process of claiming a property.

[194] Guido Cháves, Coordinador de Fomento, SINAC.

In the year 1999 this decree was repealed and complete property rights are required again. When asked about the reasons for this decision in the same interview, Mr. Cháves contended that the right to private property has a constitutional status, and because of this it should be respected.

6.4.3 Results

Due mainly to low resource availability (see 5.2.1), in most cases the interviewed landowners have neither the technical nor the financial means to perform logging as required by the government, which makes it unavoidable for them to negotiate with third parties. For example, when the landowners were asked "what did they had to do to obtain a logging permit?", only 4 contended to have taken care of the paperwork themselves (one intermediary and three loggers). In most cases the paperwork to obtain logging permits was undertaken either by forest engineers (14 cases), intermediaries (12 cases) or loggers (12 cases).

Conventional logging is the result of a voluntary agreement between landowners and loggers and/or forest engineers. This mutual agreement is based largely on a contractual relationship where the rules of logging activities are stated. Logging contracts are usually arranged with one year anticipation to logging activities.

The logger and forest engineer interviews showed that logging contracts emerged as a response of loggers to protect themselves from deals being made but never performed. Loggers contended that when a verbal contract was arranged with a landowner, it was not unusual that at the time when the deal was to be executed, the landowner had already sold the same timber to two or three other loggers who offered better prices. When the landowner interviews are revised to see how many written contracts were established, it turns out that in 26 cases written logging contracts were arranged and in 15 cases the agreement were verbal contracts. Written empowerments, in which landowners empower loggers to take care of the bureaucratic paperwork, were arranged in 35 cases (80% of the total interviews). A usual form of payment of the landowners to the loggers for cutting through the red tape succeeds in timber.

All of the landowners who said to have signed a logging contract were asked if they had a copy available. Some said to have one but not with them (at their house), while many explained they did not receive a copy of the contract even though they asked for one. Most landowners who had a copy of the logging contract available (5) agreed to show it to me to read it. This way I took notice of the basic characteristics of these logging contracts. Afterwards I asked other landowners if they signed similar contracts.

Logging contracts establish explicitly the *prices of timber, the measuring method of timber, the exclusive performance of logging activities by the signing logger, and compensations* in the case one of the parts fails to comply to the deal. It was characteristic of the logging contracts that almost none included compensations for either inflation or the currency devaluation.[195] Compensations include in most cases the payment of the incurred costs on the side of the logger, and a lump-sum valid for both parts. Following, these issues will be explained in more detail.

The prices of standing timber

Commercial timber is mostly classified in three major groups; soft timber, hard, and semi-hard timber. In the Osa, the interviews showed that hard and precious timber are considered the same. The lowest prices accrue to soft timber, while the highest prices are paid for hard timber. Besides its commercial classification, other factors also affect the prices of standing timber like quality, distance between the sawmill and the logging site and access difficulties to the logging site itself. The prices of standing timber used throughout this research are the ones published by the 'Cámara Costarricense Forestal, CCF' for the different regions of the country is the CCF. These regions are mainly three, Atlantic, North and South Pacific. These prices are not exactly the result of a market process, i.e., of a competitive process and the consequent interaction of demand and offer. Nonetheless, CCF average prices are used here as synonym of – local – market prices. According to the CCF, the published prices are calculated on the basis of the information obtained from three sources, landowners in the different regions, loggers, and a log landing in San José that receives timber from the Atlantic and the South Pacific.[196] Also, 95% of the information stems from the associates of the CCF. All of the interviewed loggers admitted to know the CCF prices for the South Pacific. An expert from CATIE said that the prices of standing timber are usually determined in a 'backwards' process, that is, by taking initially the price of sawn wood and resting the costs of transport, extraction, etc. until the standing tree.[197] The logger is mostly the one performing the calculus. The interviews showed that in few cases some timber species were paid separately as 'other semi-hard', this is mostly the case of 'cedro'.[198] But because these cases are very few, only the three major groups are included in the analysis.

Of the interviewed landowners, more than half (25) admitted to ignore the prices of standing timber at the moment they signed the logging contract, while 9 obtained information from other loggers, forest engineers, neighbors or a local organization (SIPRAICO). The neighbors are not necessarily a reliable source of information because some informed themselves through their neighbors and still became prices below those of the CCF. Six landowners said

---

[195] It can be fairly assumed that in a country like Costa Rica, e.g., a small open economy with a strong component of imported inputs, local inflation is strongly influenced by the rate of devaluation that, between 1998 and 1999 was of 11%.

[196] Ing. Mariela Herrera Morera, Directora de la Unidad de Comercialización de la CCF, personal communication.

[197] Manuel Gómez, personal communication.

[198] There are several species in the Osa of which the word 'cedro' is also a part of the name like 'cedro amargo' (*Cedrela odorata*), 'cedro caracolito' (*Ruptilocarpon caracolito*), 'cedro dulce' (*Tapirira myriantha*), 'cedro maría' (*Calophyllum brasiliense, Calophyllum longifollium*).

to know the price distribution because they had personal experience in the logging trade and four others refrained from giving any comments.

Table 13. Landowners' answers to the question: Did you know the prices of timber?

			Yes, from what source?						
	Total	*%*	*From another logger*	*From a forest engineer*	*He is an intermediary*	*Neighbors*	*He is a COVIRENA*	*I am a logger*	*Through SIPRAICO*
Yes	**15**	**34**	4	1	1	3	1	3	1
No	**25**	**57**							
Nd	**4**	**9**							

Source: Own elaboration based on landowner interviews performed in the Osa peninsula between March 9 and May 20 2001.

An additional difficulty that landowners in the Osa are most likely to face when they negotiate timber is that they do not necessarily know what timber specie belongs to what category, because tree diversity in the Osa is very high.[199] There are of course some exceptions because there are tree species known to almost everyone, like the 'nazareno' (*Peltogyne purpurea*), that can be immediately identified for the purpled color of its wood. This specie is regionally endemic, known to exist only between Nicaragua and Panama, and it is endangered because overexploitation. Moreover, other four tree species – also regionally endemic – are endangered due to overexploitation (Jiménez 1999, cited in Barrantes et al. 1999: 40).[200]

Additional to the classification of commercial trees in the Osa – and observed by other researchers in forest management plans – is that many trees are classified wrong, and that the same vulgar name is given to different tree species (Jiménez 1996: 32-3; Barrantes et al. 1999: 37-42).[201] Barrantes et al. (1999: 42, 50) argue that the purpose of – illegally – exploiting protected tree species can be behind the false identification of species in forest management plans, i.e., by giving protected species vulgar names of other species and/or giving the same name to different species, though they also admit that this can be the result of the lack of dendrological knowledge of forest engineers. They also argue that the classification of timber after its hardness (i.e. soft, semi-hard, hard) is flaw, because this classification fails to acknowledge the value derived from different commercial uses of timber – e.g. furniture, musical instruments etc. (see also Dahms 1956: 40; Jiménez 1996: 34). They

[199] According to Barrantes et al. (1999) there are at least 700 tree species in the Osa.

[200] Besides the 'nazareno', these species are: 'chiricano triste' (*Vantanea barbourii*), 'ajo' (*Caryocar costarricense*), chiricano alegre (*Humiriastrum diguense*), and 'reseco' (*Tachigali vesicolor*).

[201] The forest inventories in management plans include vulgar names instead of scientific names.

also criticize that only three species are considered precious (i.e. hard),[202] while other species – so-called semi-hard – are given a lower value even though their timber is as fine as those acknowledged as precious (Barrantes et al. 1999: 48). The landowners and the interviewed loggers said that there is only one specie considered – and paid as – 'precious' in the Osa, namely 'cristóbal' (*Platymiscium curuense*).[203] Due to the complexity and apparent confusion around the classification of timber, one cannot exclude the possibility that a logger will cheat on the landowner – by paying semi-hard timber as if it were a soft timber and so on – if he realizes that the landowner is not aware of 'what is what'. Likewise, one cannot rule out that the logger will take advantage of the use of vulgar names on several species and of wrong classifications to cheat on the AFE by taking different trees than the ones supposedly approved for logging.

Now, assuming that the interviewed landowners did sell their timber for what it really was (i.e., soft, semi-hard, hard), a case-by-case analysis of the interviews showed that in the case of soft timber, all of the landowners (except one, a landowner-logger from Pérez Zeledón) became prices under the average prices reported by the CCF (see Graphic 5).[204] The landowner-logger reported – in all three timber categories – extreme high prices in comparison to the prices reported by the CCF because he reported the prices of the timber at the sawmill, since he also transported the timber. Nonetheless the analysis concentrates on the prices for standing timber. Two other landowner-loggers – belonging to the group with forest management plans during 1999 – were also interviewed, but they refrained from giving information on the prices they received. One of them comes from Cartago (some 300 km away from the Osa) and the other from Pérez Zeledón (some 200 km away from the Osa).

In the case of semi-hard timber, the price distribution shows that 12 landowners (excluding the landowner-logger) obtained prices equal or higher than the average price reported by the CCF (see Graphic 6). Of these landowners, eight informed themselves either through other loggers or had some previous knowledge of the logging trade, the resting four landowners said not to know the prices at all. It is somewhat puzzling that these eight landowners mentioned above became prices under the CCF average price for soft timber, since they are supposed to 'have information'. There are three possible explanations for this. First, they consider soft timber as worthless and will accept any price for it, second, they simply do not know and are only aware of the prices of those species more familiar to them – i.e. semi-hard timber that is relatively abundant and more valuable – and third, their sources provided only partially accurate information. All the other landowners who said not to know the CCF price of

---

202 'Cedro amargo' (*Cedrela odorata*), cristobal (*Platysinum sp*), and 'carey' (*Elaeoluma glabrescens*).

203 Jiménez (1996) classifies this specie as *Platymiscium polystachyum*.

204 The average prices of standing timber for the South Pacific reported by the CCF are in so-called 'Pulgadas Madereras Ticas, PMT'. Acording to the CCF, $1m^3$= 325 PMT. During the last quarter of 1998, the conversion was changed, thus $1m^3$= 362 PMT, which is equivalent to a price increase of a cubic meter of timber. This is already included in the average price depicted in the graphic.

standing timber were paid mostly prices below the CCF average price. Some landowners (5) did know the CCF price and still became a lower price, but they said, that their need was such, that they ended accepting the price offered by the logger.

Only five landowners (excluding the landowner-loggers) admitted having sold hard/precious timber (cristóbal) to loggers. Again all except one became prices under the CCF price (see Graphic 7). Again, they ignored the CCF price.

Moreover, two landowners sold their timber by 'bulk', i.e., they arranged a wholesale price with the logger after the logger had inspected the stand. They claimed that this way they would not be 'robbed' by the logger, though they were not able to give any information on what sorts of timber were actually extracted. These two men do not know how to read and write, and felt more comfortable with this kind of deal. They also said the loggers had no problem with it.

The negotiated prices for standing timber are related to the *cost of using the price mechanism*. The landowner interviews suggest that the lack of knowledge among landowners about the distribution of market prices as well as their information sources can be a major source of transaction costs, as these sources may provide either deficient information or contribute to maintain information asymmetries. Likewise, finding trading partners can be a difficult task in an area like the Osa peninsula, where access is difficult and the infrastructure poor, in which case landowners have scanty opportunities to 'hear other offers' before they acquire contractual liabilities. The interviews suggest that those landowners with experience in the timber trade, or those who inform themselves with other loggers have better chances of obtaining better prices. The interviews suggest that loggers, when negotiating with landowners who have either no experience in the logging trade or do not know the market prices of standing timber, have a strong incentive to cheat, i.e. to start bidding at prices lower than CCF prices. The interviews also suggest that another factor that can ease cheating of the logger on the landowner is that many landowners did not know what timber belonged to what groups, i.e. soft, semi-hard or hard, hence the suspicion is valid that some loggers will take advantage of this by throwing into one group timber species that may have a higher value than believed by landowners.

Graphic 5. Prices of soft timber, 1998 ($/m3)

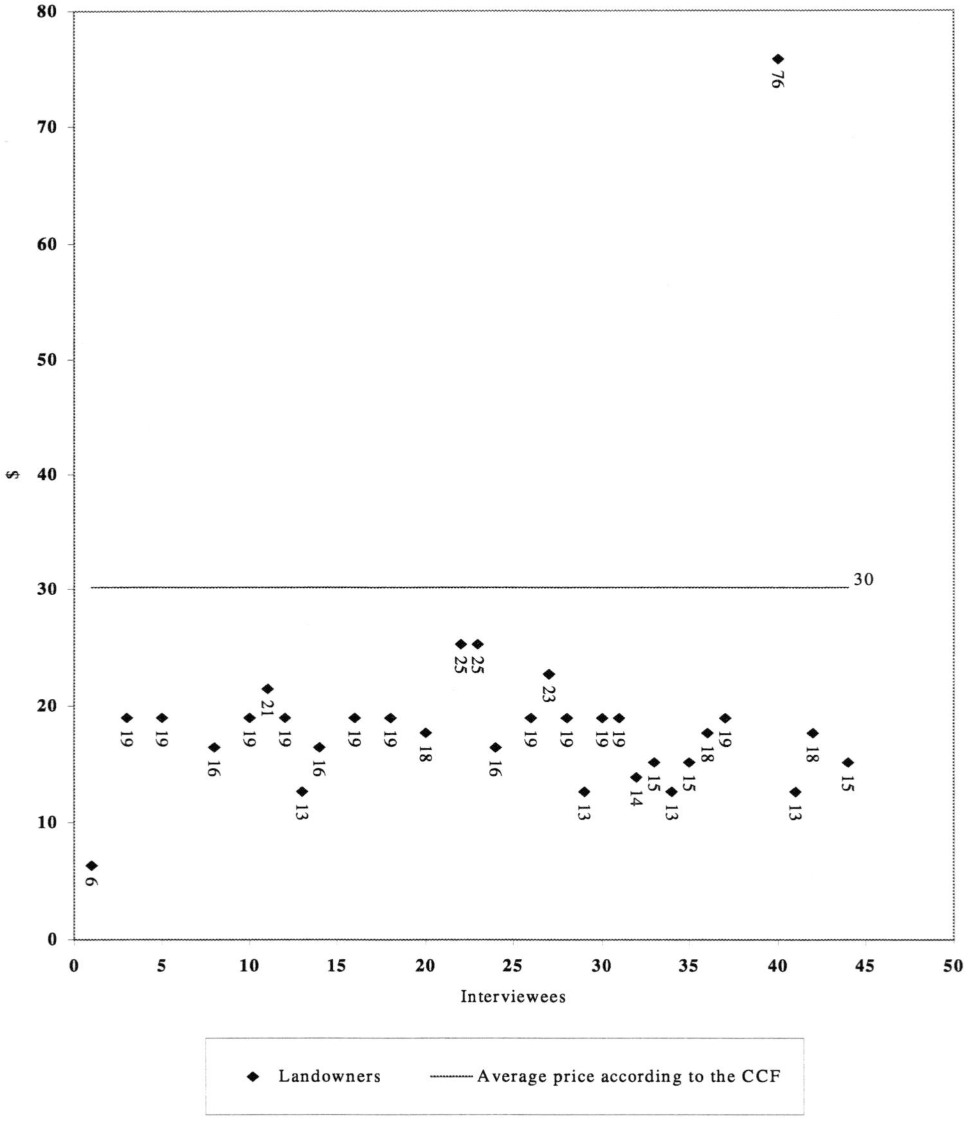

Source: own elaboration

Graphic 6. Prices of semi-hard timber, 1998 ($/m3)

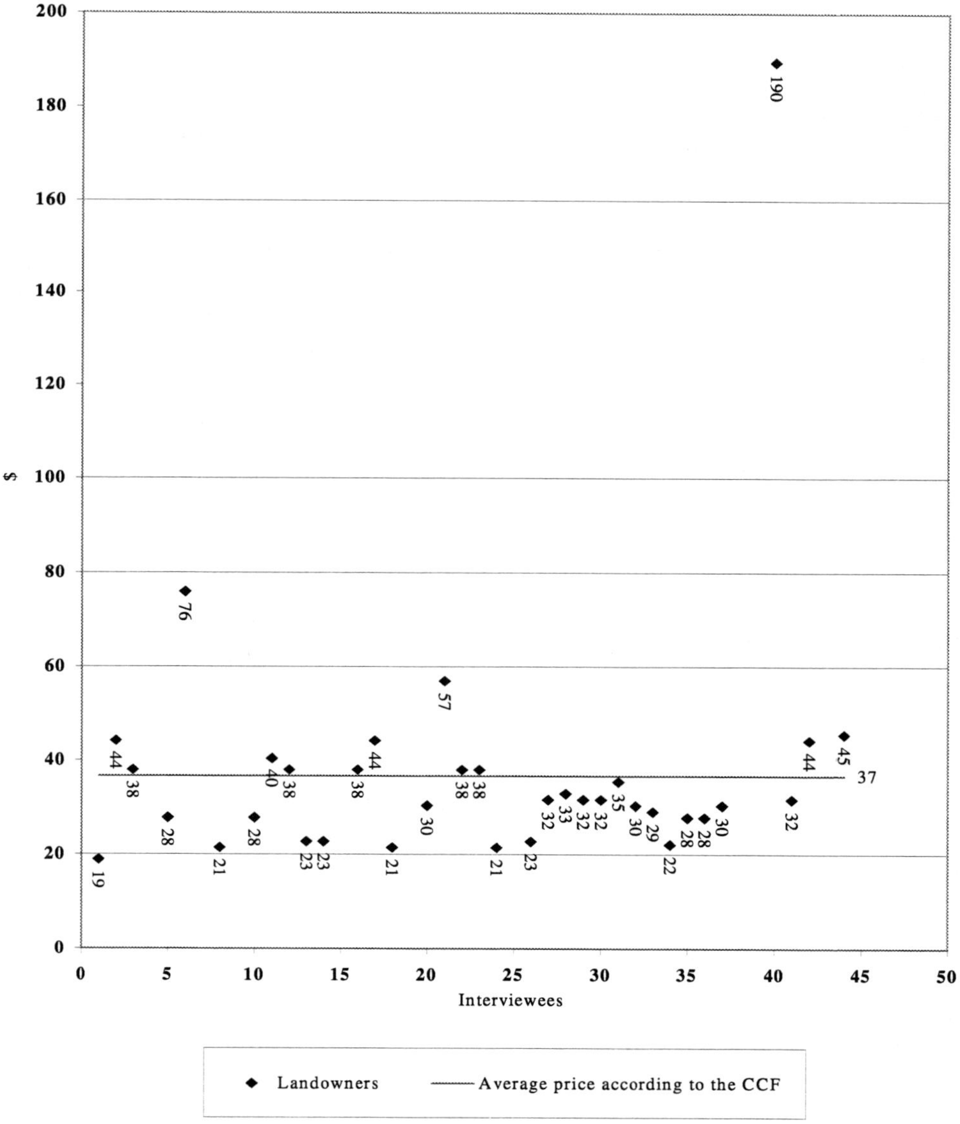

Source: own elaboration

Graphic 7. Prices of hard timber, 1998 ($/m3)

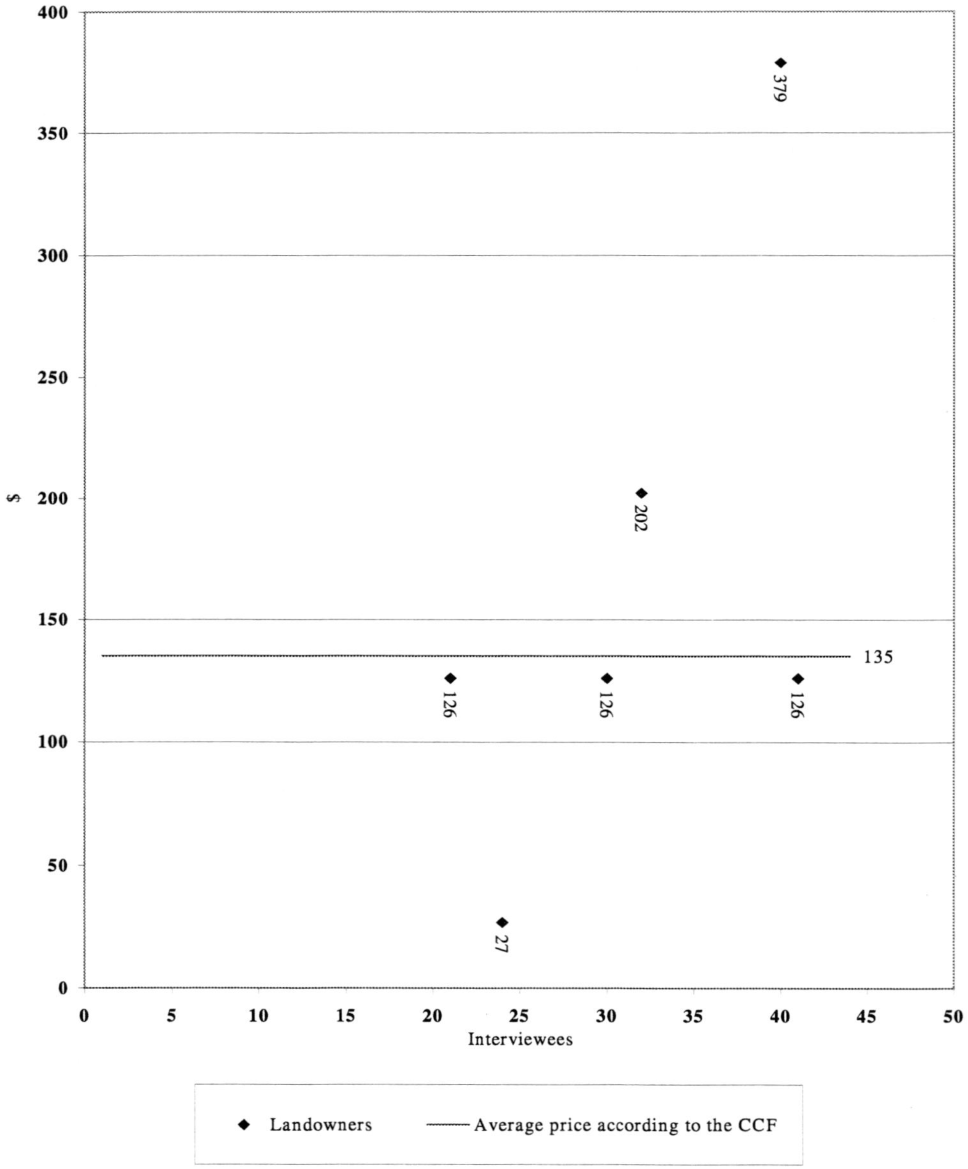

Source: own elaboration

There is also a *cost of negotiation* involved. Considering that timber prices are mostly negotiated with a year anticipation to logging – in the period t_0 – and that these prices are usually fixed contractually, it is unlikely that the landowner can renegotiate better prices when the logging activities are undertaken in t_1, should he/she become aware at a later moment of the CCF prices and/or the inflation rate. In this sense, it cannot be assumed that the negotiated prices reflect the information that the landowner needs to perform efficient transactions, that is, assuming that an efficient transaction is one in which – at least – the CCF prices are reached. In this regard it can be considered that the local timber market is relatively illiquid, because the price negotiation in t_0 does not reduce the uncertainty about market prices and bargaining is limited, affecting therefore landowners' final payoffs. The interviews suggest that asymmetric information is relevant. The *cost of negotiation* arises from the existence of asymmetric and imperfect information between the trading partners, something that strongly characterizes their negotiating styles and gives those – loggers – with accurate information on the CCF price distribution a strong incentive to push the prices down in the negotiation prior to logging.

There is a *cost of optimization* related to the effect of inflation/devaluation on the real value of timber over time, because these macroeconomic variables lead to a reduction of the real value of the traded timber for the landowner, whose main interest should be to maintain the real value of the timber he is trading. Since everyone knows that inflation exists, it is difficult to assume that the lack of inclusion of compensations for the effect of inflation is due to asymmetric information. Instead, it can be considered that the trading partners agree – explicitly or implicitly – upon no compensations in this regard. Nonetheless this is still a transaction cost imposed by macroeconomic conditions on the trading partners, but to the disadvantage of landowners. Given the fact that timber prices are fixed contractually at t_0 and that timber is paid in t_1, the landowner becomes less value for his timber and consequently the logger also pays less. Of the logging contracts I had the chance to read, there was only one where price increases were foreseen over time, but these increases were clearly behind the inflation rate, for example 3% yearly increase on the price of 'cristóbal' when the inflation rate in the country in 1998 ranged 11%.[205] In this case, the insufficient price adjustment to inflation can also be seen as an effect of monetary illusion, i.e. when economic agents fail to perceive the effect that the change of relative prices has on the real value of timber over time.

A more subtle transaction cost – related to the negotiation of timber prices – is also partially related to the *release of confidential information*, which is the loggers' knowledge of market prices. I mean 'partially related' because in principle – in a good functioning market economy – such information is not confidential at all because it is accessible to every economic agent. But confidentiality arises from the fact that in remote places like the Osa peninsula it is relatively difficult for landowners to obtain reliable information on the prices of standing

---

[205] See Banco Central de Costa Rica Internet WWW page at URL: <http://websiec.bccr.fi.cr/indicadores/Cuadro.web>

timber. In this sense, loggers can still keep their knowledge on timber prices to themselves as part of their negotiation strategy/style, and in these circumstances a confidential character of such information arises. Hence should the logger inform the landowner about the CCF prices of standing timber, he would reduce his potential benefits, and by not giving away this kind of information, loggers create a transaction cost for the landowner.

<u>The measurement method of timber</u>

In Costa Rica – like in several other Latin American countries – the generally accepted method of measuring the volume of timber relies on the formula of a cube, where:

$$V = \left(\frac{C}{4} - i\right)^2 L$$

and '*C*' is the circumference of the log that, by dividing it by four is turned into a square, and '*L*' is the length of the log.

Logging contracts establish that a log's circumference is to be measured on its thinnest end – using a string. Customarily, an inch (i = 2,54cm) is afterwards subtracted to the folded string to account for bark and deformations/imperfections of the log. The interviews (i.e. landowners, loggers and forest engineers) showed different insights to this method. Several forest engineers and many landowners argued that loggers usually subtract not only one inch, but between two or three, and that this way loggers trick landowners on the volume of timber. They also said that this string can be sometimes stretched up to two inches (depending on the weight attached to it), that way the sides of the cube are also shortened. On the other hand, loggers contended that when more than one inch is subtracted it is due to imperfections of the log and that such a practice is not unusual. When asked about the "stretching string", they said they did not do that, but probably others.

Though the method of volume measuring belongs to the basic rules (information) that should be commonly shared by the trading actors in conventional logging (landowners-loggers), to 'know' how timber is measured appears to have different intensities between the landowners. A relatively large group (13, of which 3 are loggers) said to positively know how the timber was measured, though many also added that loggers are very tricky when it comes to volume measuring. Ten landowners contended that they knew how it was done because they were at the log landings at the time the timber was measured, which does not necessarily demonstrates knowledge of the method because – when asked – they were not able explain it thoroughly. The majority (19 landowners) admitted not to know at all how the timber volume was measured.

Table 14. Landowners' answer to the question: Did you know how the timber was measured?

Answer	**Total (from 44)**	**%**
Yes	13	30
Yes, I was present	10	23
No	19	43
Nd	2	5
Total	**44**	**100%**

Source: Own elaboration based on landowner interviews performed in the Osa peninsula between March 9 and May 20 2001.

The measurement of the volume of timber is clearly related to the *cost of optimizing* because it is in the interest of the landowner to become the value of as much timber as possible to maximize his income, while it is in the logger's interest to reduce the costs of the purchased timber by paying for as less volume as possible. Like in the case of timber prices, increased *optimization costs* can be partly attributed to deficient information and partly to asymmetric information. It can be partly attributed to deficient information because in several cases landowners do not know – or know only partially – how the timber is measured, and it can be partly attributed to asymmetric information because it is in the interest of loggers to keep this information to themselves, i.e., how much timber they are really buying. Though in this case the logger has an incentive to cheat, the landowner suspects he is being tricked out.

As mentioned above, it is usual that the loggers undertake the bureaucratic paperwork for the landowner to obtain the logging permit by means of an empowerment, in which case they also usually agree with the landowner upon the payment for this service to succeed in timber. Hence – in view of the volume and price effects explained above – it is likely that many landowners end up paying more to obtain logging permits than these are really worth.

<u>The exclusive performance of logging and compensations</u>

In a broader context, the contractual negotiation of timber also involves a transaction cost for forgone *option values*. Both are closely related. Logging contracts establish that for the period for which the contract is valid (one or more years), only the signing logger can perform logging activities in the property, which means that the timber to be extracted between t_0 and t_1 belongs to the logger, not to the landowner. Likewise, the establishment of compensations – should one of the partners withdraw from the deal – restrains the room for bargaining at later periods (i.e. re-negotiation), hence they restrain property rights over standing timber. Compensations usually include a lump-sum and the incurred costs on the side of the logger. In the revised logging contracts, compensations were set at a lump sum of approximately $2000. Should the logger withdraw from the deal, the landowner is to become the lump sum. Should the landowner withdraw from the deal, he is to pay the lump sum and the operation costs to the logger.

As explained above, logging contracts emerged from the side of loggers to restrain competition and assure property rights over timber, i.e. to reduce both the risk of loosing business to other competitors and the chance of opportunistic behavior on the side of landowners. Consequently, if the landowner is offered a better deal, he cannot renegotiate his timber because of the acquired liability, which represents a forgone *option value* for the – better – deal the landowner could have performed, but is not allowed to unless he pays a compensation to the original signing logger, which is very unlikely to happen (that is of course, unless the competing logger finances everything) because for many landowners the lump-sum alone represents almost 2/3 of their yearly income. Thus compensations will preclude alternative deals on the side of landowners as long as they offset other potential benefits. But the interviews revealed that compensations can be a one way street, where the landowner is bound to pay them if he withdraws from the deal, but not necessarily the logger. Actually, if the logger breaks the agreement, the landowner should be able to follow a lawsuit against the logger, but because sometimes he does not have a copy of the contract, he refrains from doing so, or because the process of engaging a lawyer appears to him more costly than what he considers it is really worth, he does not even try. Moreover, logging contracts sometimes include a clause that says "a loaded truck is a paid truck". This means that every time a truck is loaded the landowner should become the payment for that timber. But – as several landowners argued – it has happened many times that when the logger has loaded the truck he simply takes off and does not pay to the landowner. Sometimes the landowner is paid weeks after, and sometimes he is not paid at all.

Despite the fact that compensations can be a powerful instrument to assure compliance of landowners to logging contracts, it was seen that many – i.e., 11 of 26 landowners with written contracts – never though of withdrawing from the deal, though they knew about the compensations. When the resting 15 landowners were asked about the consequence of calling off the logging contract, most of them recalled that compensations would be due, though they as well did not show signs of wishing to withdraw. In this group only one said not to know what could happen. In contrast, in the group of landowners with verbal contracts (15), six said explicitly that they did not have any intention of withdrawing from the deal, while other six said nothing would happen, and two did not know. Like in the first group, several of these landowners showed no particular signs of wishing to withdraw from the deal. But when the interviews of the landowners with written contracts are compared with those with verbal contracts, it can be seen that the landowners with verbal contracts are more aware of their bargaining power, because they are confident that if they decide to go to another logger they can force the first logger to renegotiate, which would not be possible were written contracts signed.

A model of transaction costs for conventional logging in the Osa

A numerical example might give an idea of the importance of transaction costs of – contractual – conventional logging for landowners in the Osa between 1998 and 1999. For this purpose, several strong assumptions are made:

1. That all the interviewed landowners with forest management plans in 1999 (except the three landowner-loggers and two other landowners whose management plans were stopped by ACOSA due to irregularities) arranged logging contracts. This makes n=39.

2. That the gross volume of approved timber for this group (20700 m^3) is distributed according to the model posited by Jiménez (1996) and Barrantes et al. (1999), as follows:

Table 15. Osa peninsula. Classification of timber classes according to their market value

Class	% of total	% of commercial timber
Fine (precious) timber	2,73	3,68
Hard timber	14,38	19,37
Semi hard	20,85	28,09
Soft timber	36,27	48,86
Not commercial	25,44	

Source: own elaboration based on Jiménez (1994) and Barrantes et al. (1999)

Table 15 shows on its second column the distribution of different timber classifications according to their commercial potential. Therefore, excluding the proportion of non-commercial timber, the third column shows a second distribution in which only commercial timber is accounted for.

3. The gross volume of timber (m^3) from forest management plans approved by ACOSA during 1999 is also the amount sold by landowners.[206] When an inch of bark is subtracted – according to the conventional measuring method – the volume of any log is reduced by approximately 5%, which gives a starting figure of 19577m^3. Since many landowners complained that loggers cheat on them by stretching the string with which they measure the log's circumference by more than one inch and subtract more than one inch than necessary for bark, I am assuming that one more inch bark is subtracted and that the string is stretched one more inch in all cases.[207].

The change in volume when additional inches (to bark) are subtracted from the folded string and assuming that the circumference is correctly measured (i.e. not shortened) is given by:

$$\int_{x_i}^{x} \frac{\partial V}{\partial x} dc$$

[206] The volume corresponding to three landowners who are also loggers is not included because these do not face the same transaction costs as regular landowners. Hence only the volume accruing to 41 landowners was considered.

[207] The reader must know that the reason why I am referring to inches is that landowners and loggers use this measure, even though the official measuring scale is metric. Nonetheless, in all calculations inches are converted to centimeters. One inch is equal to 2,54 cm.

where $\frac{\partial V}{\partial x}$ is the marginal change of the volume when "x" changes, $x = \frac{C}{4} - 2{,}54$ and $x_i = x - i$, and $0 \leq x_i < x$

And since the primitive of the derivative $\partial V / \partial x$ is known, all one needs to do is substitute x, and x_1 in the equation:

$$V = (x - i)^2 L$$

to approximate the reduction of volume when additional inches are subtracted.

4. The total timber approved in 1998 is extracted by the end of 1999.

5. The average CCF prices of standing timber for the years 1998 and 1999 (for the South Pacific of the country) are valid prices for the Osa, i.e., they accurately reflect the effect of distance and access difficulty to the area.[208]

6. That the prices received by landowners are the result of a bidding process between them and the loggers before the logging contract is signed, i.e. 1998 (t_0). Average prices of standing timber received by landowners in the Osa peninsula are estimated based on data obtained through landowner interviews. The prices received by the landowner-loggers are not included in the average, as they are not representative of the prices perceived by 'normal' landowners and deviate the average upwards. All the prices were converted to (current) US dollars by means of the average exchange rate used in the monetary accounts of the 'Banco Central de Costa Rica'.

According to these assumptions, the total CCF value of the approved timber for forest management plans (for logging operations in 1999) was of $727.000 in 1998 ($t_0$), i.e., the moment in time when the timber was negotiated and the logging contracts signed. At the end of the logging activities in 1999 (t_1) the approximate value perceived by landowners was $456.000. The sequence of the different transaction costs is as follows:

[208] See CCF (1998a; 1998b; 1998c), and CCF (1999a, 1999b).

CCF value	Price effect (t0)	Value perceived by landowners	Devaluation effect (t1)	Value perceived by landowners after devaluation
$ 727.122	-24,91%	$ 546.029	-10%	$ 490.237
Less one additional inch from logger		$ 508.167	-10%	$ 456.243
Measurement effect		-7%		-37%
				Transaction costs

Additional transaction costs for bureaucratic paperwork not included

This means that total transaction costs accruing to landowners represented approximately \$270.000 (37%) of the original CCF value of standing timber and results from the combined effect of:

- The average prices of standing timber perceived by landowners being lower than the CCF prices (price effect in t_0 of 25%). This transaction cost is the combined result of the *cost of using the price mechanism*, the *cost of negotiation*, the *optimization cost* and the *release of confidential information*. The cost of using the price mechanism in the Osa is most notorious because in order to obtain reliable information actors must have some connection to the logging industry, otherwise, the only way to obtain information on prices is through trading (and gaining experience) or through word of mouth. Loggers that notice that a landowner lacks reliable information have a good starting basis to negotiate to their advantage – i.e. bid at lower prices – by keeping CCF prices to themselves.

- The effect of the devaluation rate between 1998 and 1999 (10%), i.e., the *cost of optimization* imposed by the macroeconomic environment. The assumption that all the timber is extracted at the end of the period makes this assessment rather optimistic because many logging contracts extend over several years, depending on how big the management plan is. Therefore, should the logging contract last several years, the effect of the devaluation on the value of timber – hence on the real income of the landowner – is bound to be larger.

- The effect on the volume of timber when loggers cheat by stretching the string to measured the logs' circumference and when – one more – inch is subtracted from the string after dividing it by four (approximately 7%), can be associated to the *cost of optimizing* and *the cost of negotiation.*

- The exclusive performance of logging, i.e., *traded property rights, option value*. The assessment of this transaction cost could be a scenario where the landowner has an option that pays at least the CCF prices.

Information appears to be a common denominator of the variables influencing transaction costs, and its effect is large under the assumptions made for the group of landowners, but these transaction costs are also representative of the costs that a single landowner can bear when he signs a logging contract. Each of the sources of transaction costs mentioned hitherto is related in one way or another to the quality and stock of the information available to landowners. The same way that shared information is necessary for institutional stability, deficient information and information asymmetries also contribute to maintain the 'status quo' of loggers under the circumstances explained above.

Considering the general case of an income function of conventional timber trade for any landowner:

$$I_l = VP$$

More specifically, the landowner's income function can be described as:

$$I_l = V(v_{m_{(i)}})P(p_{ccf_{(i)}}, p_{dr_{(i)}})$$

Where:

- The commercial volume of traded timber $V(v_{m(i)})$ is a function of the measuring method $v_{m(i)}$, and where the final traded volume is a function of the information available to landowner. The variable $v_{m(i)}$, includes the combined effect of "the stretching string" and additional inches being subtracted from the folded string on the volume of timber.
- The price at which standing timber is negotiated $P(p_{ccf(i)}, p_{dr(i)})$ is a function of the available information to the landowner on the CCF price distribution, $p_{ccf(i)}$, and a function of the devaluation rate $p_{dr(i)}$, which are both a function of information.

Now, the impact that an increase of the information stock of a single landowner (l_x) would have on his income function from conventional timber trade would be:

$$\frac{\partial I_{l_x}}{\partial i_{l_x}} = \frac{\partial V}{\partial v_{m_{(i)}}}\frac{\partial v_{m_{(i)}}}{\partial i}P + \frac{\partial P}{\partial p_{m_{(i)}}}\frac{\partial p_{m_{(i)}}}{\partial i}\frac{\partial P}{\partial p_{dr_{(i)}}}\frac{\partial p_{dr_{(i)}}}{\partial i}V$$

Where, for example, an information change that leads the landowner to avoid being tricked out on the volume measurement of timber means:

$$\frac{\partial V}{\partial v_{m_{(i)}}}\frac{\partial v_{m_{(i)}}}{\partial i} \geq 0$$

Reliable information changes on prices should have a similar effect on the landowner's income, whereas, deficient information is bound to have the opposite effect. Changes in the information stock of the landowner are likely to have a positive impact on income stemming from timber trade. In the more general case, it is to expect that:

$$\frac{\partial I_{l_x}}{\partial i_{l_x}} \rangle 0$$

An increase of the information stock of the landowner is understood as additional (reliable) information that will increase his/her bargaining power and will lead to improved contractual conditions, hence to increased income from conventional timber trade. In the example above, the information stock has different variables (components), and depending on which variable the landowner becomes increased information, so will be the income change. In terms of the previously introduced equations, this means that if only one variable is affected – say information on market prices – the other partial derivatives become irrelevant. It appears logic to think that changes in landowner's information stock, by reducing deficient information, will also reduce information asymmetries and will make it more difficult for loggers to cheat on the landowner. The effect of a change of the information stock for the collectivity of landowners has then the following form:

$$\sum_{X=1}^{n} \frac{\partial I_{L_x}}{\partial i_{L_x}} \rangle 0$$

In the theoretical framework it was stated that transaction costs arise when economic agents exchange ownership to assets. In this chapter it has been seen that deficient information, asymmetric information and most probably guile behavior on the side of some loggers – incentivized by the expectation of obtaining higher benefits – can contribute heavily to the formation of transaction costs. There is a cost of doing business with the wrong information, this being the forgone income compared to what could have been earned should the right information had been at hand. Either because of newcomer's naive expectations or being victim of opportunist behavior, transaction costs for the landowner arise firstly through the contractual agreement, where the terms of negotiation are fixed. The less reliable the information available to the landowner, the smaller his payoff and consequently the larger the transaction costs. This does not mean that those landowners who agreed verbally on conventional logging did not bear similar transaction costs. They probably did if they had similar information deficiencies as those with written contracts. The only difference is that – if they increased their information stock – they probably had a chance to renegotiate. Nonetheless, and raising again the issue, despite how high the transaction costs might have been for the landowners, the benefits they obtained from engaging in conventional logging were probably perceived to be larger than the costs. Furthermore, the benefits they obtained from conventional logging are probably perceived higher than any other forestry activity, otherwise they would have refrained from engaging in conventional logging. A possible explanation of landowners' engagement is that many are newcomers and are therefore not aware of the transaction costs involved, and thus of the forgone income. Nonetheless, loggers do have a reputation for cheating on landowners, so despite how naive a landowner might be, he will probably suspect he will be cheated upon. The threat of sanctions probably does not play such a relevant role since more than half of the interviewees did not think of withdrawing from the deal. Either due to deficient or asymmetric information, landowners bear significant transaction costs from conventional logging, and since they appear to be unorganized it is also unlikely that they might be able to coordinate their negotiation strategy towards a better equilibrium, consequently landowners will probably continue complying to the institutional arrangements set by conventional logging if they can maintain their expectation of maximizing their payoffs, i.e. of meeting their goals.

A model of the break even point of a conventional logger

Now to approximate the business reasons behind a logger's strategic and/or opportunistic behavior, it is useful to take a look at the break-even point of a single logger, that is, to assess how much timber (m^3) must be extracted so that the logger's benefit is equal to zero. For this exercise, I am assuming a simple logger, who owns some of the machinery to perform logging but does not own the trucks to transport timber nor a sawmill. The prices of roundwood at the sawmill are also those obtained from the CCF. The distribution of timber follows the model presented above. For this exercise, I selected arbitrarily a single management plan[209] and the information on costs with which the figures are calculated were obtained from different loggers and forest engineers. The landowner to whom the farm belongs said to ignore the market prices of standing timber. According to the data obtained from ACOSA, the timber volume approved for extraction in this management plan is of 3170 m^3, and the net traded volume – following the figure introduced above – is of 2950 m^3.

The benefit function of the logger is

$$(1) \qquad B = TI_{\log g} - TC_{\log g}$$

where the total income from logging is

$$(2) \qquad TI_{\log g} = P_T Q_T$$

and P_T is the CCF price of timber at the sawmill, Q_T is the volume of timber bought from the landowner. The total cost of logging is given by the equation,

$$(3) \qquad TC_{\log g} = FC_{\log g} + VC_{\log g}$$

where $FC_{\log g}$ is the fixed cost of logging and $VC_{\log g}$ is the variable cost of logging. The variable cost is given by the price of standing timber paid to the landowner. Regarding fixed

[209] Forest management plan Number 101AR in the ACOSA listing.

costs, loggers and forest engineers gave information on extraction costs on a weekly basis, therefore, if the logger knows how big the management plan is, he can also assess in advance how much its execution is going to cost. Considering that the logger can plan the logging activities with one year in advance, I am assuming that all the other costs – i.e. except timber – are fixed. The weekly fixed costs – excluding transport costs – are estimated to be $1 400. The fixed costs include the logger's salary, which I am arbitrarily setting at $500 a week. Transport costs depend on the volume of timber to be transported – independent of the class of timber. For this management plan transport costs amount to approximately $56 000. The estimated time for the execution of this management plan is 9 weeks.[210] Hence the total fixed costs amount to some $78 000. The logger's variable cost function has the following form:

$$(4) \qquad VC_{\log g} = p_l Q_T$$

Where p_l is the price loggers pay to landowners for standing timber.

Therefore, substituting (2), (3) and (4) in (1), one has

$$(5) \qquad B = P_T Q_T - FC_{\log g} - p_l Q_T$$

The break-even point is therefore given by,

$$(6) \qquad Q_T = \frac{FC_{\log g}}{P_T - p_l}$$

With the data obtained from the logger and forest engineer interviews, and according to the model of distribution of timber for the Osa, I assessed the logger's break-even point separately for each of the different timber classifications. The results are depicted in Graphic 8. The first part of the Graphic shows how much timber there is available according to the model of distribution of commercial timber in the Osa. The following columns depict the break even points for each timber class alone because, first, it is not possible to show all the possible break-even combinations of timber, and second, because this way the commercial relevance for the logger of each timber class becomes clear.

[210] Actually it should be 8 weeks, but an extra week is considered to account for heavy weather and/or machinery failures.

Graphic 8. Logger's break-even point

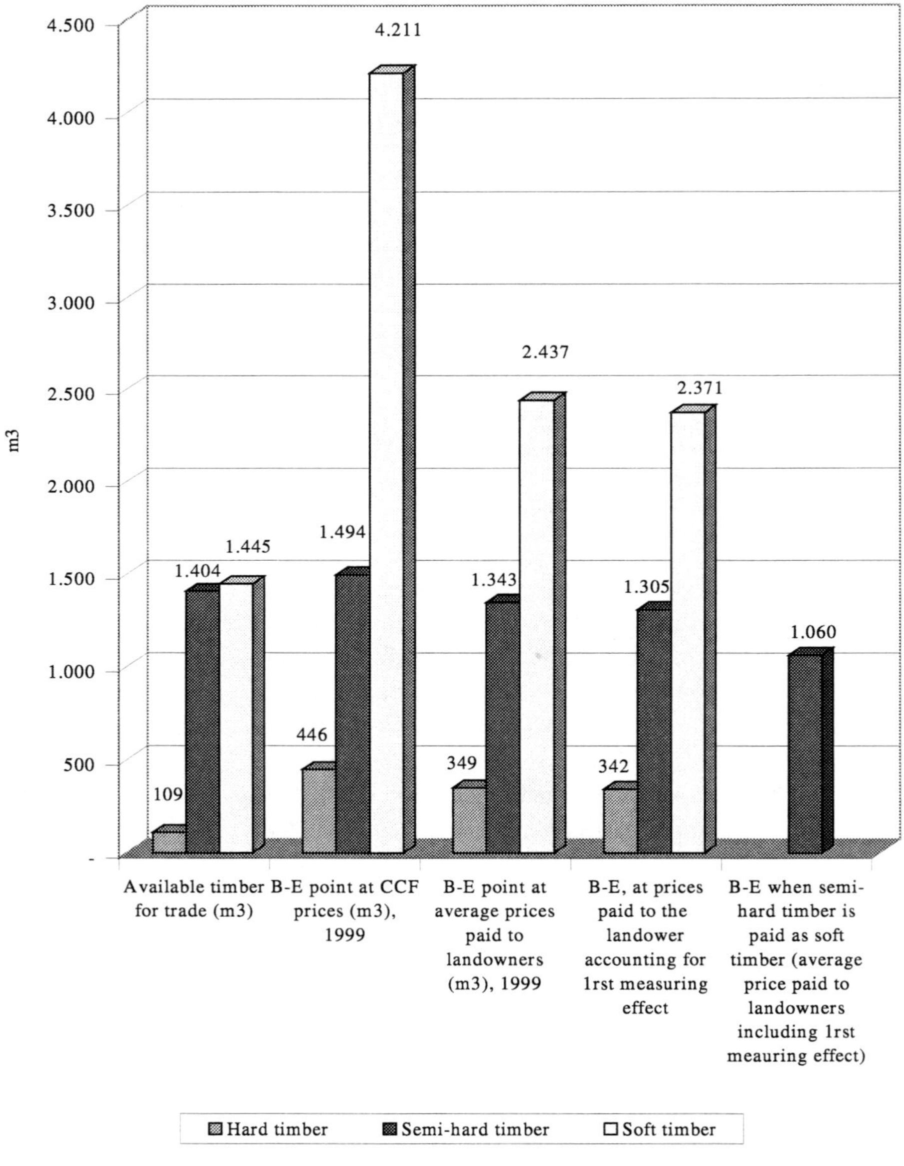

Source: own elaboration

Under the assumptions made, a rational logger – i.e., one who maximizes his benefits – will always be primarily interested in extracting a combination of hard and semi-hard timber rather than soft timber because – at CCF prices – he will need more than double soft timber than semi hard and hard timber to cover his operation costs. In the cases of soft and semi-hard timber, Graphic 8 illustrates how the logger can reduce his break-even point progressively when he;

1. pays prices to landowners lower than those of the CCF
2. cheats on the volume of timber by paying for less timber than he is actually taking. What I mean with the first measuring effect in Graphic 8 is when the logger subtracts another inch (2,54 cm) additional to bark – assuming that the quality of the log does not demand additional inches to be subtracted. In this case, paying for less volume is the equivalent of reducing the price by the percentage the logger is not paying for, which is 6%, and
3. by paying semi-hard timber as if it were soft timber.

During the interviews, several landowners complained that loggers sometimes did not cut all of the trees foreseen for felling in the forest management plan – or sometimes they did, but left them lying on the ground – and that they neither took them nor paid them as agreed. On top of this, even though the logger breaks the agreement, landowners seldom become the compensation foreseen in the contract because they refrain from following a lawsuit.

From the loggers' point of view, only when they pay lower prices for soft timber – than CCF prices – is soft timber commercially appealing, and considering the sawmill prices for hard and semi-hard timber, the logger's main concern must be to extract as much hard and semi-hard timber as possible. Additionally, if it is possible for the logger to pay semi-hard timber as if it were soft, then he will be more rapidly over his break even point. Looking at this example, opportunistic behavior of loggers to maximize their profits is understandable, though not excusable.

In the theoretical approach I introduced the game of chicken as a form to characterize the timber trade in the Osa. The game of chicken is a cooperation game, and I use it in this case because conventional logging succeeds on a voluntary basis. Thus one can expect that loggers – during the negotiation of timber – would prefer that landowners sell their timber as cheap as possible, while landowners are seeking the highest income possible, but many landowners have a weak position to negotiate a fair price because, first, their information is deficient and second, they need money as fast as possible. Consequently, loggers have an advantage during the negotiation, i.e., they have more bargaining power than landowners as they are not as affected by delays because they have more resources to support themselves than landowners. For example, they can always bid at lower prices than those of the CCF and still make concessions over prices as long as the CCF price is not exceeded, and landowners are rather willing to negotiate and obtain some value of their timber than nothing at all in an economic surrounding where income sources are scarce. Considering the fact that these economic agents act under bound rationality, it is clear that information asymmetries and deficient information definitely play an important role in allowing loggers to obtain larger payoffs and maintain their status quo as long as they negotiate with their – less informed – counterpart, the landowners. Therefore, as long as the landowners cannot do better by pursuing a different negotiation strategy they will continue to have an incentive to comply to conventional logging. That is, the landowners would rather do a bad deal than no deal at all.

Coming back to the complain of landowners about loggers not taking all the timber agreed in the contract. Lets suppose the logger has already cut the trees and he is with the landowner at the log landing discussing the payment. The landowner complains that there are still marked logs lying on the field and that the logger should also take them as agreed. The logger explains to the landowner his position regarding the operation costs and the value of timber at the sawmill, and that if he takes the soft timber he will be incurring a loss hence he can only take what is really worth selling. Even if the landowner understands the logger's point of view he will try to stick to the agreement because it is in his own interest. Should the landowner further complain about the logger taking only the timber he wishes and not all of it as initially agreed, the logger can confront the landowner with "I will only take what I can really use, and that is my final offer, take it or leave it". The landowner could consider that the logger is breaking the original agreement, but if he really is in need of cash (and landowners in the Osa usually are) he will probably not maintain an inflexible position because, first, to take the logger to court will require time and money, second – even if the landowner expects to win the lawsuit – if the compensation is not high enough to offset the costs of the process he will have to invest the value of the timber in covering the costs, which can significantly reduce his income. The costs of the process will depend – among other things – on how much time it will take, and the landowner cannot know this in advance. Consequently, if the landowner is risk-averse, he is bound to refrain from following a law suit against the logger, and so the landowner is chicken. A similar argumentation can be used if the landowner tries to renegotiate the prices and/or the volume of timber, in that case, the landowner would be the deal-breaker. The logger will only let go if the landowner can pay to the logger, but the payment of the compensation plus the operation costs will reduce the chances of achieving the goals that the landowner had originally set himself. The risk aversion of landowners is good exemplified by a saying that several landowners brought up during the interviews; 'I will rather make a bad deal than to have a good fight'.

<u>The commitment to engage in conventional logging activities and landowners' satisfaction derived from logging</u>

Though it is often assumed (by some environmentalists and academicians) that landowners are systematically sought and convinced of engaging in conventional logging by loggers and/or forest engineers, the landowner interviews showed that in most cases (63%) logging came about because the landowner took the initiative, and he looked for either a logger, an intermediary, a forest engineer or an organization (usually SIPRAICO) to help him undertake logging. The interviews showed that loggers looked directly for landowners only in 4 cases.

Forest engineers contacted landowners to perform logging in only one case. Conventional logging can happen in many fashions, either the landowner looks for a logger or vice-versa, or an intermediary looks for a landowner and even a forest engineer can bring the parties together. But according to the interviews, conventional logging takes place primarily because of landowners' initiative. The role of timber intermediaries (usually persons living in the area) was found to be substantially more relevant because they had an active role in convincing landowners of logging in 10 cases. In this case, the landowner is bound to receive even lower prices than when he/she negotiates directly with the logger, but the volume of timber he/she gets paid for can be higher than otherwise, because the income of the intermediary depends from the volume sold to the logger. Nonetheless, this does not necessarily leave the landowner in a better position if the additional value of the increased volume is offset by an even lower price.

Intermediaries play an important role in conventional logging. One of the interviewed loggers admitted openly that he is constantly informed by local intermediaries of who in the peninsula is looking for a logger, so he does not have much trouble in finding landowners to do business with. Since most loggers live far away from the Osa, intermediaries are a valuable information source for loggers.

But if logging is actually more a consequence of the landowners' initiative, then what reasons move landowners engage in conventional logging? The most usual reason was to obtain rapid cash (10). Nine landowners revealed their wish to obtain cash for productive activities that actually compete directly with forests (agriculture and/or cattle ranching). Seven landowners wished to buy another property elsewhere, while six others wanted to assure their rights to the property, i.e. finish the inscription of the property in the land registry. Five wished to build/repair their houses. Five others wished to continue engaged in conventional logging on a regular basis (including the three landowner-loggers). Only one landowner had the intention of starting another business that might help him make a living without depending on forest resources (see Graphic 9).

Graphic 9. Landowners' motivations to engage in conventional logging

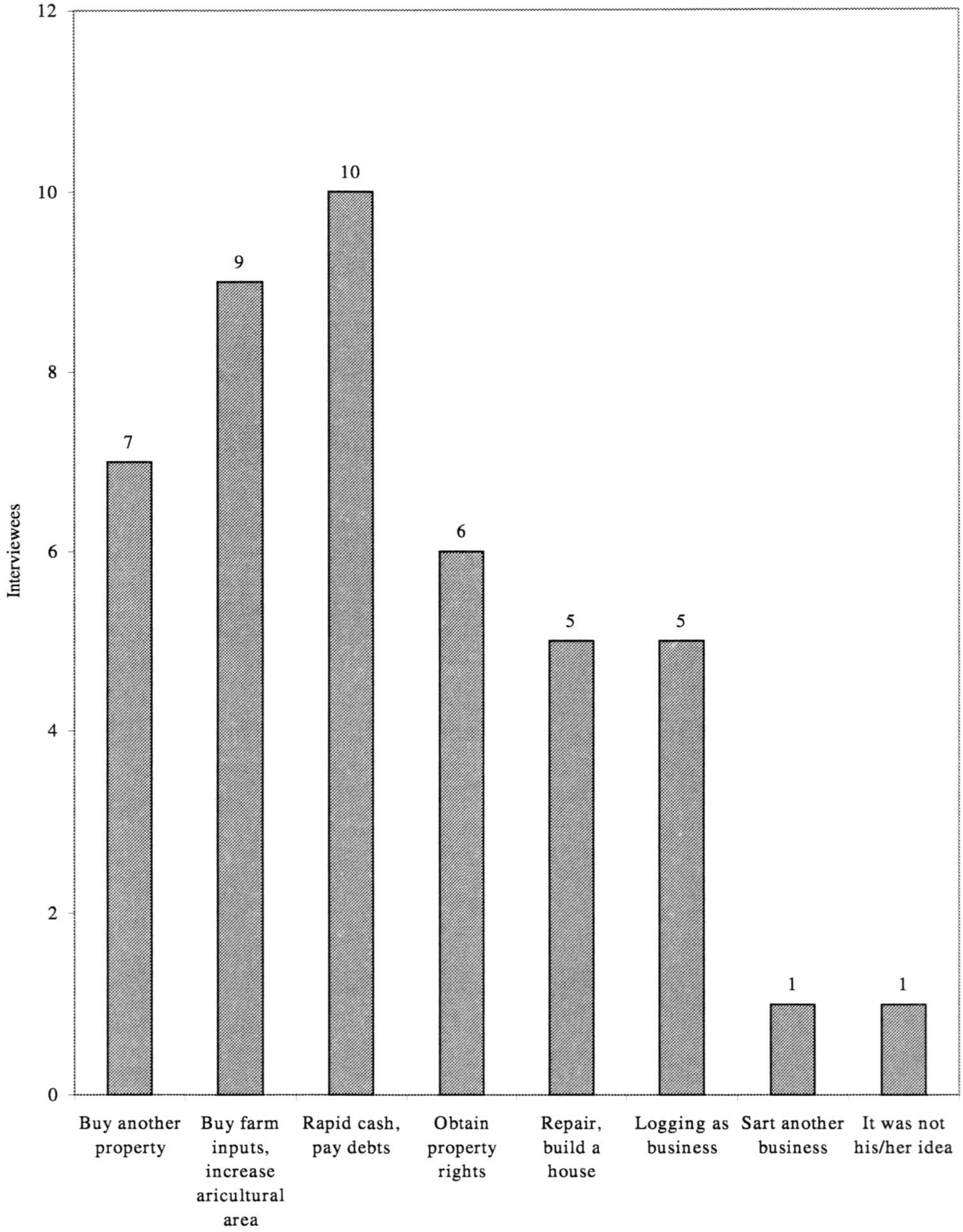

Source: own elaboration

A widely accepted fact among academicians and environmentalists is that landowners engage in conventional logging because it provides them with the financial means to satisfy short-term needs. While this is the case of those seeking to obtain rapid cash and/or to pay debts, the other reasons are not necessarily short-term, nonetheless they can also be considered to attend basic needs of these rural households like assuring property rights, repair the existing house (or build one) and buy inputs for the farm. In view of this, it is unlikely that the achievement of the goals pursued at this stage by the interviewed landowners will reduce the pressure on forest resources because their achievement does not contribute to the formation of productive capital that might play a role in, first, a long-term improvement of their socio-economic profile (except maybe for assuring property rights), and second, they do not bring landowners to engage in productive activities that do not compete directly with forest resources. I mean 'at this stage' because investments in productive activities that are compatible with and/or do not compete directly with forest resources can only be expected to happen when basic needs can be surely satisfied in the long-term, not before, and when landowners show a disposition to engage in such alternative productive activities, which cannot be observed in this group. Additionally, it is most likely that landowners lack the know-how on how to start/engage in such alternative activities. Consequently, it is questionable that landowners' motivations – and their achievement – may contribute to the establishment of forest-friendly activities and the development of a forest culture. Likewise, the contribution of conventional logging to the creation of a forest culture in the Osa is markedly limited because landowners' role remains that of mere spectators.

The ensuing question is therefore, did the landowners achieve their goals after engaging in conventional logging? According to the interviews, more than half of the group (24 landowners) had success in achieving their objectives, while 12 landowners reached them partially and 8 did not meet their goals.

Though landowners are part and parcel of conventional logging in the Osa, one basic factor stands directly in the way to the achievement of their goals, which is the unreliability of the information with which they negotiate. This should be no surprise because the quality of information available to an actor depends heavily on how he/she is related to the logging industry, and most landowners in the Osa do not have strong commercial links to the logging industry other than occasionally selling standing timber. On the other hand, loggers have a more structured and reliable information network about the landowners – attended partly by local intermediaries, who know their neighbors, their problems and therefore their willingness to engage in conventional logging. This sets the conditions for conventional logging to bring together complementary intentions between actors that will end up making business. But his does not mean that conventional logging makes everyone happy.

Landowners were also asked about their satisfaction with logging. Here their positions are somewhat polarized since 21 landowners were either very unsatisfied (11) or unsatisfied (10) with logging because they either could not meet their goals and/or felt swindled by their trading partners, or because they said that logging had actually destroyed much of the forest in their property and considered that a loss. The other half of the group said to be either satisfied (16) or very satisfied (6) with logging because they met their goals, and were able to use what belongs to them, i.e. the forest in their properties.

This brings up a related topic, which is the satisfaction of the landowners with their actual ownership of forest. More than half of the group said to be either very unsatisfied (5) or unsatisfied (19) with forest ownership, because it does not pay anything to own it since they cannot use it at their will. Paradoxically, this includes several landowners (13) who would like to protect the forest and receive forestry incentives, but cannot access them because they have either partial property rights or none. A small group was either satisfied (2) or very satisfied with forest protection (4). These landowners are protecting small forest patches between 12 and 44 ha. mainly to protect water springs inside their properties. Only one said to have 160 ha, and the reasons that move him to protect the forest are similar. A larger group was either satisfied (7) or very satisfied (5) because they were able to engage in logging and were expecting to perform more logging in the future.

When satisfaction with logging and forest ownership are taken together and looked at case-by-case, some interesting relationships in four clearly defined groups can be observed.

The members of the first group (10 landowners) are satisfied both with forest ownership and with conventional logging. Landowners' main goals were logging as a business itself, pay debts, buy farm inputs and repair the house. All of them achieved their goals and were happy to have access to the resources in their properties.

The members of the second group (9 landowners) are satisfied with forest ownership but unsatisfied with logging activities. Even though almost everyone achieved their goals (pay debts, build a house, buy another property, start a business and obtain property rights), their dissatisfaction originates from damages to the forest, i.e. to the property.

The members of the third group (11 landowners) are unsatisfied with forest ownership but satisfied with logging. Half achieved their goals (perform logging, obtain partial property rights, buy farm inputs, buy another property, obtain rapid cash), while the other half achieved them partially (get rid of the forest for cattle, pay debts, buy farm inputs, obtain rapid cash). Their dissatisfaction with forest ownership has its origin in their frustration of wanting to use the forest (what they say is theirs), but only after going through much trouble.

The members of the fourth – and larger – group (13 landowners) are unsatisfied both with forest ownership and logging. Only one of them achieved his goal, which was to pay debts. The rest achieved either partially their goals (obtain property rights, build a house), or did not achieve them at all (rapid cash, buy farm inputs, build/repair the house, obtain property rights). Dissatisfaction originates in this group also from the frustration of not being able to use the forest at their will, and from having made a bad deal.

Regarding the dissatisfaction with both forest ownership and logging I must come back to the issue of monitoring and landowners' perception of fairness of the formal enforcement mechanism, because many landowners actually hold against the government not acting consequently when denounces against irregular logging are followed. First, landowners contend that they cannot efficiently monitor loggers on the field. They engage the logger to perform a job and they must largely count on the logger to do it right, and should something go wrong – e.g. that the logging permit is misused by the logger – it is not the logger the one who suffers the consequences, but the landowner. Landowners also say that it is illusory to expect them to go and file complaints against people that are actually giving them access to resources that they would otherwise not have. Of course there are exceptions to this, for example, when the landowner is sure that he is being robbed by the logger he will do anything to get rid of him. But if logging occurs on a friendly basis, it is doubtful that the landowner will pester the logger with complaints before the AFE. Landowners also hold against the government treating actors differently according to their wealth, that is, that those landowners and loggers with enough material resources and influences have better chances of misusing a logging permit and getting away with it than other landowners relatively worse off.

Differentiated treatment of the better-off by governmental actors is a usual claim throughout society in almost any part of the world. Examples are abundant and can be found in almost any newspaper everyday. In Europe for example, members of the Italian ministry of justice have raised heavy arguments against president Berlusconi for holding back investigations involving him and his enterprises.[211] Likewise in France, the Judge Eric Halpen resigned to his position due to sabotage of his work related to the questioning of Jaques Chirac in relation to corruption affairs. In this regard he said that 'in France one has the sensation that justice is not equal for all, and while influential and rich people are not even bound to be investigated, common thieves are'.[212] The point I wish to make is that the fact that the better-off get preferential treatment from governmental organizations should not be played down by assuming it to be commonplace because such 'double moral' directly erodes the reputation of governmental organizations and the credibility of formal institutions, and if formal institutions loose their credibility some actors will have an increased incentive not to comply to them, and even to rebel against them if they find them bad enough.

Back to the Osa, it can be seen that the sources of landowners' dissatisfaction with logging arise either from damages to the forest, not meeting their goals, making bad deals and from the perception of being discriminated by corrupt governmental agencies. On the one hand, damages to the forest are the direct consequence of conventional logging. First, heavy machinery is always used and logging is very selective, second vines connecting tree crowns are seldom cut, because to cut them takes more work and time and time is money. Consequently, this source of dissatisfaction can be partially attributed to naive expectations on

---

211 See Badische Zeitung, Montag 14 Januar 2002, p.2.

212 See Badische Zeitung, Dienstag 15. Januar 2002, p.5.

the side of the landowners awaiting minimal damages to occur to their properties. The second and third sources (not meeting their goals, making bad deals) are probably a combination of having high (naive) expectations and negotiating with imperfect information and under asymmetric information with loggers. The last source of dissatisfaction actively erodes the credibility of formal arrangements and act as a disincentive for landowners to comply to them.

7 Discussion

7.1 Addressing the research questions

7.1.1 How do informal arrangements support the stability of conventional logging in opposition to formal arrangements?

Chapters 5 and 6 provided an extended insight to the first and second research questions posed at the beginning of this research study. There, the rules, behavior codex and enforcement mechanisms supporting conventional logging on the side of private as well as of governmental actors are pictured, as well as the dominant objectives influencing landowners' forest use decisions. In Chapter 6 it can be seen that while conventional logging takes place within the formal normative arrangements, other informal norms come constantly into play, like strategic – opportunistic – behavior grounded on information deficiencies and asymmetries during timber trade. These norms of strategic behavior are observable in the process prior to logging itself, that is, they take place during the negotiation of timber, whereas enforcement mechanisms arise either during or after logging.

This research study shows that on the side of landowners, informal norms of behavior support conventional logging in at least two ways. First, there is a local willingness to engage in conventional logging favored by the formal framework as it hinders institutional diversity, i.e. other arrangements that may be locally preferred to suit local needs, e.g., small scale logging. Second, landowners' engagement in conventional logging is also a result of their lack of bargaining power to influence institutional change, i.e., to propose and implement rules that match local needs and circumstances. In this sense, landowners comply to conventional logging because they lack better alternative choices, i.e., because conventional logging represents their second-best choice, and consequently they are willing to comply to its rules as long as they expect positive payoffs despite the relatively large transaction costs that they – implicitly or explicitly – accept.

Now, to deepen on how informal arrangements support the stability of conventional logging in opposition to formal arrangements, it is necessary to evaluate the 'robustness' of formal arrangements, hence one must look closely at the governance system. The weaknesses of the formal governance system will contribute to strengthen the informal norms supporting conventional logging by giving private actors the chance to act opportunistically, which can also be conceived as a parallel informal governance system. I will elaborate my arguments following Ostrom's theory of governance.

While recent institutional changes aim to the holistic management of forest resources, the instruments selected by the Costa Rican government rely largely on the use of a financial mechanism (the PES) as the main instrument to guide/influence the behavior of private actors towards specific forest uses, together with a monitoring system that pursues to involve private actors – mainly forest engineers, landowners and COVIRENA – in the monitoring of logging activities. Both instruments show several weaknesses while at the same time, governmental authorities show a flimsy presence both in the areas of monitoring and community relations.

Despite the official acknowledgement of the forest environmental services, the formal framework fails to contribute to establish *clearly defined boundaries* about what rights accrue to landowners regarding the use of collective goods – i.e. appropriation and provision – hence at the same time it fails to establish a *congruence between appropriation and provision rules.* The forest environmental services acknowledged by the Forest Law became partially nonfungible because landowners can exchange them for money with only one actor, the state. But at the same time the formal acknowledgement of forest environmental services tends to introduce uneasiness among landowners who say 'if my forest produces the so-called environmental services, why am I not being paid for them'? This circumstance tends to increase the asymmetry between the costs that landowners have to bear by securing forest environmental services and the benefits that society – the appropriator – perceives. In this regard, if the forest environmental services are acknowledged by law, then any landowner/forest-owner (independently of small, medium or large) that contributes to society's welfare by providing these goods and services – in one form or another – is entitled to receive the PES, because the law says so. Now if the state claims it cannot attend the demand for PES because it lacks the financial resources to supply for them – or for some other reason – does not that make the state a free-rider? This brings the state indeed – either willingly or unwillingly – into a twilight concerning its performance to induce collective action. Those who refrain themselves from applying to the PES can be considered to be donating these services to the general wellbeing and pose no problem whatsoever. But if the government free-rides on the other actors, there are two related effects that can be derived from the theory on collective action. First, the state looses credibility on its commitment to engage in the payment for the production of collective goods. Second, the other actors will also have an incentive to deceive, as repeated rounds of 'the game' – e.g. every additional year – teaches them that the state is not trustworthy because it fails to follow its own rules.

Despite the large reliance of the Costa Rican State on the financial instrument of the PES, it can be seen that in the case of collective goods like the forest environmental services, the PES do not necessarily contribute to the formation of 'well defined property rights', which eases free-riding. First, the PES do not provide more *comprehensiveness* (nor *transferability*) to the forest environmental services, i.e. they do not enhance the right of the providers to use and dispose of those collective goods according to the law, because a monopsonic appropriator – the state – fails to pay for the collective goods being provided. Second, the slacking performance of the state in relation to the PES implies that the costs, but not all the benefits derived from the provision of the forest environmental services accrue to the landowners, i.e., the PES are not providing the forest environmental services with more *exclusiveness*. Third, the *enforceability* of the rights over the provision of forest environmental services is a one-way street, because the landowners cannot force the state to pay for the appropriation of those services, but the state can force them to continue providing them. In this regard, the management that the state performs of the PES shows strong limitations in allowing private landowners to realize the monetary benefits that allegedly stem from these services, hence to induce them to collective action.

The empirical evidence shows that a weakness of the local governance system is that landowners – e.g. in the Osa – do not perceive a *congruence between appropriation rules and local conditions*. While there is evidence that some landowners wish to perform small-scale logging instead of conventional logging, the formal framework hinders such institutional flexibility by maintaining appropriation costs of timber disproportionately high for landowners wishing to engage in small-scale logging. This is because the formal framework – as defined for the whole country – fails to create room enough to account for local conditions despite the intention of promoting local participation as the new Forest Law proclaims. This shows that the actors affected by the *operational rules of collective arrangements* cannot participate in modifying these rules. This shows not only that the so-called decentralization of SINAC is far from being achieved since local offices of SINAC, e.g. ACOSA, cannot negotiate/tailor the rules with local actors, it also shows that either local participation is not being taken as seriously as it should, or its role has not been fully understood by governmental authorities. In either case, this throws a shadow on the governmental willingness to *recognize the rights of participants to organize around the use of resources*.

The governmental organizations in charge of the management of natural resources have undergone a process of institutional change after the second half of the 90s, and one of the most important changes in the monitoring of logging activities is that there has been a partial transfer of responsibilities from the public to the private sector. Thus part of the responsibility accrues now to a third – and presumably – independent/neutral party, the forest engineer, who is endowed with public faith. An evident unintended consequence of this arrangement is that it does not necessarily improve collective action towards the production and maintenance of the collective goods that allegedly stem from sustainable forest management, because it does not provide them any incentive to *actively engage in monitoring*. The reason is that, as an independent actor, no one can impede a forest engineer to work directly for – or in a partnership with – a logger, and if that happens the forest engineer is no longer a neutral actor, because he will look after his own interests and those of his employer/partner, that is, he will behave strategically to maximize his payoffs and take advantage of his public faith. The moment that forest engineers are endowed with 'public faith' they turn into key actors of the governance system, but if they are no longer able to remain neutral, the governance system has automatically a leak. A circumstance that leads to this failure is that the monitoring responsibilities are not separated during the management of forest resources. For example, one of the most basic principles of financial control is that certain activities should not be performed by the same person, e.g., – for evident reasons – someone employed as a cashier should not be in charge of the bookkeeping. Similarly, the failure in the monitoring system of the AFE can be observed by the fact that the same forest engineer who writes the management plan also certifies duly completion of logging activities before the AFE. In view of this, there are sound reasons to doubt the neutrality of forest engineers working in this fashion, not only because some may work directly for/or with the logger, but also because they are – more or less – forced to keep inspections limited to reduce loggers' operation costs. Hence after logging has taken place the forest engineer cannot reverse the errors committed by the logger and his team, and since he does not supervise the whole execution of the management plan to prevent errors before they happen, he is rather forced to justify errors and changes of his forest management plan instead of disclosing negligent performance. In this regard the forest engineer behaves rationally because the payoffs of justifying errors are larger than disclosing negligent performance of the logger after the management plan has been finished, because he would expose himself to formal sanctions. Finally, if he denounces the logger he will make himself a bad reputation among other loggers, and will bring himself in danger of loosing his clientele.

Likewise, several factors hinder landowners from an *active participation in monitoring*. Why should a landowner denounce the logger that helps him access financial resources? It is hard to find a reason except that – according to the Forest Law – if he refrains from reporting irregularities, he will be breaking the law by being accessory to an environmental crime (pretty much like the forest engineer), but if he files denounce against the logger for irregularities he will jeopardize his future income, and since the AFE is bound to monitor a management plan rather when a denounce is filed, the landowner will be prone to take the risk.

The AFE's officials/functionaries also face similar problems. Allegedly, due to lack of material and human resources they are not able to monitor every management plan neither *ex ante*, during logging, nor *ex post*. Maybe the larger problem source for them is *ex ante* because if – due to lack of field inspections – they approve a plan that contains trees that should have never been fallen, it would take a very courageous employee to file denounce against himself, and make others aware of his own error.

Another weakness of the formal governance system is that sanctions for *rule offenders* are perceived unfair by landowners, who feel disadvantaged in comparison to loggers, the ones actually performing logging, and with whom many have a written contract. Landowners resent the fact that they are more likely to be punished than loggers and, even though the law foresees gradual sanctions according to the deed, landowners still find this unfair because they are passive actors in the process of logging. To put it in Ostrom's words, rule offenders are not likely to be punished depending of the seriousness of their offense.

Moreover, local enforcement mechanisms are successful in holding local actors back from monitoring, because informal sanctions are credible. Hence, landowners and other local actors sometimes find it worthwhile to rebel against those local actors in charge of monitoring (COVIRENAS) and to actively pursue to deprive them from their credibility and authority before other local actors.

In view of this, while private actors perceive that the payoffs of complying to conventional logging are higher than those they can obtain from observing formal rules, the weaknesses of the formal enforcement mechanisms can – and do – arise the expectation among private actors that they can break the rules and get away with it.

Probably policy makers could have – *ceteris paribus* – included loggers in the governance system more effectively by making use of incentive measures that compel them to stick to the formal framework, for example, by introducing performance bonds and setting a lump-sum per hectare. Thus, if logging performance is demonstrated deficient/negligent, the logger shall not receive back the deposit he made. And if he performs logging as expected, he should receive his deposit plus interests. But this instrument requires that the AFE can effectively inspect logging stands *ex ante* and *ex post*, and/or monitoring forest engineers without any business relationship with the logger. But considering that the CCF played an important role in lobbying the new Forest Law, it is understandable that such instruments were not considered. That is, the logging industry negotiated a formal framework that contributes to maintain its *status quo*.

7.1.2 How do informal arrangements influence the achievement of formal forest policy goals (sustainable forest management and forest protection)?

The influence of informal arrangements in the achievement of formal forest policy goals depends on how far informal and formal goals coincide, hence they will positively influence the achievement of formal ends if they are coupled, and will hinder their achievement if formal and informal arrangements are decoupled. Forest protection excludes by definition conventional logging, and the decision to protect the forest does not contradict formal ends. Conventional logging might prove different though, because the goals pursued by private actors are complementary and rather detached from formal ends, making them a substantial factor that, by supporting conventional logging, hinder the achievement of some formal ends. The main goal pursued by loggers is to stay in their business, that is to continue logging conventionally, which is only tangentially related to the achievement of formal ends concerning natural forest management because of the technology used and the limited local socioeconomic impact it has. Likewise, the motivations that move landowners to engage in conventional logging do not have a direct connection to formal ends. The informal norms that support conventional logging and hamper the achievement of formal ends are mainly – on the side of loggers – opportunistic behavior and the expectation of impunity due to scanty monitoring, and – on the side of landowners – individualism related to the use of private property and also conflict avoidance with loggers, who have more resources than landowners and therefore more bargaining power. Moreover, informal norms are effectively supported by local enforcement mechanisms. The instability of formal requirements on the side of the government is also a factor that contributes to strengthen informal norms.

The Costa Rican state maintains that if logging activities are duly attended by private actors, formal ends will be achieved. While this may be true, the evidence obtained for this research indicate that in the case of conventional logging this is only partially true because of several reasons.

The weaknesses of the governance system pinpointed above indicate that the formal framework cannot guarantee that private actors will comply to formal rules on the field, because the design of formal arrangements still makes the payoffs expected from non-compliance larger than those of compliance, which stalls collective action towards formal ends. This eases opportunistic behavior and raises the expectation of impunity on the side of loggers. Landowners are rather spectators when it comes to conventional logging, so their compliance to formal norms will depend mainly on the role they wish to assume in monitoring of logging activities. But landowners may have strong reasons to refrain from assuming this role because they would be putting their own well being at stake, first, because they may endanger their own income – hence their wish of doing something they want with their property – and second because they may damage their social relations with their neighbors and the local community. This means that the payoffs that landowners can expect from complying to formal norms are smaller than those they can receive from not doing so. In the case of loggers, it is doubtful that they will want to fully comply to formal arrangements because that would mean for them an increase of their operation costs. The case of forest engineers and government officials/functionaries was also depicted above.

Much of the discussion around the achievement of forest policy ends in Costa Rica turns around the sustainability of conventional logging. But in spite of the argumentation of the government and logger organizations, who insist that conventional logging is sustainable because after some time everything is 'green' again, it is difficult for them to argue convincingly that conventional logging and sustainable forest management are the same thing. The studies revised for this research point to a much more complicated reality than the argument brought up above, namely, that one of the immediate impacts of conventional logging is damage to the soil, and connected to that is the increased runoff. Moreover, in places where conventional logging has taken place over a long period of time, an impact on biodiversity has been observed. As an economist – and single researcher – I do not pretend to make it my task here to demonstrate the ecological sustainability or unsustainability of conventional logging. Though sustainability at any level cannot be conclusively proven, I think that there are founded reasons to doubt that conventional logging is ecologically and socially sustainable. Nonetheless, it would be naive to expect logging not to have an impact on forest resources, but the point I wish to make in relation to the achievement of formal ends is that as long as conventional logging continues to take place, a tradeoff between specific collective goods will also take place – for example more CO_2 fixation and less biodiversity or vice-versa, and so the achievement of formal ends is only partial. But then one will probably not be able to continue calling it 'sustainable' forest management. Instead, it would be less confusing to talk about partial sustainability, where some environmental functions of the forest are maintained, but at the expense of others. However, throughout this research I found no evidence that the government or logger organizations are willing to change their discourse in such a direction, and they have good reasons for that.

How a group understands sustainability is directly related to the interests the group may have. The logging industry has evidently a stake in making conventional logging look sustainable, because long-term external financing for the industry – from the World Bank, for example – depends on that. Likewise, the government has also a stake in convincing donor agencies that formal ends are being achieved. For that matter, the Costa Rican state has built a coalition with the logging industry and has engaged in a process of institutional change that includes the acknowledgement of forest environmental services, the decentralization of governmental agencies, innovations of the monitoring of logging activities, etc.

The concept of path dependence is helpful to better understand this process of institutional change. Conventional logging stems from a period when forest lands in Costa Rica were intensively cleared for agriculture. In this period no particular value was assigned to forest resources other than being a cheap source of timber, that is, in the best case, in the worse scenario the timber was just burned down. During this time, a particular cost-minimizing technology for land use change (chainsaws, and heavy machinery primarily designed for the construction branch, but also useful for clearing forest lands) makes its way into the logging industry and is locked-in in what I call a case of second-degree path dependence. It is a second-degree case because at the time this happens, society's general conception of forest resources lacks largely information on the overall relevance of these resources, rather, the Costa Rican society is concerned with 'agricultural development'. Consequently, the inferiority of the technology being locked-in at that time by the incipient logging industry is not seriously questioned by policy-makers, only by very few academicians. As an aftermath of the Rio Conference, the concept of sustainability occupies the agenda of almost every country in the world, and of course of Costa Rica too, partly because financial resources for sustainable development were made available by industrialized countries and donor agencies. I am not saying that money is the only interest of the Costa Rican state behind sustainability, but I do assign it an important role. For example, after the UNFCCC, Costa Rica comes up with innovative initiatives (like Joint Implementation and Certifiable Tradable Offsets, that capture the attention of conflicting interests around the convention) that strategically position the country in a 'clean development field' that allows the expectation to access 'healthy' financial resources for an economy with a history of internal and external deficit. Today, the World Bank's forest strategy seeks to introduce a conditionality approach in its lending programs, that is, the WB should only lend to governments already committed to reform in the forest sector. In this context the Costa Rican state engages in the institutional reform of the forest sector and makes a strategic alliance with the logging industry.

But despite how good the institutional reform might be, the state cannot hinder the logging industry from behaving strategically and look after the interests of its members. Thus, the formal framework has changed, forest management plans have been introduced, but the technology used by the forest sector remains pretty much the same despite forest management plans which means that they are only partially attended. For example, the training of forest workers in low-impact logging techniques is lacking and consequently its field application too.

On top of this, in this research I find little evidence that local actors and communities are being given a chance to participate in the proposal and innovation of institutional arrangements adapted to local conditions. This can be explained through a vested interest of the logging industry in keeping their sources of raw material from natural forests, therefore the informal arrangements that have traditionally supported conventional logging prevail. To present a forest management plan before the AFE does not necessarily mean that something is changing on the field. I am not contending that forest management plans are good or bad because, as such, they are only an instrument that can be used appropriately or not, and can and should be further improved. This research gives several insights of the problems bound to forest management plans, and these are indeed related to their lax implementation and to how the process of logging is monitored. In view of this I consider that the Costa Rican forest sector is walking a sort of tight-rope where, on the one side institutional changes have been undertaken to try to correct regrettable institutional outcomes from the past, and on the other side – since this change is also costly for the logging industry and demands more sophisticated logging technology – its members are introducing changes at a sluggish pace, if at all. Therefore, the country is in real danger of going into a third-degree path dependence case because with the information available, it can be assessed *ex ante* that the maintenance of conventional logging as it is today, is bound to deliver a suboptimal outcome in socioeconomic and environmental terms. Consequently, should conventional logging prevail, and as long as the formal framework precludes local initiatives of alternative natural forest management, a transition to a third degree path dependence case is imaginable.

Small-scale logging will surely demand a different approach of forest management plans and will necessarily give rise to other transaction costs related to the monitoring of such activities, but if local needs can be addressed through such an approach and local actors stop being spectators and perceive this activity – or other arrangements – as theirs, there may be increased chances to couple informal norms with formal norms. I am not saying – and not even suggesting – that conventional logging should be banned. But conventional logging should be urgently revised, and the formal framework should be flexible enough to allow small-scale logging as a legitimate forest use, so that those who wish to engage in it can. Small-scale logging is more likely to contribute to the creation of a local forest culture than conventional logging because it has the potential to bring the interested local actors inside forest issues, instead of keeping them outside. Now, someone could argue that the new Forest Law does give the chance to private actors to engage in small-scale logging because the definition of forest adopted by the new Forest Law opens a wide range of forest resources – like secondary forests and heavy intervened forests – for private landowners. But the formal framework has in this regard a major failure which is, that it fails to acknowledge these resources as forests, consequently, the formal framework does not give private actors any particular reason to change their traditional point of view towards these forests resources, and consider them anything else than idle fallows and useless lands.

The instability of formal norms contributes to the creation of unstable future expectations. For example, the declarations given by the representative of MINAE for this research are quite revealing regarding the change of requisites from complete property rights to partial, and back to complete property rights to award logging permits. First, MINAE raises an argument anchored on a concept of social justice, namely, that partial property rights are allowed for logging permits to "give those with scarce economic opportunities an option to improve their economic situation through sustainable forest management". Following, MINAE justifies the change of requisites back to complete property rights based on a constitutional argument, namely, "that the right to private property has a constitutional rank, and because of this it should be duly respected". Both arguments can be probably justified, but on different levels, which renders the argumentation line of MINAE inconsistent, and because of this it contributes to the formation of uncertain expectations among landowners concerning the access to forest resources. This is most delicate in areas where landowners are awaiting expropriation, because the creation of uncertain expectations contributes to increase the discount rate of landowners and drives them to use forest resources as fast as possible before they loose access to what they consider theirs. This inconsistency of formal norms weakens the achievement of formal ends and strengthens informal norms supporting conventional logging, while allowing it to operate – officially – as "sustainable forest management" as long as it complies to bureaucratic requisites.

7.1.3 How does the institutional framework (formal and informal) structure benefit distribution among private actors?

Chapter 6 gave an insight to the transaction costs carried by private landowners in conventional logging. It suggests that these costs are relatively high compared to the CCF value of standing timber. The importance of shedding light on this issue is that transaction costs are an indicator of the institutional efficiency in distributing benefits among trading partners.

Transaction costs can originate from the need to develop, monitor and enforce contracts, but they also originate from the existence of asymmetric and deficient information – hence from opportunistic behavior – which allows that one partner can impose unnecessary costs on the other as a means to increase benefits. Chapter 6 focuses mainly on this last source of transaction costs and, following the results, formal and informal institutional arrangements ruling conventional logging are rather inefficient and skew benefit distribution to the advantage of loggers and other better-off actors. The additional costs carried by landowners are at the same time the additional benefits of loggers.

As landowners have bad chances of making efficient transactions because of a lack of information, efforts could be directed to the achievement of an information network, so that landowners share at least the same information on timber prices and volume measurement as their trading partners. This is not an insurmountable task, and for the government a rather easy one. But the formal framework has assigned this function to the private sector, namely to the logging industry, and because loggers have a stake in maintaining their *status quo* it is not in their interest to establish such an information network, and the Osa is a good example of that.

Additionally, looking back at the socioeconomic profile of the interviewed landowners and the main reasons that drove them to engage in conventional logging, it is doubtful that the financial resources that they obtained from timber trade might contribute either to an improvement of their socioeconomic situation or to a reduction of the pressure on forest resources, which throws reasonable doubt on the social, human and economic sustainability of conventional logging. This group faces awkward economic conditions and difficult access to public services including health and education, and according to this study, neither the government nor other private agents seem to effectively contribute to an improvement of these areas. Probably, had the landowners been aware of the CCF prices of standing timber and of the volume measurement method, their gross income would have been larger. But since these financial resources are not invested in productive activities that might bring them closer to economic stability and contribute to curve the pressure on forest resources, but rather in activities with short term horizons or to address basic needs, it seems rather a matter of time before the landowners find themselves in a situation equal or worse than the one they had before they engaged in conventional logging. This suggests a vicious circle that might lead – in the medium- to long-term – to increased forest degradation and worsening socioeconomic conditions.

Policy makers have the choice to transmit (or not) information to incentive particular forms of forest use. The main goals of the Costa Rican forest policy have been (for more than a decade) the achievement of sustainable forest management and forest conservation. Social sustainability is also part of a strategy of sustainable forest use and conservation, but the data on which this research is based do not suggest that conventional logging – as performed under the formal framework – is contributing to social sustainability in the Osa. Likewise, the analysis on how the PES influences the profitability of forest protection from a private point of view does not suggest that this may be an attractive forest use for small landowners in areas where this land use is desired, like in buffer zones of national parks, forest reserves, etc.

If one admits that information plays a key role regarding the benefit distribution of the commercial use of forest resources, then one must also recognize that information also goes beyond the simple transmission of market data and engineering formulas. To have people informed requires an effort of many years of active involvement of governmental and non-governmental organizations and demands principally the direct involvement of local landowners and communities in the development and implementation of local institutional arrangements. It requires education, but in rural areas where the education level is low (like in the Osa) it is unlikely that one might school again all the landowners. This study finds evidence that landowners are still closer to agriculture than to the forest, and in this regard coincides with the point of view of the CCT (1992: 3), Gottfried et al. (1994: 111), Segura et al. (1997a: 117, 124) and Watson et al. (1998: 57-58) in that an agricultural culture persists. Following the results of this study, this is partly due to the weak performance of governmental agencies in establishing and furthering stable relationships with landowners and communities to introduce, discuss and negotiate forest related issues. To develop a forest culture, local actors are rather faced with a task of learning by doing, so if people find way to make a decent living while owning a forest, there might be a chance to effectively develop that forest culture, and because there is no recipe whatsoever, the local partake in the development, tailoring and implementation of norms that locally regulate forest use is crucial. But this research study finds that, additional to the governmental performance, the same formal framework hinders this development by first, hindering alternative local forest uses, and second, by maintaining a centralized system of decision making that impedes that regional governmental agencies negotiate the kind of tailoring of the formal framework needed to address local needs. The long-term instability of formal norms does not help to achieve this either.

Because landowners are used to trading with loggers, and an effective informal information network exists that brings these actors together, the expectations built around conventional logging are stable, even though the level of trust between the partners is low. Thus as long as the formal framework is maintained as it is, this business partnership is likely to continue, because from a landowner point of view conventional logging is the second-best choice. For good or bad, loggers have a starring role in the process that allows landowners access to logging permits, simply because landowners cannot take the bulk of red tape and loggers can. This is a key issue in the whole process. It is rather puzzling that locally based NGOs throughout the country have not taken the initiative in this regard. An exception to the rule is found in ACA-HN, and ACCVC where locally strong NGOs are present and apparently do undertake those tasks, though it is not clear what transaction costs arise for the landowner during that process. Nonetheless, this kind of service would offer the opportunity to work with local landowners and provide them not only with accurate information but also to pursue educational aims that, in the log-run, may contribute to improve socioeconomic conditions and arrest human pressure on forest resources. This way – and assuming stable formal institutions – the local business culture could be positively influenced.

The formal framework attempts – through the acknowledgement of forest environmental services – to move private actors towards sustainable forest management and forest protection and for that matter relies on a financial instrument, the PES. As seen in chapter 5, the PES has the problem that it is socially selective, and tends to leave outside the weaker actors, even though they can be as relevant as any other for the achievement of policy goals. In this regard, while one can fairly consider that the institutional change introduced by the acknowledgement of forest environmental services is a positive development of the formal framework, this institutional change is also rather superficial, because by maintaining the same structure that underpinned the old forestry incentive system, it still fails to duly address the social objectives allegedly targeted, as the socioeconomic situation of the worse-off – i.e., small landowners –

under the PES tends to remain similar to that existing before the new Forest Law was approved.

Therefore, the maintenance of the old incentive structure for the PES is a barrier itself for the achievement of specific policy goals. In spite of the evidence provided by several researchers that suggest that there are tradeoffs between environmental services depending on what forestry activity is undertaken, the formal framework gives the impression that all of the environmental services included in the law are equally important. But if a forestry activity receives higher PES than the other while enhancing the production of specific environmental services at the expense of others, the supposition of equal importance can no longer be held. Indeed the actual structure of the PES suggests the contrary, namely, that implicitly it is given preference to those environmental services for which financing is available, hence carbon fixation is strongly incentivized while the tradeoff with other environmental services – like biodiversity, landscape and soil protection – is neglected by the government and by logger organizations, who insist these are also being attained in the same areas where conventional logging takes place. Consequently, if private actors seek to maximize their income, they will prefer the logging activities that render higher profits, and so not only the tradeoff of environmental services will continue to take place, but also conventional logging will continue to be preferred by landowners who will in turn continue to carry the burden of unnecessarily high transaction costs to the advantage of the logging industry.

7.2 Concluding remarks

One of the achievements of this research is that it sheds light and deepens on issues and causal relationships mentioned by other authors for Costa Rica.

In this research it is explained why landowners refrain from participating in sustainable forest management, something that Howard and Valerio (1996) attribute to a lack of basic information on technical requirements and potential stable returns as well as scarce familiarity with the periodic nature of cash flows from forest management. While this may be partially true, this research shows that the formal institutional framework actually contributes to maintain landowners as passive actors when it comes to the management of natural forests, and in that regard it strengthens informal norms that have traditionally underpinned conventional logging. This coincides partially with the observations made by Gottfried et al. (1994) about the institutional and political environment (a highly interventionist regulatory system) being a source that discourages the adoption of sustainable natural forest management techniques. Likewise, Richards et al. (1996: 11) contend that "*in Costa Rica in the forest sector, decentralization has been more administrative than political, with regional structures replicating central ones but most decision-making power being retained in the centre*". In this regard, the findings of these authors strengthen the observation made in this research that the institutional change in the forest sector tends to be superficial because despite the attempts of governmental decentralization and the inclusion of the private sector, decisive conditions that can move landowners to participate in – and increase their payoffs from – sustainable forestry activities are still not met.

Indeed the case of the decentralization of SINAC shows – in the case of the Osa – that decision-making processes within governmental agencies are still strongly centralized, which hinders 'norm tailoring', hence to induce local participation. This finding contrasts with the arguments of de Camino et al. (2000), who refer positively to the process of governmental decentralization and institutional change, especially regarding the transference of responsibilities from the public to the private sector. In this respect, they describe positively the role assigned to the ONF, the CRA, and forest engineers. In contrast, this research finds that the performance of the private sector towards landowners is poor because its presence does not contribute to reduce imperfect and asymmetric information among landowners so that they are able to perform more efficient transactions. On the contrary, the strong involvement of the private sector contributes to the maintenance of the *status quo* of the logging industry. While de Camino et al. (2000) mention the role of the CRA as relevant, the evidence found from ACOSA did not reveal such relevant role of this group as a proponent of forest policy. Likewise, this research observes critically the role of forest engineers as independent actors, particularly the evident strategic failure of concentrating planning, execution and certification of logging activities in one single independent actor.

This research brings forward evidence that one of the motivations of landowners to engage in conventional logging still is the expectation of securing property rights. Peuker (1991), Kishor and Constantino (1993), and Gottfried et al. (1994) make similar observations, though under other formal framework conditions, and they observe how the incentive to obtain property rights drives the process of deforestation. Today, land use change is indeed banned, but landowners still maintain the expectation that conventional logging can contribute to the achievement of property rights by providing them with the financial resources necessary to finally inscribe their properties acquired under the old law that granted property rights to those peacefully occupying abandoned lands.

One of the insights found in this research refers to the role that loggers play in the way that private landowners decide to use their forests. While Gottfried et al. (1994) make similar observations as those found in this research about loggers paying much lower prices for standing timber than those the local market actually sets, this research provides a deeper insight into the negotiation process of timber and throws light on significant sources of transaction costs for landowners.

This research study finds that the maintenance of the old incentive structure for the PES hampers the accomplishment of specific policy goals, like the maintenance of biodiversity and the achievement of social goals. While Chomitz et al. (1998) contend that a difficulty to target biodiversity is the fact that it yields no revenue, this study complements that assertion by showing that one of the reasons that probably contributed to the maintenance of the old incentive structure is the maintenance of a market oriented focus that implicitly finances those environmental services for which there are 'environmental markets' (like carbon fixation); but then this renders the aspiration of the Costa Rican state of enhancing the production of all forest environmental services inconsistent. Furthermore, while Chomitz et al. (1998) see an advantage in the role of the state as a monopsonic agent (and as an intermediary that further sells these services to other agents, like in the case of CO_2) that can use revenues to secure biodiversity services, this research discusses the problems arising from an 'undisciplined' monopsonic agent, namely, the loss of credibility of the state in its commitment to secure these services and the negative effect that this has on collective action.

This research also matches the observation made by several authors (for example Gottfried et al. 1994; Watson et al. 1998) in that bureaucratic requisites marginalize small landowners from accessing financial incentives, and shows that besides this fact, the actual financial incentives, i.e. the PES, tend to discourage small landowners from opting specific forest uses in strategic areas (like forest protection in buffer zones of national parks). This is likely to be the case when loggers take care of the paperwork. In this regard, the PES system gives landowners a clear signal to prefer some forest use over other – probably – more desirable in some specific areas. As a result, it is also highlighted how the design of PES for different forestry activities contribute rather partially to the achievement of formal ends.

Additionally, the evidence found here is complementary of the findings of other authors like Schelhas (1996) and Jantzi et al. (1999) regarding the environmental services that landowners recognize in their forests, and suggest that landowners tend to recognize those environmental services related to the maintenance of their farms.

The research complements the findings of Silva (1997), who finds that the private sector (mainly through the CCF) successfully lobbied the hindrance of the approval of grassroots legislation that would have put the logging industry at disadvantage (i.e. reduced their payoffs) prior to the approval of the new Forest Law. In this regard, this dissertation offers some insights on the role of the government as planner and proposer of institutional reform. This research shows how the private sector effectively lobbied for legislation that gives the logging industry an advantage in the access to forest resources and in the monitoring of logging activities. It shows that the government does not act alone as a proposer of institutional change, but that it can – and will – act strategically and undergo coalitions with other actors as long as this can contribute to position the country internationally. It can also be seen that this strategic behavior is not conflict-free, because while the country seeks to profit from its international image, at home things look pretty much the same as usual because the coalition partner also acts strategically by taking reform on the paper but not on the field, and takes advantage of the government's inefficacy to effectively monitor. Of course this shows two different realities, the one that the country proclaims in international forums, and the one that a researcher can observe on the field.

Finally, I would like to address the issue of how appropriate the theory of the NIE is to tackle the issues addressed in this research study.

I find that the NIE presents an appropriate framework to address the issues discussed in this research. First, the theory provides a framework that allows an explanation of how institutions arise and change by comprising power relationships and strategic behavior of stakeholders as posited by Elster (1986), North (1990), Knight (1992) and Khan (1995), which allows the explanation of the coalition between the state and the private sector in Costa Rica. The concept of path dependence, as explained by Liebowitz and Margolis (1995) is particularly useful to clarify why the institutional change in the Costa Rican forest sector takes the form it has. Additionally, the NIE provides a useful background to analyze the potential of recent institutional arrangements to induce collective behavior of private actors in the Osa as stated by Hardin (1982), Elster (1989) and Tuomela (1992). Ostrom's theory of governance proves to be a useful instrument to analyze how the design of formal enforcement mechanisms provides stability to formal arrangements, and, by contradiction, how the weakness of these mechanisms strengthen informal arrangements that underpin conventional logging.

Particularly useful for the analysis presented in Chapter 6 is the theory on transaction costs (Kerr and Maré 1996; 1998) together with the assumption of bound rationality and opportunistic behavior (Simon [1983]1993; Sen and van Kooten 2001). The evidence obtained for this research study provides a reasonable basis to assume that opportunistic behavior is characteristic of economic environments where the level of trust is low (due to a business culture where opportunistic behavior is usual) and incomplete and asymmetric information are present. This position is different to the point of view defended by Cartier (1994: cited in Sen and Van Kooten 2001: 71), who says "*it is evident that laziness, cheating, absenteeism, pilfering and misappropriation, abuse and exploitation exist, and may be induced if the original contract were made under duress; but to postulate a general principle of shirking rests on a view of human behavior and a lack of objectivity which does not contribute to serious analysis*". A general assumption of opportunistic behavior is probably not appropriate for every agent in every economic environment, since opportunism is likely to vary according to the economic, social and cultural setting. The findings of this research study refer mainly to a rural area – like so many in Costa Rica and Central America – with difficult access, scarce infrastructure and whose inhabitants face stringent economic and social conditions. The findings in this research indeed suggest that opportunistic behavior does play an important role as a source of transaction costs in timber trade in this rural setting, and not to recognize this economic behavior would deliver a rather naive economic analysis.

8 Literature

Adger, Neil W., and Katrina Brown. 1994. *Land use and the causes of global warming.* Sussex: John Wiley & Sons Ltd.

Alvarado, Alfredo and Ricardo Monge. 1997. *Costa Rica 1997-cohort 6. Chapter IV. An Overview of the Agricultural Sector in Costa Rica.* LEAD. Internet WWW page, at URL: <http://globe.lead.org/lead/session/costarica/97/docs/chapter4.htm> (version current as of July 30, 1998).

Anderson, Robert and Robert Schneider. No date. *Sustainability, Yield Loss and Inmediatismo: Choice of Technique at the Frontier.* World Bank, LAC Dissemination Note I.

Angelsen, Arild and David Kaimowitz. 1999. "Rethinking the causes of deforestation". *The World Bank Research Observer* 14(1): 73-98.

Araya, Mena Yadira y Gerardo Artavia Zamora. 1998. *Sistema Nacional de Areas de Conservación. Parques Nacionales y otras Areas Silvestres Protegidas.* MINAE/ACDI/WWF/SINAC. Heredia: Conlith S.A.

Arias, Guillermo. 1998. "El desarrollo forestal futuro y el sector privado". In *Foro Nacional sobre Análisis de Politicas Forestales y de Recursos Naturales de Costa Rica.* Hotel Corobicí, 8 y 9 de Octubre. Oficina Nacional Forestal, Universidad para la Paz. San José, Costa Rica.

Arnold, Michael J.E. 2001. *Forestry, Poverty and Aid.* CIFOR, Occasional Paper No. 33. August.

Barahona, Jiménez Luis. 1975. *El gran incógnito.* San José: Editorial Costa Rica.

Barrantes, Gilbert, Quírico Jiménez, Jorge Lobo, Tirso Maldonado, Mauricio Quesada y Ruperto Quesada. 1999. *Evaluación de los planes de manejo forestal autorizados en el período 1997-1999 en la Península de Osa. Cumplimiento de normas técnicas, ambientales en impacto sobre el bosque natural.* Informe para la Fundación Cecropia. Julio.

Barry, Deborah, Hernan Rosa, Nelson Cuéllar. 1997. Políticas Forestales en El Salvador. Análisis de las Restricciones para el Desarrollo del Sector Forestal." In Segura, Olman, David Kaimowitz and Jorge Rodríguez eds., *Políticas forestales en Centro América. Análisis de las restricciones para en desarrollo del sector forestal.* San Salvador, El Salvador: EDICPSA.

Bates, Robert H. 1995. "An Assessment of the New Institutionalism." In Harriss, John, Janet Hunter and Colin M. Lewis, eds., *The New Institutional Economics and Third World Development.* London: Routledge.

Becker, Michel. 2000. *Perspectivas de Mercado para Madeira Certificada na Europa.* XI Seminario de Atualização sobre Sistemas de Colheita de Madeira e Transporte Florestal. Pinhais – Paraná – Brasil.

Bertie, L. Sylvia. 2000. *Effects of roads on erosion in a wet tropical forest in the Río Riyito watershed, Peninsula de Osa, Costa Rica.* In partial fulfillment of the requirements for the degree of Master of Science. Colorado State University. Department of Earth Resources. Fort Collins, CO.

Biesanz, Mavis Hiltunen de, Richard Biesanz and Karen Zubris de Biesanz. 1979. *Los Costarricenses.* San José, Costa Rica: Editorial Universidad Estatal a Distancia (EUNED).

Bolaños, Rojas Luis Alberto. 1998. *El Sistema Nacional de Areas de Conservación en el Desarrollo Forestal de Costa Rica.* Documento a presentar en: Foro nacional sobre análisis de las políticas forestales y recursos naturales de Costa Rica con miras al futuro. Ministerio del Ambiente y Energía. Sistema Nacional de Areas de Conservación. 8-9 de octubre.

Buchanan, James and Gordon Tullock. [1965] 1982. *The Calculus of Consent. Logical Fundations of Constitutional Democracy.* Ann Arbor: The University of Michigan Press.

Cálix, Isabel de, y Lizardo Sosa. 1997. Políticas Forestales en Guatemala. Análisis de las Restricciones para el Desarrollo del Sector Forestal." In Segura, Olman, David Kaimowitz and Jorge Rodríguez eds., *Políticas forestales en Centro América. Análisis de las restricciones para en desarrollo del sector forestal.* San Salvador, El Salvador: EDICPSA.

Cámara Costarricense Forestal (CCF). 1998a. *Desde el Bosque.* Organo Informativo Oficial de la Cámara Costarricense Forestal. Año 1. Número 2. Enero-Febrero.

CCF. 1998b. *Desde el Bosque.* Organo Informativo Oficial de la Cámara Costarricense Forestal. Año 1. Número 3. Marzo-Abril.

CCF. 1998c. *Desde el Bosque.* Organo Informativo Oficial de la Cámara Costarricense Forestal. Año 1. Número 4. IV Trimestre.

CCF. 1999a. *Desde el Bosque.* Organo Informativo Oficial de la Cámara Costarricense Forestal. Año 2. Número 1. I Cuatrimestre.

CCF. 1999b. *Desde el Bosque.* Organo Informativo Oficial de la Cámara Costarricense Forestal. Año 2. Número 4. III Cuatrimestre.

Campos, Arce José Joaquín, Marlen Camacho Calvo, Róger Villalobos Soto, Carlos Manuel Rodríguez, Manuel Gómez Flores. 2001. *La tala ilegal en Costa Rica. Un análisis para la discusión.* Informe elaborado por el Centro Agronómico Tropical de Investigación y Enseñanza (CATIE) a solicitud de la Comisión de Seguimiento del Plan Nacional de Desarrollo Forestal. Turrialba.

Casson, Mark. 1991. *The Economics of Business Culture. Game Theory, Transaction Costs and Economic Performance.* Oxford: Claredon Press.

Castle, Emery N. 1996. "Pluralism and Pragmatism in the Pursuit of Sustainable Development". In Adamowicz, W.L., P. Boxfall, M. K. Luckert, W. E. Phillips, W.

A. White, eds., *Forestry, Economics and the Environment*. Wallingford, Oxon: CAB International.

Castro, Salazar René y Guillermo Arias Murillo. 1998. *Costa Rica: Hacia la Sostenibilidad de sus Recursos Naturales*. MINAE/FONAFIFO.

Centro Científico Tropical (CCT). 1992. *Política forestal para Costa Rica*. CCT, San José, Costa Rica.

Centro Científico Tropical, Centro de Investigaciones en Desarrollo Sostenible (CCT/CIEDES). 1998. *Estudio de Cobertura Forestal Actual (1996/97) y de Cambio de Cobertura para el Periodo entre 1986/87 y 1996/97 para Costa Rica* (presentado al Fondo Nacional de Financiamiento Forestal, FONAFIFO). San José, Costa Rica. Abril.

CEPAL/FAO/OIT. 1980. *Tenencia de la Tierra y Desarrollo Rural en Centroamérica*. Colección Seis. Ciudad Universitaria Rodrigo Facio, Costa Rica: Editorial Universitaria Centroamericana (EDUCA).

Chomitz, Kenneth M. and David A. Gray. 1996. "Roads, Land Use, and Deforestation: A Spatial Model Applied to Belize." *The World Bank Economic Review* 10(3): 487-512.

Chomitz, Kenneth M., Esteban Brenes and Luis Constantino. 1998. *Financing Environmental Services: The Costa Rican Experience and Its implications*. World Bank.

Clarence-Smith W.G. 1995. "Cocoa Plantations in the Third World, 1870s-1914. The political economy of inefficiency." In Harriss, John, Janet Hunter and Colin M. Lewis, eds., *The New Institutional Economics and Third World Development*. London: Routledge.

Crossley, R.A., T. Lent, D. Propper de Callejon and C. Sethare. 1997. "Innovative financing for sustainable forestry." *Unasylva*. No. 188, 48 (1): 23-31.

Current, Dean. 1994. *Agroforestry for Sustainable Development: Policy Lessons from Central America and Panama*. Department of Forest Resources, University of Minnesota. Working Paper No. 18.

Dahms, Klaus Günther. 1956. *Forst und Holz in Mittel- und Südamerika*. Stuttgart: Holz-Zentralblatt Verlags-GmbH.

Dasgupta, Partha. 1996. "The Economics of the Environment". *Proceedings of the British Academy*. Vol. 90: 165-221. Internet WWW page, at URL: <http://www.britac.ac.uk/pubs/src/keynes95/00index.html> (version current as of January 18 2002).

de Camino, Ronnie and Marielos Alfaro. 1998. *Certification in Latin America: Experience To Date*. Rural Development Forestry Network. Network Paper 23c, summer. Overseas Development Institute.

de Camino, Ronnie, Olman Segura, Luis Guillermo Arias and Isaac Pérez. 2000. *Forest Policy and the Evolution of Land Use: An Evaluation of Costa Rica's Forest*

Development and World Bank Assistance (preliminary report). Operations Evaluation Department. World Bank.

Deutsche Bischofskonferenz. 1997. *Soziale Sicherungssysteme als Elemente der Armutsbekämpfung in Entwicklungsländern.* Eine Studie der Sachverständigtengruppe "Weltwirtschaft und Sozialethik". Bonn.

Dubash, Navroz K. and Frances Seymour. No date. *The Political Economy of "Environmental Adjustment": The World Bank as Midwife of Forest Policy Reform.* Paper presented at a conference on "International Institutions: Global Processes ~ Domestic Consequences" at Duke University. April 9-11.

Eggertsson, Thraínn. 1990. *Economic behavior and institutions.* Cambridge: Cambridge University Press.

Eisenberg, Andrea. 1999. *Die Lösungen sozialer Dilemmata und der Wandel informeller Institutionen.* Diskussionsbeitrag 04-99. Max-Planck-Institut zur Erforschung von Wirtschaftswissenschaftssystemen. Abteilung Institutionenökonomik und Wirtschaftspolitik.

Elster, Jon. 1989. *Nuts and Bolts for the Social Sciences.* Cambridge: Cambridge University Press.

Elster, Jon. 1989a. *Solomonic Judgements.* Cambridge: Cambridge University Press.

Elton, Charlotte, Jesús Almancía, Irving Díaz, Ricardo Almanza, Javier Morón, Francisco Herrera, Pablo Torrealba, Carlos Bellido. 1997. "Políticas Forestales an Panamá. Análisis de las Restricciones para el Desarrollo del Sector Forestal." In Segura, Olman, David Kaimowitz and Jorge Rodríguez eds., *Políticas forestales en Centro América. Análisis de las restricciones para en desarrollo del sector forestal.* San Salvador, El Salvador: EDICPSA.

Farris, Robert. 1999. *Deforestation and Land Use on the Evolving Frontier: An Empirical Assessment.* Development Discussion Paper No. 678. Central America Project Series. Harvard Institute for International Development. Harvard University.

Ferraro, Paul. 2001. "Cost-Effective Conservation: A review of What Works to Preserve Biodiversity". *Resources* 17(142): 17-20.

Finegan Brian. 1992. "The management potential of neotropical secondary lowland rain forest." *Forest Ecology and Management* 47: 295-321.

Fondo Nacional de Financiamiento Forestal. 1996. *Pago de Servicios Ambientales e Incentivos forestales.*

Fondo Nacional de Financiamiento Forestal, Ministerio del Ambiente y Energía. 1997. *Los Servicios Ambientales: Una Alternativa para la Conservación de los Bosques Naturales y el Manejo de las Plantaciones Forestales.*

Food and Agriculture Organization (FAO). 1995. *State of the World's Forests.* Rome. Internet WWW page, at URL: <http://www.fao.org/DOCREP/003/X6953E/ X6953E00.htm> (Version current as of July 10, 2002)

FAO. 2001. *State of the World's Forests*. Rome. Internet WWW page, at URL: <http://www.fao.org/docrep/003/y0900e/y0900e00.htm> (Version current as of August 2, 2002)

Gillis, Malcolm. 1992. "Economic Policies and Tropical Deforestation." *Advances in Economic Botany* 9: 129-142.

Goodland, Robert. 2002. "Sustainability, Human, Social, Economic and Environmental." In Munn, Ted and Peter Timmerman, eds., *Encyclopedia of Global Environmental Change*. Volume 5. New York: John Wiley and Sons. Internet WWW page, at URL: <http://www.wiley.co.uk/wileychi/egec/pdf/ga811-w.pdf> (version current as of September 9, 2002).

Gottfried, Robert R., Charles D. Brockett, William C. Davis. 1994. "Models of sustainable development and forest resource management in Costa Rica." *Ecological Economics* 9: 107-120.

Greenhill, G. Robert. 1995. "State Intervention in the Brazilian Coffee Trade During the 1920s: A Case Study for the New Institutional Economics?" In Harriss, John, Janet Hunter and Colin M. Lewis, eds., *The New Institutional Economics and Third World Development*. London: Routledge.

Greif, Avner. 1998. "Cultural Beliefs and the Organization of Society: A Historical and Theoretical Reflection on Collectivist and Individualist Societies." In Brinton, Mary C. and Victor Nee, eds., *The New Institutionalism in Sociology*. New York: Russell Sage Foundation.

Gudmunson, Lowell. 1983. *Hacendados, políticos y precaristas: La ganadería y el latifundismo Guanacasteco (1800-1950)*. San José: Editorial Costa Rica.

Gudynas, Eduardo. 1998. "Conservación, Sustentabilidad Ecológica y la Articulación entre Comercio y Ambiente." *Ciencias Ambientales* 14: 48-61.

Hardin, Russell. 1982. *Collective Action*. Resources for the Future. Baltimore: Johns Hopkins University Press.

Harsanyi, John C. 1962. "Measurement of Social Power, Opportunity Costs, and The Theory of Two Person Bargaining Games." Behavioral Science 1: 67-80. In Abel, Peter, ed. 1991. *Rational Choice Theory*. – (Schools of thought in sociology, no. 8). Cambridge: Cambridge University Press.

Heckathorn, Douglas D. 1988. "Collective Sanctions and the Creation of Prisioner's Dilemma Norms." *American Journal of Sociology* 94(3): 535-62. In Abel, Peter, ed. 1991. *Rational Choice Theory*. – (Schools of thought in sociology, no. 8). Cambridge: Cambridge University Press.

Heindrichs, Thomas. 1997. *Instrumentos de financiamiento innovadores en el sector forestal y de conservación de la naturaleza de Costa Rica*. Proyecto sectorial de la GTZ "Apoyo a Programas Internacionales para el Bosque Tropical (TWRP)". Area de trabajo Manejo Forestal y Conservación de la Naturaleza. Eschborn, Alemania.

Hinkelammert, Franz. 1998. "Circuito Económico, Sacrificidad y Alternativas al Capitalismo." *Ciencias Ambientales* 14: 38-47.

Howard, Andrew. 1995. "Price trends for stumpage and selected agricultural products in Costa Rica." *Forest Ecology and Management* 75: 101-110.

Howard, Andrew F. and Juvenal Valerio. 1996. "Financial returns from sustainable forest management and selected agricultural land use options in Costa Rica." *Forest Ecology and Management* 81: 35-49.

International Institute for Sustainable Development (IISD). 1999. "Global workshop on addressing the underlying causes of deforestation and forest degradation." 18-22 January 1999. San José, Costa Rica. *Sustainable Development* 21(1). Internet WWW page, at URL: <http://www.iisd.ca/sd/sanjose/sdvol21no1e.html> (version current as of September 25, 2002).

Jantzi, Terrence, John Schelhas and James P. Lassoie. 1999. "Environmental values and forest patch conservation in a rural Costa Rican community." *Agriculture and Human Values* 16: 29-39.

Jenkins, Edwin. 2001. *La Osa Productos Forestales (Recopilación de Información).* Informe de consultoría para el Consejo Nacional de Cooperativas (CONACOOP). Enero 2001.

Jiménez M., Juan José. 1996. *Diagnóstico del Mercado de Maderas de la Península de Osa.* Fundación Neotrópica, Agua Buena de Osa, Marzo.

Kaimowitz, David, Erwidodo O. Ndoye, P. Pacheco and W. Sunderlin. 1998. "Considering the impact of structural adjustment policies on forests in Bolivia, Cameroon and Indonesia." *Unasylva*. 194(49): 57-64.

Keipi, Kari. 2001. "Forest Investments in Latin America and the Caribbean". In Palo, Matti and Jussi Uusivuori, eds., *World Forests, Markets and Policies.* Dordrecht: Kluwer Academic Publishers.

Kerr Suzi C. and David Maré. 1996. "Efficient Regulation Through Tradable Permit Markets: The United States Lead Phasedown". Department of Agricultural and Resource Economics, University of Maryland at College Park, Working Paper 96-06.

Kerr, Suzi and David Maré. 1998. *Transaction Costs and Tradable Permit Markets: The United States Lead Phasedown*, Presented at Environmental Economics Seminar, Stanford University, March. Internet WWW page, at URL: <http://www.motu.org.nz/pdf/transaction_costs.pdf> (version current as of January 13, 2001).

Khan, Mushtaq. 1995. "State Failure in Weak States. A critique of the new institutionalist explanations." In Harriss, John, Janet Hunter and Colin M. Lewis, eds., *The New Institutional Economics and Third World Development.* London: Routledge.

Kishor, Nalin M., and Luis F. Constantino 1993. *Forest Management and Competing Land uses: An Economic Analysis for Costa Rica.* LATEN Dissemination Note #7, The world Bank, Latin America Technical Department, Environment Division, October.

Knight, Jack. 1992. *Institutions and Social Conflict*. Cambridge: Cambridge University Press.

Knight, Jack and Jean Ensminger. 1995. "Conflict over Changing Social Norms: Bargaining, Ideology and Enforcement." In Brinton, Mary C. and Victor Nee, eds., *The New Institutionalism in Sociology*. New York: Russell Sage Foundation.

Kvale, Steiner. 1996. *InterViews: An Introduction to qualitative research interviewing*. California: Sage Publications, Inc.

La Hoja. Volumen 1. Números 1-9. COVIRENA, La Palma. Costa Rica 1998.

Landes, David. 1998. *Wohlstand und Armut der Nationen. Warum die einen reich und die anderen arm sind*. Berlin: Siedler Verlag.

Láscaris, Constantino. 1977. *El Costarricense*. San José, Costa Rica: Editorial Universitaria Centroamericana (EDUCA).

Liebowitz, L. J. and Stephen E. Margolis. 1995. "Path Dependence, Lock-in, and History." *Journal of Law, Economics and Organization* 11 (1): 205-226.

Lindegaard, Klaus and Olman Segura. 1998. "Trade offs in joint implementation strategies." In Arler, Finn and Ingeborn Svennevig, eds., *Cross-Cultural Protection of Nature and the Environment*. Odensee: University Press.

Luzurriaga, Carlos. 1997. *Costa Rica, Evaluation of the Joint Implementation Program*. Deutsche Gesellschaft für Technische Zusammenarbeit.

Mahar, Dennis and Robert Schneider. 1994. "Incentives for tropical deforestation: some examples from Latin America". In Brown, Katrina and David Pearce, eds., *The Causes of Tropical Deforestation. The economic and statistical analysis of factors giving rise to the loss of the tropical forests*. London: UCL Press Limited.

Marwell, Gerald and Ruth E. Ames. 1981. "Economists Free Ride, Does Anyone Else?" *Journal of Public Economics* 15: 295-310.

Mena, Araya Yadira y Gerardo Artavia Mora. 1998. *Sistema Nacional de Areas de Conservación. Parques Nacionales y otras Areas Silvestres Protegidas de Costa Rica*. Ministerio del Ambiente y Energía (MINAE).

Méndez G., Johnny A. No Date. *Costos de las actividades de aprovechamiento forestal, en el bosque natural de la zona norte de Costa Rica*. Proyecto Manejo Integrado de Bosque Natural DFID/CODEFORSA/MINAE/ITCR, Colección Técnica Manejo de Bosque Natural - N°1, Ciudad Quesada, Costa Rica.

Mery, Gerardo, Sebastiao Kengen and Concepción Luján. 2001. "Forest-Based Development in Brazil, Chile and Mexico". In Palo, Matti and Jussi Uusivuori, eds., *World Forests, Markets and Policies*. Dordrecht: Kluwer Academic Publishers.

Ministerio del Ambiente y Energía, Sistema Nacional de Areas de Conservación, Area de Conservación Osa, Programa de Educación Ambiental. 1999. *Estrategia Regional de Educación y Extensión Ambiental*.

Ministerio del Ambiente y Energía, Oficina de Sociedad Civil, Area de Conservación Osa (MINAE/ACOSA). 2000. *Listado de proyectos para Pago de Servicios Ambientales (PSA).* Información suministrada por el Fondo Nacional de Financiamiento Forestal (FONAFIFO).

Ministerio del Ambiente y Energía (MINAE), Programa de las Naciones Unidas para el Desarrollo (PNUD), Oficina Nacional Forestal (ONF). 2001. *Plan Nacional de Desarrollo Forestal.* San José, Costa Rica.

Morton, Julia. 1987. *Fruits of Warm Climates.* Winterville: Creative Resource Systems. Internet WWW page, at URL: <http://www.hort.purdue.edu/newcrop/morton/pejibaye.html> (version current as of August 05, 2002).

Müller, Eva y Manuel Solís. 1997. "Estudio de Caso: Los Bosques Secundarios de Costa Rica." *Memorias del Taller Internacional sobre el Estado Actual y Potencial de Manejo y Desarrollo del Bosque Secundario Tropical en América Latina.* Pucallpa – Perú, 2 al 6 de junio: 149-157.

Mummert, Annette. 1998. *Selbstorganisation in informellen Siedlungen: Möglichkeiten und Grenzen außerlegaler Regelsysteme.* Diskussionsbeitrag 07-98. Max-Planck-Institut zur Erforschung von Wirtschaftssystemen. Abteilung Institutionenökonomik und Wirtschaftspolitik. Jena.

Mummert, Uwe. 1999. *Informal Institutions and Institutional Policy – Shedding Light on the Myth of Institutional Conflict.* Diskussionsbeitrag 02-99. Max-Planck-Institut zur Erforschung von Wirtschaftssystemen. Abteilung Institutionenökonomik und Wirtschaftspolitik. Jena.

Muranaga, Jun, and Tokiko Shimizu. 1999. *Market Microstructure and market liquidity.* Bank of Japan. Internet WWW page, at URL: <http://www.bis.org/publ/cgfs11mura_a.pdf> (version current as of October 06. 2001).

Muranaga, Jun. No date. *Dynamics of market liquidity of Japanese stocks: An analysis of tick-by-tick data of the Tokyo Stock Exchange.* Bank of Japan. Internet WWW page, at URL: <http://www.bis.org/publ/cgfs11muran.pdf> (version current as of October 06. 2001).

Muschler, R.G., and A. Bonnemann. 1997. "Potentials and limitations of agroforestry for changing land-use in the tropics: experiences from Central America." *Forest Ecology and Management* 91: 61-73.

Naranjo, Carmen. 1977. *Cinco temas en busca de un pensador.* Ministerio de Cultura Juventud y Deportes. San José, Costa Rica.

Nee, Victor. 1998. "Norms and Networks in Economic and Organizational Performance." *The American Economic Review* 88(2): 85-9.

Nee, Victor. 1998a. "Sources of the New Institutionalism." In Brinton, Mary C. and Victor Nee, eds., *The New Institutionalism in Sociology.* New York: Russell Sage Foundation.

Nee, Victor and Paul Ingram. 1998. "Embeddedness and Beyond: Institutions, Exchange, and Social Structure. In Brinton, Mary C. and Victor Nee, eds., *The New Institutionalism in Sociology*. New York: Russell Sage Foundation.

Nießlein, Erwin. 1985. *Forstpolitik. Ein Grundriß sektoraler Politik.* Pareys Studientexte 47. Hamburg, Berlin: Verlag Paul Parey.

North, Douglass. 1989. "A Transaction Cost Approach to the Historical development of Polities and Economics." *Journal of Institutional and Theoretical Economics* 145: 661-8.

North, Douglass. 1990. *Institutions, Institutional Change and Economic Performance.* Cambridge: Cambridge University Press.

North, Douglass. 1995. "The New Institutional Economics and Third World Development." In Harriss, John, Janet Hunter and Colin M. Lewis, eds., *The New Institutional Economics and Third World Development*. London: Routledge.

North, Douglass. 1998. "Economic Performance Through Time." In Brinton, Mary C. and Victor Nee, eds., *The New Institutionalism in Sociology*. New York: Russell Sage Foundation.

Olson, Mancur. 1968. "Economics, Sociology and the Best of all Possible Worlds." *Public Interest*. Summer: 96-118. In Abel, Peter. 1991. *Rational Choice Theory*. – (Schools of thought in sociology, no. 8). Cambridge: Cambridge University Press.

Organization for Economic Co-operation and Development (OECD). 1999. *Handbook of Incentive Measures for Biodiversity. Design and Implementation*. Paris: OECD.

Ostrom, Elinor. 1990. *Governing the Commons. The evolution of institutions for collective action*. Cambridge: Cambridge University Press.

Ostrom, Elinor. 1995. "Designing Complexity to Govern Complexity." In Hanna, Susan and Mohan Munasinghe. 1995. *Property rights and the Environment*. Washington D.C.: Beijer International Institute of Ecological Economics and the World Bank.

Ostrom, Elinor. 1999. *Self-Governance and Forest Resources*. CIFOR: Occasional Paper No. 20.

Panayotis, Varangis N., Rachel Crossley, Carlos A. Primo Braga. 1995. *Is There a Commercial Case for Tropical Timber Certification?* Policy Research Working Paper 1479. The World Bank International Economics Department. Commodity Policy and Analysis Unit. June.

Pearce David, and Katrina Brown. 1994. "Saving the world's tropical forests." In Brown, Katrina and David Pearce, eds., *The causes of tropical deforestation. The economic and statistical analysis of factors giving rise to the loss of the tropical forests.* CSERGE, UCL Press.

Pearce, David. 1996. "Global Environmental Value and the Tropical Forests: Demonstration and Capture." In Adamowicz, W.L., P. Boxall. M. K. Luckert. W. E. Phillips and W.

A. White, eds., *Forestry, Economics and the Environment*. Wallingford: CAB International.

Peuker, Axel. 1991. "Public Policies and Deforestation in Costa Rica." Draft. *LATEN*. World Bank, May 7.

Pierce Colfer, Carol J., Ravi Prabhu and Eva Wollenberg. 1995. *Principles, Criteria and Indicators: Applying Ockham's Razor to the People-Forestry Link*. CIFOR Working Paper No. 8.

Porras, Anabelle y Beatriz Villareal. 1993. *Deforestación en Costa Rica: implicaciones sociales, económicas y legales*. San José: Editorial Costa Rica.

Putz, Francis E. 1994. *Approaches to Sustainable Forest Management*. CIFOR Working paper No. 4. September.

Quirós, Brunilda Hilje. 1993. *La colonización agrícola de Costa Rica*. Nuestra Historia, fascículo 10. San José, Costa Rica: Editorial Universidad Estatal a Distancia.

Repetto, Robert. 1993. "How to Account for Environmental Degradation". In Adamowicz, W.L., W. White and W.E. Phillips, eds., *Forestry and the Environment: Economic Perspectives*. Wallingford, Oxon: CAB International.

Resor, J.P. 1997. "Debt-for Nature Swaps: a decade of experience and new directions for the future". *Unasylva*. No. 188, 48(1): 15-22.

Richards, Michael, Guillermo Navarro, Alberto Vargas and Jonathan Davies. 1996. *Decentralizing Forest Management and Conservation in Central America*. London: Overseas Development Institute. Working Paper 93.

Richards, Michael and Pedro Moura Costa. 1999. "Can tropical forestry be made more profitable by internalising the externalities?" *Natural Resource perspectives*. Number 46, October. London: Overseas Development Institute.

Richards, Michael. 1999. *Internalising the Externalities of Tropical Forestry: A Review of Innovative Financing and Incentive Mechanisms*. London: Overseas Development Institute.

Richards, Michael. 2000. "Can Sustainable Tropical Forestry be Made Profitable? The Potentials and Limitations of Innovative Incentive Mechanisms. *World Development* 28(6): 1001-16.

Rivera, Roy. 1986. *Política y Distribución de Tierras en Costa Rica*. 1a. ed. Ciudad Universitaria Rodrigo Facio, Costa Rica: Editorial Alma Mater.

Robertson, Nina. 2000. *Following the Greenbacks. Socio-Economic Aspects of the Degradation of Green Macaw Habitat in the Northern Zone of Costa Rica*. Stanford University. Internet WWW page, at URL: <http://www.stanford.edu/~ninar/Costarica-macaw.htm> (version current as of August 5, 2002).

Robinson, Joan. [1970] 1975. *Libertad y Necesidad*. México: Siglo Veintiuno Editores S.A.

Rodríguez, Jorge. 1997. "Aspectos Políticos e Institucionales de los Bosques Secundarios Tropicales de América Central." *Memorias del Taller Internacional sobre el Estado Actual y Potencial de Manejo y Desarrollo del Bosque Secundario Tropical en América Latina*. Pucallpa – Perú, 2 al 6 de junio: 141-8.

Román, Vega Isabel y Roy Rivera Araya. 1990. *Tierra con fronteras (Treinta años de política de distribución de tierras en Costa Rica)*. Centro de Estudios para la Acción Social (CEPAS). Documento de Análisis No. 14.

Sader, S. A., T. Sever, J.C. Smoot, and M. Richards. 1994. "Forest Change Estimates for the Northern Petén Region of Guatemala – 1986-1990." *Human Ecology* 22(3): 317-332.

Schelhas, John. 1996. "Land use Choice and Change: Intensification and Diversification in the Lowland Tropics of Costa Rica." *Human Organization* 55(3): 298-306.

Scherr, Sara. 1999. "The economic context for agroforestry development: evidence from Central America and the Caribbean." *Outlook on Agriculture* 28(3): 163-170.

Segura, Olman, David Kaimowitz y Jorge Rodríguez eds. 1997. *Políticas forestales en Centro América. Análisis de las restricciones para en desarrollo del sector forestal*. San Salvador, El Salvador: EDICPSA.

Segura, Olman, Robin Gottfried, Miriam Miranda y Luis Gómez. 1997a. "Políticas forestales en Costa Rica. Análisis de las restricciones para en desarrollo del sector forestal." In Segura, Olman, David Kaimowitz and Jorge Rodríguez eds., *Políticas forestales en Centro América. Análisis de las restricciones para en desarrollo del sector forestal*. San Salvador, El Salvador: EDICPSA.

Segura, Olman and Bjorn Johnson. 1998. *Forest Services and Property Rights from an Innovation Point of View: The Case of Costa Rica*. Paper prepared for presentation at the Fifth Biennial Meeting of the International Society for Ecological Economics (ISEE), November 15-19, Santiago de Chile.

Segura, Olman and Leiner Vargas. 1999. "Institutional Innovation and Policy Learning in Costa Rica." Universidad Nacional. International Centre on Economic Policy for Sustainable Development (CINPE). Paper 19 for the book "*Networks of Innovation in Latin America. Towards a Triple Helix of University-Industry-Government Relationships*".

Seligson, M. 1984. *El Campesino y el Capitalismo Agrario de Costa Rica*. San José: Editorial Costa Rica.

Sen, Wang, and G. Cornelis van Kooten. 2001. *Forestry and the New Institutional Economics. An application of contract theory to forest silvicultural investment*. England: Ashgate.

Seymour, Frances J., Navroz K. Dubash, Jake Brunner, Francois Ekoko, Colin Filer, Hariadi Kartodihardjo and John Mugabe. 2000. *The Right Conditions. The World Bank,*

Structural Adjustment, and Forest Policy Reform. Washington D.C.: World Resources Institute.

Shión, Miguel y Rosario Ambrogui. 1997. Políticas Forestales en Nicaragua. Análisis de las Restricciones para el Desarrollo del Sector Forestal." In Segura, Olman, David Kaimowitz and Jorge Rodríguez eds., *Políticas forestales en Centro América. Análisis de las restricciones para en desarrollo del sector forestal.* San Salvador, El Salvador: EDICPSA.

Silva, Eduardo. 1997. "The Politics of Sustainable Development: Native Forest Policy in Chile, Venezuela, Costa Rica and Mexico." *Journal of Latin American Studies* 29: 457-493.

Simon, Herbert A. [1983]1993. *Homo rationalis: die Vernunft im menschlichen Leben.* Frankfurt/Main: Campus Verlag.

Simon, Lola, Elias Awe y Oscar Rosado. 1997. Políticas Forestales en Belice. Análisis de las Restricciones para el Desarrollo del Sector Forestal." In Segura, Olman, David Kaimowitz and Jorge Rodríguez eds., *Políticas forestales en Centro América. Análisis de las restricciones para en desarrollo del sector forestal.* San Salvador, El Salvador: EDICPSA.

Sistema Nacional de Areas de Conservación (SINAC). 1999. *Análisis operativo de los planes de manejo evaluados en ACOSA durante el período 1997-1999.* SINAC, Componente de Control y Protección.

Smith, Joyotee, César Sabogal, Wil de Jong y David Kaimowitz. 1997. *Bosques secundarios como recurso para el desarrollo y la conservación ambiental en los trópicos de América Latina.* CIFOR Occasional Paper No. 13. December.

Solórzano, Raúl. 1990. *Economía y política forestal para Costa Rica.* Centro Científico Tropical, Notas Técnicas y Económicas N°6, San José, Costa Rica.

Solórzano, Raúl, Ronnie de Camino, Richard Woodward, Joseph Tosi, Vicente Watson, Alexis Vásquez, Carlos Villalobos, Jorge Jiménez, Robert Repetto y Wilfrido Cruz. 1991. *La Depreciación de los Recursos Naturales en Costa Rica y su Relación con el Sistema de Cuentas Nacionales.* Centro Científico Tropical, World Resources Institute.

Steele, Paul. 1999. *An economic analysis of collective management for natural resources; with case studies of small scale irrigation and fisheries is South Asia* (preliminary draft). Centre for Social and Economic Research on the Environment (CSERGE), University College London.

Stinchcombe, Arthur, L. 1986. "Reason and Rationality." *Sociological Theory* 4: 151-166. In Abel, Peter, ed. 1991. *Rational Choice Theory.* – (Schools of thought in sociology, no. 8). Cambridge: Cambridge University Press.

Stonich, Susan, Douglas L. Murray, and Peter Rosset. 1994. "Enduring Crises: The Human and Environmental Consequences of Nontraditional Export Growth in Central America." *Research in Economic Antropology* 15: 239-274.

Stork, N. E., T. J. B. Boyle, V. Dale, H. Eeley, B. Finegan, M. Lawes, N. Manokaran, R. Prabhu and J. Soberon. 1997. *Criteria and Indicators for Assesing the Sustainability of Forest Management: Conservation of Biodiversity.* CIFOR Working Paper No. 17. August.

Suazo, Jenny N., Ian Walker, Miguel Ramos, Sergio Zelaya. 1997. Políticas Forestales en Honduras. Análisis de las Restricciones para el Desarrollo del Sector Forestal." In Segura, Olman, David Kaimowitz and Jorge Rodríguez eds., *Políticas forestales en Centro América. Análisis de las restricciones para en desarrollo del sector forestal.* IICA-Holanda/Laderas C.A., CCAB-AP, San Salvador, El Salvador

Thiele, Rainer und Manfred Wiebelt. 1996. *Tropenwaldmanagement – En Balanceakt zwischen Schutz und Raubbau.* Kieler Diskussionsbeiträge. Oktober.

Tipper, Richard. 1998. "Forests, Carbon and Climate Change". *Tropical Forest Update* 8(1): 2-4.

Torres, Leopoldo. 1998. *Las instituciones y el desarrollo forestal futuro. Ponencia del sector privado*, in: Foro Nacional sobre Análisis de Políticas Forestales y de Recursos Naturales de Costa Rica. Hotel Corobicí, 8 y 9 de Octubre de 1998. Oficina Nacional Forestal, Universidad para la Paz. San José, Costa Rica.

Toye, John. 1995. "The New Institutional Economics and its Implications for Development Theory." In Harriss, John, Janet Hunter and Colin M. Lewis, eds., *The New Institutional Economics and Third World Development.* London: Routledge.

Trochim, William M. 2000. *The research methods Knowledge Base.* 2nd Edition. Internet WWW page, at URL: <http://trochim.human.cornell.edu/kb/index.htm> (version current as of September 19, 2002).

Tuomela, Raimo. 1992. "On the Structural Aspects of Collective Action and Free-Riding." *Theory and Decision* 32: 165-202.

Utting, Peter. 1993. *Trees, people and Power. Social dimensions of deforestation and forest protection in Central America.* London: Earthscan Publications Ltd.

Uusivuori, Jussi and Susanna Laaksonen-Craig. 2001. "Internationalization of Forest Industries". In Palo, Matti and Jussi Uusivuori, eds., *World Forests, Markets and Policies.* Dordrecht: Kluwer Academic Pulibshers.

van den Homberg, Elena. 1999. *Guerreros del Golfo Dulce: Industria forestal y conflicto en la Península de Osa, Costa Rica.* 1a. ed. San José, Costa Rica: Editorial Departamento Ecuménico de Investigaciones (DEI).

Vayda, A. P. 1996. Methods and explanations in the study of human actions and their environmental effects. CIFOR/WWF special publication. Jakarta, Indonesia.

Volz, Karl-Reinhard. 1997. "Waldnutzungskonzepte und ihre forstpolitische Bewertung." *Forstw. Cbl.* 116: 291-300.

Watson, Vicente, Sonia Cervantes, César Castro, Leonardo Mora, Magda Solís, Ina T. Porras y Beatriz Cornejo. 1998. *Abriendo espacios para una mejor actividad forestal.* Proyecto: Políticas exitosas para los bosques y la gente. 1a. ed., Centro Científico Tropical, San José, Costa Rica.

Weingast, Barry R. 1989. "The Political Institutions of Representative Government." *Journal of Institutional and Theoretical Economics* 145: 693-703.

Williamson, Oliver E. 1984. "The Economics of Governance." *Journal of Institutional and Theoretical Economics* 140: 195-223.

Williamson, Oliver. 1998. "The Institutions of Governance." *The American Economic Review* 88(2): 75-9.

World Bank. 2000. *A review of the World Bank's 1991 Forest Strategy and it's Implementation*. Operations Evaluation Department. Preliminary Report. January 13.

Wunder, Sven. "Poverty alleviation and tropical forests – what scope for synergies?" *World Development* 29(11): 1817-1833.

Yin, Robert. 1994. *Case study research: design and methods.* 2nd ed. California: SAGE Publications, Inc.

Zafirovski, Milan. 2001. *Exchange, Action, and Social Structure. Elements of Economic Sociology.* Contributions in Sociology, Number 134. Westport, Connecticut: Greenwood Press.

Laws and Bylaws

Criterios e Indicadores para el Manejo Forestal y la Certificación en Costa Rica. Decreto Número 27388-MINAE. In *La Gaceta*, N° 212. Lunes 2 de noviembre de 1998, p. 5-9.

Decreto Ejecutivo 8494-A del 26 de abril de 1978, en: la Gaceta número 104 del 01 de junio de 1978

Decreto Ejecutivo 9388-A del 30 de noviembre de 1978, en: la Gaceta número 239 del 15 de diciembre de 1978

Decreto Ejecutivo 10142-A del 12 de junio de 1979, en: la Gaceta número 119 del 27 de junio de 1979

Ley Forestal. Ley Número 7174 del 28 de junio de 1990.

Ley Orgánica del Ambiente. Ley número 7554 del 4 de octubre de 1995. In Zeledón, Ricardo. 2001. *Código Ambiental.* Editorial Porvenir, San José, Costa Rica.

Ley Forestal. Ley número 7575 del 5 de febrero de 1996, reformada por leyes Nos. 7609 del 11 de junio de 1996, 7761 del 2 de abril de 1998 y 7788 del 30 de abril de 1998. In Zeledón, Ricardo. 2001. *Código Ambiental.* Editorial Porvenir, San José, Costa Rica.

Ley de Biodiversidad. Ley número 7788 del 30 de abril de 1998. In Zeledón, Ricardo. 2001. *Código Ambiental*. Editorial Porvenir, San José, Costa Rica.

Plan de Ordenamiento Territorial. Decreto Número 29393 – MINAE. In *Alcance N° 34 a La Gaceta* del martes 15 de mayo del 2001. Imprenta Nacional.

Reglamento a la Ley Forestal. Decreto Número 25721-MINAE. In *La Gaceta*. N° 16. Jueves 23 de enero de 1997, p. 35-42.

Sala Constitucional de la Corte Suprema de Justicia: Recurso de Amparo No. 3605-V-92, Sindicato de Productores Independientes del Cantón de Osa, Ministerio de Recursos Naturales Energía y Minas y otros. Expediente 3605-92, 2456-97.

Newspapers

Badische Zeitung

El Sol de Osa

La Nación. Internet WWW page at URL: <http://www.nacion.co.cr>

The Tico Times

Other internet resources:

International Tropical Timber Organization (ITTO). 1993. Guidelines on The Conservation of Biological Diversity in Tropical Production Forests. Internet WWW page, at URL: <http://www.itto.or.jp/policy/pds5/contents.html> (version current as of April 28, 2002).

ITTO. 1993a. Manual for the application of criteria and indicators for sustainable management of natural tropical forests. Internet WWW page, at URL: <http://www.itto.or.jp/policy/pds10/contents.html> (version current as of April 28, 2002).

Proyecto Estado de la Nación. Internet www page, at URL: <http://www.estadonación. or.cr>

The Governance Working Group of the International Institute of Administrative Sciences. 1996. *Governance: A Working Definition*. Internet WWW page, at URL: <http://www.gdrc.org/u-gov/work-def.html> (version current as of September 26, 2002).

United Nations. 1992. *Agenda 21 – Combating Deforestation*. Chapter 11. Internet WWW page, at URL: <http://www.unep.org/Documents/Default.asp?DocumentID =52&ArticleID=59> (version current as of April 03, 2002).

United Nations. 1992a. *Report of the United nations Conference on Environment and Development. Forest Principles*. Rio de Janeiro, 3-14 June 1992. Internet WWW page, at URL: <http://www.un.org/documents/ga/conf151/aconf15126-3annex 3.htm> (version current as of April 30, 2002).

United Nations. 1992b. *United Nations Framework Convention on Climate Change.* Internet WWW page, at URL: <http://unfccc.int/resource/docs/convkp/conveng.pdf> (version current as of September 21, 2002).